The Con Game

A Failure of Trust

T. S. Laham

ISBN: 978-1-4834-1723-3 (sc)
ISBN: 978-1-4834-1722-6 (e)

Lulu Publishing Services rev. date: 10/29/2014

For LIAH

Contents

PART II: ELDER MISTREATMENT

CHAPTER 3: ELDER NEGLECT AND ABUSE 39

CHAPTER 4: ELDER EXPLOITATION 62

PART III: CONSERVATORSHIP SYSTEM

CHAPTER 5: THE PAPER CHASE 97

PART IV: CHANGE AGENTS

CHAPTER 8: THE ADVOCATES 189

CHAPTER 9: THE AGENCIES 212

EPILOGUE 231

REFERENCES..233

INDEX..259

FOREWORD

As a practicing attorney specializing in estates and trusts for the past 30 years, I have had firsthand experience in administering many conservatorship estates. The problems the author highlights in *The Con Game* are issues of which I have personal knowledge. My career in estate planning has led me to face other family structures with cracks that might have been avoided with sufficient preliminary planning. These types of legal issues are increasing because of the extended longevity of the human race. Additionally, families are no longer "centralized"; children marry and move away, frequently leaving the elderly isolated. Who, then, is responsible? If seniors gather the necessary knowledge and take time to create a program to ensure their care while still mentally, physically, and financially capable, many pitfalls can be avoided.

In this book, the example given is a woman who had only one immediate family tie, yet many siblings, nieces, and nephews became engaged in her physical care and in the managing of her estate. The woman's son and relatives in this example do not share the same concern for the elderly woman's care. The disagreement becomes so heated that the Probate Court must eventually intervene. Once the matter advances to the supervision of the Court, the number of professionals associated with the case grows at an alarming rate. This, of course, leads to enormous costs and fees as well as severe emotional stress.

The Con Game offers a vivid picture of just such a family feud and its resulting chaos. The author zeroes in on the many estate planning strategies that might curtail or even eliminate such conflict and, ultimately, help all parties involved avoid the emotional and financial price tag that typically follows. The book is easy reading, and if readers follow the author's recommendations, they can avoid the pain and cost that often accompany conservatorship disputes.

Kirk McIntosh, Esq.
Costa Mesa, California
November 27, 2013

ACKNOWLEDGMENTS

I owe a debt of gratitude to several people who inspired and championed the evolution of this work. I would like to express my sincere appreciation to my colleague and friend Professor Carolyn Seefer for her keen editorial skills as my copyeditor and proofreader. Also, I want to thank legal consultants Kirk McIntosh and Scott Dallas whose insights and feedback were invaluable in the preparation of this book. I am equally indebted to clinical nurse and palliative care expert Kathleen Adlard for her contributions to this work and for her continuous encouragement.

Extra special thanks are due to David Adlard for his courage of conviction and his willingness to fight the good fight. I am also most grateful to Nadim Bikhazi who, as always, has encouraged me to keep writing.

Last but not least, I would like to thank my family and friends for their rallying support and many kindnesses, with special thanks owed to the Adlard and the Foster families.

INTRODUCTION

In classical Greek philosopher Plato's renowned work *The Republic*, Plato carried out a dramatic dialogue with Socrates and other philosophers, where they debated philosophical and moral views on a variety of subjects, such as the meaning of justice, the immortality of the soul, and successful aging. On the latter, Plato shared a story about an exchange that he had with Greek poet Sophocles. Plato asked Sophocles if he felt the sting of old age in the form of a loss of interest or pleasure in life. Sophocles replied that he had escaped this feeling and instead had achieved tranquility during his twilight years. From this Plato surmised, "For certainly old age has a great sense of calm and freedom; when the passions relax their hold, then, as Sophocles says, we are freed from the grasp not of one mad master only, but of many...for he who is of a calm and happy nature will hardly feel the pressure of age, but to him who is of an opposite disposition, youth and age are equally a burden." As far back as 380 BC, even Plato believed that you are as old as you feel and think.

Age is relative, yet the difficulties of aging can be universal. Many older adults lead happy, healthy, and independent lives, while others do not; those who do not must often depend on others for their care and assistance. This is especially true for the dependent elderly who suffer from aging-associated diseases such as Alzheimer's disease and related dementias. As a population, the dependent elderly are at greater risk of mistreatment, including psychological and physical abuse, neglect, exploitation, abandonment, and isolation. The sad and shocking truth is that perpetrators of elder mistreatment are most often family members.

Every family keeps secrets. One of the deadliest family secrets is that of elder mistreatment. In America, an older parent, relative, or friend is physically, emotionally, or sexually abused or financially exploited every five seconds. Yet more than 80 percent of elder mistreatment goes unreported.

In instances where elders are being abused, neglected, or exploited, families often turn to the courts for help by seeking a conservatorship to protect their elderly loved ones. As a legal concept, a conservatorship protects and manages the personal care and/or financial affairs of a vulnerable or dependent adult. In its practical application, however, a conservatorship is the most restrictive alternative and most intrusive option to addressing a situation. Also, a conservatorship can create new problems and even perpetuate the abuse when a court-appointed protector seizes "supreme control" over a conserved elder. Along the way, a conservatorship can strip an elder of his or her basic freedoms—sometimes in just a matter of minutes. The elder is then reduced to the status of an infant with as few rights as a felon. In most cases, there is no exit strategy: the conservatorship ends when the conserved elder dies or runs out of money.

As a general researcher and writer, I was drawn to the study of elder mistreatment when a close friend shared a heart-wrenching story about an elderly relative who was stricken with dementia and became a victim of elder mistreatment in her own household. The tragic and macabre story contained all the gritty elements of a news segment that could be featured on Bill Kurtis's *Investigative Reports*, including intrigue, predation, betrayal, injustice, misappropriation, and debasement. The dreadful situation tore her immediate family apart, and led to a bitter family feud that played out in a courthouse.

After a decade-long exploration of the subject matter, I realized that even though researchers, clinicians, and other professionals engaged in a robust dialogue on elder mistreatment, a public discussion of the topic was still limited in scope. To expand the dialogue and make the information easier for people to consume, I mined and distilled a huge body of data to gain meaningful insights on the topic. This book represents the culmination of these efforts.

The book is divided into four parts. Part I explores aging in America by delving into how people think, feel, and act from one generation to the next, with a focus on older generations. Key cohort groups, including the Silent Generation, Baby Boomers, and Generation X, are highlighted in the framework of their roles and relationships in an aging society.

Part II examines the social phenomenon of elder mistreatment in America. The different types of risk factors for elder mistreatment are addressed, as well as the common characteristics of abuse victims and their perpetrators. In addition, the nature and prevalence of elder exploitation are explored, with special attention given to elder fraud and different types of influence.

Part III presents an in-depth probe into the conservatorship system. Different types of conservatorships, the formation of a conservatorship, and the pros and cons of a conservatorship are featured. Also, the duties and responsibilities of conservators and the standards of decision making used in making surrogate decisions are explained. Finally, the dark side of conservatorships is exposed.

Part IV provides resources people can consult for assistance and support to prevent and stop elder neglect, abuse, and exploitation. This section also covers alternatives to a conservatorship and offers a wide range of information and resources on a variety of elder issues.

Winning the war against elder mistreatment is everyone's responsibility. Robbing the elderly of their dignity and respect, trampling on their rights and autonomy, and denying them proper care and treatment harms and dehumanizes them. Treating our elders with dignity and respect begins in the home. Parents must teach their children that elders are valuable and vital members of our society. In the words of Plato, "Let parents bequeath to their children not riches, but the spirit of reverence."

T. S. Laham
Oakland, California
November 2014

LIST OF PLAYERS AND PARTIES

To guide you through the main plot and weaving subplots of the legal story highlighted in the book, a list of key players and parties is provided. The list is divided into groupings according to *family members* who were directly embroiled in the main character's situation; *professional fiduciaries* who were appointed by the court; and *attorneys* involved in the conservatorship case.

Family Members	
Selma	The matriarch of the Lyon family. Selma, a widow, shared a household with her son Zachary and one of her sisters, Minerva.
Minerva	Selma's sister. She ran the Lyon household until she died. Her death set the stage for the family melodrama.
Zachary	Selma's son. Zachary was married to Sybil, who provides home care.
Sybil	Zachary's wife. Sybil was at the center of the Lyon family feud.
Livingston	Selma's nephew, who is a lawyer and Selma's court-appointed conservator of the estate.
Noah	Selma's nephew, who is a medical specialist.
Mason	Selma's nephew, who is a family practice physician.

Harper	Mason's wife, who is a clinical nurse and a palliative care expert.
Agatha	Selma's niece, who is a lobbyist.

Professional Fiduciaries	
Mr. Gaines	Selma's court-appointed conservator of the person
Mr. Powell	Selma's court-appointed trustee and co-conservator of the estate

Attorneys	
Attorney Forte (aka Forte)	Livingston's conservatorship attorney
Attorney Young (aka Young)	Agatha's elder law attorney in Northern California
Attorney Armstrong (aka Armstrong)	Agatha's estate planning attorney in Southern California
Attorney Hall (aka Hall)	Selma's court-appointed attorney
Attorney Wright (aka Wright)	Selma's estate planning attorney discharged by Zachary
Attorney Gilroy (aka Gilroy)	Selma's attorney retained by Zachary for Selma
Attorney Walker (aka Walker)	Zachary's attorney hired for the settlement negotiations

PART I
Aging America

CHAPTER 1

Coming of Age

If you grew up listening to crooners like Bing Crosby or Frank Sinatra or watching Frank Capra films like the Clark Gable-Claudette Colbert romantic comedy *It Happened One Night*, you were probably born sometime between 1925 and 1945, making you a member of the Silent Generation. If you attended a Janis Joplin or a Jimi Hendrix concert or went to the cinema to catch Stanley Kubrick's existentially trippy film *2001: A Space Odyssey*, you were likely born between 1946 and 1964, making you a member of the Baby Boom Generation. If you remember getting body slammed in a mosh pit at a Nirvana concert or got hooked on the cult film *Office Space*, you were probably born sometime between 1965 and 1981, making you a member of Generation X. Finally, if you were eagerly anticipating each installment of *The Lord of the Rings* trilogy or queuing up to buy the latest Xbox, you were probably born sometime between 1982 and 2000, making you a member of Generation Y, also known as the Millennial Generation.

When you think of the Silent Generation, what famous names come to mind? If you said former vice president Walter Mondale; author Gore Vidal; magazine publisher Hugh Hefner; civil rights leader Martin Luther King, Jr.; or author and feminist Gloria Steinem, you'd be right. Now try naming some famous Boomers. U.S. President Barack Obama; career politician Hillary Clinton; the former governor of Massachusetts Mitt Romney; Microsoft founder Bill Gates; and the "Queen of Talk" Oprah Winfrey are Boomers. Next, when you read stories about the Google Boys Sergey Brin and Larry Page; social entrepreneur and founder of TOMS Shoes Blake Mycoskie; basketball great Shaquille O'Neal; rapper Eminem; or comic actor Adam Sandler, you're reading about Gen X newsmakers. Finally, if you follow singer-songwriter Lady Gaga, Facebook founder Mark Zuckerberg, or teen pop sensation Justin Bieber on Twitter, you're getting updates from a Generation Y influencer.

In this chapter, we'll define what generational cohorts are, as well as their importance in shaping our lives and our thoughts. Next, we'll discuss the Silent Generation, which is the largest living elderly group. After that, we'll examine sociocultural attitudes toward aging. Finally, we'll take a closer look at seniors' concerns and future challenges.

What Are Generational Cohorts?

Authors William Strauss and Neil Howe rewrote American history as a progression of generations in their ambitious book *Generations: The History of America's Future, 1584 to 2069*. As a core idea, Strauss and Howe propose that each generation travels through time, with each presenting "a distinctive sense of self."

So what exactly is a *generation*? According to Strauss and Howe, a generation is a special cohort. A generation arrives in a cycle. Each cycle has its own *peer personality*, a generational persona galvanized by common age markers, beliefs, behaviors, and group memberships. A generational cohort is, then, bound by a *social moment*, or an era, "when people perceive that historic events are radically altering their social environment." For example, the Silent Generation experienced at least two defining social moments: the Great Depression and World War II, while the Baby Boom Generation experienced at least four major social moments: the Vietnam War, the Cold War, the sexual revolution, and the civil rights movement.

2

While social moments vary depending on a generation's unique place in history, cohort life cycles do not. According to Strauss and Howe, as a "cluster of age-based social roles," each cohort life cycle includes four basic life phases:

Life Phase	Age Bracket	Central Role
Youth	0 to 21	dependence, growing, learning, accepting protection and nurture, avoiding harm, acquiring values
Rising adulthood	22 to 43	activity, working, starting families and livelihoods, serving institutions, testing values
Midlife	44 to 65	leadership, parenting, teaching, directing institutions, using values
Elderhood	66 and up	stewardship, supervising, mentoring, channeling endowments, passing on values

In a situational context, let's bring the narrative to life by describing six living generational cohorts: *Silent Generation, Baby Boom Generation, Generation X, Generation Y, Generation Z,* and *Generation Alpha.* First, members of the *Silent Generation,* also known as the *Silents,* (people born between 1925 and 1945) represent approximately 11.3 percent, or 35 million, of the U.S. population, according to 2010 census data. Silents were impacted by the Great Depression; two wars (World War II and the Korean War); the New Deal; the Golden Age of Radio and Silver Screen; and the postwar rise of labor unions. Silents share a set of core values, including a strong work ethic, a sense of conformity, respect for authority, and putting duty before pleasure. If your parents or grandparents are Silents, you know that they tend to be savers, they often reminisce about the good old days, and, as one author put it, "They believe in logic, not in magic." Consider Selma Lyon, the Lyon family matriarch. Selma was born in the 1920s, which places her on the cusp of the Silent Generation and the G.I. Generation (people born between 1901 and 1924). Like others in her peer group, Selma lived through the Great Depression and World War II. Selma has been described as a traditionalist who shared the same core values as those of her peer group, including a sturdy work ethic, frugality, stoicism, conscientiousness, and family dedication.

Second, Silents' children are the not-so-silent *Baby Boomers*, often simply called *Boomers*. Boomers (people born between 1946 and 1964) represent about 27 percent, or 84 million, of the U.S. population, according to 2010 census data. If you're a member of this cohort, you were probably a teenager when hippie music was popular; Flower Children tiptoed through the tulips; birth control pills were distributed as widely as Milk Duds; and student protests against the Vietnam War reached a fever pitch. Nearly all Boomers remember where they were and what they were doing the day that President John F. Kennedy was shot in 1963. The oldest Boomers became senior citizens in 2011. Incidentally, in the United States, if you're more than 60 years of age, you're usually considered a senior citizen. Three living presidents, Bill Clinton, George W. Bush, and Barack Obama, are Boomers. Boomers' core values include optimism, an esprit de corps, a desire to stay young, a need for instant gratification, a sense of personal achievement, and an urge to "go the extra mile."

Third, Boomers started their own families but not in the same numbers as their parents. Boomers' children are known as the *Generation X (Gen Xers)*. Gen Xers (people born between 1965 and 1981) make up roughly 21 percent, or 68 million, of the U.S. population, according to 2010 census data. Gen Xers have lived through one of the worst times in modern history mainly because of stagflation, the Stock Market Crash of 1987, the Challenger disaster, and Operation Desert Storm. As a result of higher divorce rates, many Gen Xers were raised by single parents and were often left home alone to fend for themselves—hence, the term "latchkey kids."

Gen Xers' core values include social consciousness, a concern for the environment, self-reliance, and finding joy in the simple things.

Fourth, the demographic cohort that followed Generation X is *Generation Y*, also called the *Millennials*. Generation Y (people born between 1982 and 2000) make up about 25 percent, or 79 million, of the U.S. population, according to 2010 census data. Generation Y came of age during the economic boom of the 1990s and also during a period of civic unrest marked by school violence and the Oklahoma City bombing. They are tech-savvy, embrace girl power, and have adopted multiculturalism. Their core values include confidence, a sense of civic duty, a need for achievement, and collectivism. According to one source, Millennials are "both optimistic about the future and realistic about the present."

Fifth, the new big kid on the block is *Generation Z*, whose birth years are subject to debate. Some authors suggest that Generation Z, also called *Gen Zers*, came on the scene somewhere between the mid to late 1990s, and thus overlap with Generation Y, and the mid-2000s to 2010, with an estimated population of 23 million and rising rapidly. Gen Zers' lives have been shaped by social media, the Great Recession of 2008-09, terrorism, environmental concerns, and technology. This generation is "constantly multitasking" and stays "actively connected," toggling from one digital device to the next, from smartphones to video game consoles and tablets to laptops. In fact, an astonishing 100 percent of Gen Zers are digitally connected (checking e-mail, texts, tweets, etcetera) for one hour or more per day, and about one half (46 percent) are connected 10 hours or longer per day, according to a survey conducted by Wikia. Tech savvy and globally connected, Gen Zers are flexible thinkers who are "tolerant of diverse cultures." According to one source, using IQ scores as a measure, Gen Zers are smarter than previous generations.

But wait, the story of generational cohorts continues to evolve. The rise of *Generation Alpha* is in its infancy—literally, as this cohort is composed of babies born from 2010 onwards. About 11.9 million births occurred between 2010 and 2012, according to birth data furnished by the Centers for Disease Control and Prevention (CDC).

Generation Alpha's history is just being written. The prognosis is that Generation Alpha will be more tech savvy, better educated, and more materialistic, as compared to previous generations.

Now let's become better acquainted with the Silent Generation.

Meet the Silents

In an article that appeared in *The Washington Post*, Neil Howe and William Strauss wrote that one of the historic nonevents for the Silent Generation was the lack of a president to be elected to the Oval Office. The authors argue that the Silent Generation came of age "too late to be a World War II hero and just too early to be a Vietnam-era student radical...have never been able to shake their Joe McCarthy-era label, invented to describe an elder-pleasing conformism...[and] are well on their way to becoming the first American generation never to produce a president." To support the authors' contention, George H.W. Bush was born in 1924, a year before the Silent Generation began, while Bill Clinton and George W. Bush were both born in 1946, the year after the Silent Generation ended.

But that hasn't stopped Silents from becoming wingmen to U.S. presidents, such as vice presidents Walter Mondale and Joe Biden, and first ladies, such as Jacqueline Kennedy, Rosalynn Carter, and Barbara Bush. In addition, this generation has had its fair share of movers and shakers. Consider the "Oracle of Omaha" Warren Buffet, one of America's richest businessmen and world's savviest investors; Michael Bloomberg, New York City's former mayor; George Soros, hedge fund legend; and Jacqueline Mars, a third-generation candy heiress.

Although Silents may not have moved mountains, like the Prudential Rock, they have inspired strength and security. According to Strauss and Howe:

> "Having come of age amid stultifying conformism,
> the Silents have spent a lifetime adding complexity to

6

a world they found over-simple, diversity to a culture they found monochromatic and openness to an elder establishment they consider too closed. These traits have made theirs the kindest generation of the 20th century."

Next, let's explore the demographics of aging.

Demographics of Aging

One good way to study generational cohorts is through *demographic trends*. *Demography* is the study of human populations in terms of age, income, household size, occupation, ethnicity, gender, education, and so on. Let's explore the demographics of aging.

- *Seniors are a growing population.* Probably one of the biggest demographic shifts is an aging of the U.S. population. According to the U.S. Census Bureau, the U.S. median age is the highest ever, rising from 35.3 years in 2000 to 37.1 years in 2012. According to the Administration on Aging (AoA), in 2009, people aged 65 years and older totaled 39.6 million, or 12.9 percent of the U.S. population. By 2030 that figure is expected to rise to 72.1 million older Americans, or 19 percent of the population.
- *Many seniors are well-off, while many are barely getting by.* Seniors are a commanding consumer market, representing $2.3 trillion in disposable income. According to the U.S. Census Bureau, households led by persons 65 and older reported a median income of $48,538 in 2011. According to the results from Gallup's Economy and Personal Finance survey conducted in April 2013, the major sources of income for retirees are Social Security (61 percent); pension plans (36 percent); 401(k)s, IRAs, or other retirement savings accounts (23 percent); and home equity (20 percent). Take Selma Lyon,

who was an older retiree. Selma's income was over double that of the median income for most seniors. She reportedly received income from a combination of sources, including a state pension, money market securities, Social Security benefits, investment property, and other sources. While many seniors like Selma are financially healthy, others are not. Almost 3.5 million elderly persons (8.7 percent) lived below the poverty level in 2010. According to the U.S. Census Bureau, in 2011, the poverty threshold for elderly individuals aged 65 years and over was $10,788.

- *Seniors are on the move.* Seniors tend to migrate to states with mild climates. For example, snowbirds from the Northeast often flock to places like Florida. States with a high concentration of seniors include California, Florida, and Texas.

- *Seniors are a diverse population.* Minorities will comprise 42 percent of the 65 and older population by 2050, more than doubling from the current proportion (21 percent), according to a Census Bureau report. By 2050 one third (33 percent) of the population aged 85 and older will be minorities.

- *Senior women take the cake.* According to the Administration on Aging, in 2010, senior women outnumbered senior men (23.0 million older women versus 17.5 million older men). This translates into a gender ratio of 132 women for every 100 men.

- *Seniors have the force with them.* Seniors who reach age 65 have an average life expectancy of an additional 18.8 years, with 20 years for females and 17.3 years for males, according to the Administration on Aging. Today, women outlive men (80.51 years versus 75.35 years). For instance, Selma's husband died in his 70s, while Selma lived past 90 years of age. In 2010, 53,364 persons aged 100 and older were living, a 53 percent increase from 1990.

- *Seniors are marriage material.* More older men are married than older women (72 percent of older men versus 42 percent

8

of older women). A key reason for the lower marriage rates among older women is that women live longer than men. In fact, 40 percent of older women were widows in 2010.

- *Seniors are home alone.* Older persons living alone in a domestic setting accounted for about 29 percent of the older population, or 11.3 million, with more women living alone than men (8.1 million women versus 3.2 million men). Nearly half of all older women (47 percent) aged 75 and older live alone.

Next, let's study how older consumers behave in the marketplace and how businesses are courting them.

The Mature Market

Today's so-called "mature market" flouts conventional stereotypes. After all, the image of a frail, grumpy elder is passé. For instance, take a look at pharmaceutical advertisements aimed at the mature market. While the ads focus on common ailments related to aging, such as arthritis, the people shown in the ads are vital, active, and engaged.

Let's face it, age is just a number. In fact, 60 percent of adults aged 65 and over said they feel younger than their actual age, and 78 percent said that they don't "feel old," according to a Pew Research Center Social & Demographic Trends survey. In marketing terms, these findings suggest that businesses should reformulate their marketing strategies to attract older consumers. Some companies are doing just that. For instance, in Ameriprise Financial's "Dreams Don't Retire" commercial, actor Dennis Hopper (himself a Silent) dispels conventional attitudes toward retirement. In the ad, Hopper says, "Your generation is definitely not headed for Bingo night." The ad then talks about the Ameriprise Dream Book that offers a financial strategy to make retirement dreams come true.

To avoid ageism in marketing, then, companies should consider *cognitive age* and not chronological age in the development of their marketing strategies. Cognitive age, also called *subjective age*, is the age that you feel. Consider the American Association of Retired Persons (AARP). If you've turned 50, the AARP has probably already sent you a direct mail package aimed at getting you to join. The organization tries to appeal to a wide audience, which presents an interesting challenge: communication messages intended for 50-somethings won't resonate with 80-somethings and vice versa. So the AARP developed ads that feature older adults at various life stages and that explain how the AARP's lifestyle-oriented information and services fit into their lives.

Another way to avoid ageism in marketing is to address *consumer lifestyles*. A *lifestyle* reflects how you spend your time and money. One fun example is the Taco Bell Super Bowl commercial, "Viva Young." In the ad, a pack of rebellious elders sneaks out of their retirement home to experience a night out on the town. They play pranks, go clubbing, make out, get tattooed, and, of course, stop for Taco Bell.

Having said all that, a stereotype that won't ever change is that of being a grandparent. According to Grandparents.com, grandparents are a growing market, now standing at 69.6 million. That figure is expected to climb by another 11 percent by 2015. According to research done by The Nielsen Company, grandparent households spend 4.4 percent more per year than all other households, or $300 per year, on purchases for grandchildren. Health insurer Humana developed an advertising campaign, "Relationships and Screenings," that displays the special relationship between grandparents and their grandchildren. In the ads, Humana encourages grandparents to stay healthy through annual checkups and screenings.

Finally, businesses must keep in mind that older consumers tend to be cautious spenders due in part to their Depression-era mentality. As a result, these consumers don't easily part with their money. So marketing strategies should *stress superior customer value* to get seniors to open their wallets.

Public Perceptions and Attitudes Toward Aging

When does old age start? At age 68, according to one survey. When people say age is relative, they're right! According to research conducted by the Pew Research Center, people under 30 believe that old age strikes before the average person turns 60, but only 6 percent of adults aged 65 or older agree with them. In addition, gender made a difference in the findings. On average, women said that a person becomes old at age 70, whereas men said that the magic number is closer to 66 years of age. Let's take a closer look at what it means to age in America.

Princeton University researchers have explored the graying of the population as well as intergenerational tensions in the United States. In seeking explanations for ageism, or age discrimination, the researchers examined *prescriptive ageist prejudices*, which are beliefs about how older adults differ from others. For example, when older adults do not conform to these beliefs, they are punished by people who discriminate against them. The researchers explain that prescriptive stereotypes are rooted in three main issues:

> *Succession*—the notion that older adults should get out of the way and make room for younger people. The thought is that seniors should relinquish well-paying jobs and key social roles to give way to younger people.
>
> *Identity*—the opinion that older people should act their age and not try to act younger than their age.
>
> *Consumption*—the belief that seniors should not consume scarce resources like health care.

A surprising finding on ageism is that it can physically injure the elderly. One study found that older people who held negative stereotypes toward aging were far more likely to experience heart attacks or strokes (25 percent), as compared to people who did not share these views (13 percent). A few explanations are given for this phenomenon. First, negative expectations can become "self-fulfilling prophecies." In other words, when an elder believes that older people are vital and vibrant, he or she is more apt to take care of him- or herself. In contrast, when an elder believes that aging equates to sickness and infirmity, he or she may subconsciously become sick and infirm. Second, genetics may play a role in people's perceptions of aging. For example, people who witnessed their parents age gracefully may have inherited good genes and also developed healthy attitudes and habits.

According to an NBC News report, whether ageism will become better or worse as more Boomers hit old age is unclear. To highlight that aging doesn't mean crippling old age, the report shared the story of a 74-year-old Duke University professor who has written several books on aging. The professor says, "One can say unequivocally that older people are getting smarter, richer and healthier as time goes on." The professor is living proof that aging doesn't mean sitting in a rocking chair on a porch; he skydives, whitewater rafts, cycles, and gets tattoos. "What makes me mad is how aging, in our language and culture, is equated with deterioration and impairment. I don't know how we're going to root that out, except by making people more aware of it," says the professor.

A discussion on aging isn't complete without a conversation on *age discrimination*. In 2012, 22,857 age discrimination complaints were filed, according to the U.S. Equal Employment Opportunity Commission. We probably all know someone age 50 or older who was put to pasture through forced retirement. Over 20 percent of American workers are subjected to forced retirement due to layoffs, cutbacks, and shutdowns at any given time, according to a Sun Life Financial study.

In addition to ageism in the workplace, prejudice against the elderly appears in the health care system. The elderly tend to receive less preventive care than other populations. According to an Alliance for Aging Research report, the elderly often aren't given access to doctors who are trained in serving elders' particular needs. This is largely because only about 10 percent of U.S. medical education requires training in geriatric medicine. In fact, only about 7,600 physicians nationwide are certified as geriatric specialists, which is well below the 36,000 geriatrists that society will need by 2030, according to the American Geriatrics Society.

The frontiers of aging are not all gloom and doom. After all, 60 is the new 40! Take a look at older female role models: plucky actress, director, producer, and screenwriter Diane Keaton; age-defying celebrity and former fitness guru Jane Fonda; actress and activist Susan Sarandon; and iconic international beauty Sophia Loren. According to a columnist for *The Seattle Times*, Liz Taylor, "most of us age accidentally." Taylor recommends that we embrace aging. She also thinks we should drop euphemisms for aging, such as "old," "seniors," "elders," and "older." She adds that Boomers, many of whom are now seniors, do not respond well to these terms. Some organizations have figured that out. For example, many senior centers are now called "community centers."

Seniors' Top Concerns

If you're an older American who is concerned about being able to afford and getting adequate health care; maintaining your health and mobility; sustaining social interactions; and remaining independent, you're not alone. In a survey conducted by Senior Journal.com, seniors said their chief concerns are:

- Keeping up with health care news (80 percent)
- Maintaining health and well-being (69 percent)
- Developing Alzheimer's disease (22 percent)
- Maintaining mobility (62 percent)
- Being able to afford prescription drugs (55 percent)
- Preserving spiritual well-being (58 percent)
- Achieving peace before death (45 percent)

- Receiving adequate care in old age (56 percent)
- Managing personal finances (52 percent)
- Maintaining social relationships (48 percent)
- Dealing with depression (32 percent)
- Dealing with loneliness (31 percent)

In another survey, the majority of seniors 65 and older (74 percent) said "staying physically active is a major challenge," according to Home Instead Senior Care Network. Seniors also feared these situations:

- Loss of independence
- Failing health
- Running out of money
- Not being able to remain at home
- Death of a spouse or another family member
- Not being able to take care of basic needs
- Not being able to drive
- Becoming isolated or lonely
- Relying on strangers for care
- Falling or getting hurt

Selma's fears included the above-mentioned concerns. According to Selma's relatives, Selma was worried that she would be unable to take care of herself, which would make her dependent on others for her care. She was also afraid of losing her independence. But her greatest fear was being involuntarily placed in an institutional setting like a nursing home. Thus Selma insisted on remaining in her home where she had lived for over a half century, no matter what.

Other study findings reveal that many seniors fear not being able to pay basic living expenses, a fear that seems to be justified. Over 9 million older Americans can't pay their bills, according to a study conducted by Wider Opportunities for Women. For example, many seniors say that they can't always afford to see a doctor or buy prescribed medications. About one in five people over age 50 said that they had to switch to cheaper medications or pass on costly medications, as well as skip doctor's appointments.

Let's take a moment to discuss seniors' medical concerns. According to the Centers for Disease Control and Prevention (CDC), the top elderly issues and conditions are as follows:

- *Heart disease*, which is the number one cause of death among the elderly
- *Strokes*, which are the third leading cause of death among the elderly
- *Alzheimer's disease*, which is a key cause of death among the elderly
- *Renal disease*, which is the fifth leading cause of death among the elderly
- *Infectious disease*, such as the flu and pneumonia, which is a key health problem for the elderly
- *Diabetes*, which is another leading cause of death among the elderly
- *Accidents and injuries*, which are serious problems for the elderly
- Other chronic illnesses, such as asthma, emphysema, arthritis, and ulcers, which are frequently present in the elderly population

For instance, according to Selma's brother, Selma, who had been extremely healthy during her adulthood, battled several medical conditions during her elderhood. These included hypertension, stroke, dementia, congestive heart failure, diabetes, and arthritis, among other things.

Finally, many seniors are worried that they won't get adequate help at home. According to a survey conducted by the National Council on Aging (NCOA), United Healthcare, and *USA Today*, at least 13 percent of seniors age 70 and over need assistance with their activities of daily living.

Seniors' Future Challenges

Older Americans are of two minds about the future. On one hand, "they are confident they will be able to maintain their health and think they manage stress effectively," according to a survey performed by the National Council on Aging (NCOA), medical insurer United Healthcare, and the newspaper *USA Today*. On the other hand, nearly half of low- and middle-income seniors don't know how they'll make ends meet in the next five to ten years. Other survey findings include:

- About a third of older Americans aren't able to afford long-term care.
- One in five seniors would be fiscally toppled by one major financial event.
- Lower-income seniors are more likely to suffer from chronic illnesses and less likely to exercise.
- Seventy-two percent of seniors live with a lingering health problem.
- Nearly 20 percent of seniors over 65 continue to work either full- or part-time.
- Over 25 percent of seniors don't know how to access community resources and facilities to help them live independently.

Now let's look at new and continuing developments on the horizon that will affect older Americans. Based on a report published by the Federal Interagency Forum on Aging-Related Statistics, here's what's coming down the pike.

- *Here Comes the Boom.* The arrival of the "silver tsunami" (aging Boomers) will change the demographics of aging forever. The fresh infusion of older Americans will be more racially diverse and better educated than past generations of seniors.
- *A Rising Tide Does Not Lift All Boats.* Most older Americans are benefiting from greater prosperity than their predecessors, with

a sharp increase in the number of high-net-worth households. On average, net worth has risen by an astronomical 80 percent for older Americans over the past 20 years. However, elders with limited education and African-American elders continue to struggle under economic inequality.

- *Live Long and Prosper.* The good news is that Americans are living longer. The not-so-good news is that old age increases the risk of getting certain age-associated diseases and disorders, such as arthritis, cardiovascular disease, cancer, hypertension, and Alzheimer's disease.

- *The Economics of Aging.* Seniors continue to pay more for health care. According to a Journal of General Internal Medicine report, over 75 percent of Medicare-eligible households are $10,000 out of pocket for health care.

- *Diversity Is the Spice of Life.* One of the fastest-growing segments of the American population is Hispanics. By 2050 the older population will be composed of 59 percent non-Hispanic whites, 20 percent Hispanics, 12 percent blacks, and 9 percent Asians, according to population projections.

- *The Politics of Aging.* Pundits say that every elder should be prepared for four major "aging shocks": prescription drugs that won't be covered by Medicare or private insurance; medical care that won't be paid by Medicare or private insurance; private insurance costs that won't be affordable; and long-term care costs that won't be affordable.

- *The Dynamics of Dependency.* The percentage of elderly older than 85 years who are unable to take care of their basic needs due to impairments or because of institutionalization is more than six times the rate of 65- to 74-year-olds. For example, as Selma's dementia progressed and her dependent care needs increased, Selma's worst fear became a reality: she was institutionalized in a locked Alzheimer's and dementia care facility for a time. Over the period from 2000 through 2005, there was a 9 percent increase in the number of noninstitutionalized people aged 65 and older who said that they have trouble taking care of their basic needs, such as bathing and dressing, according to a *U.S. News and World Report.*

- *A Beautiful Mind.* The new crop of seniors is twice as likely to have graduated from college than the previous generation, according to the U.S. Department of Education. Interestingly, there's a link between educational attainment and disability rates. The disability rate for college graduates is about half of that of high school dropouts.

- *The Bionic Woman and Man.* Seniors benefit from advancements in medicine and medical technology, such as joint replacement surgery and heart surgery, which allow them to lead healthier, longer lives. Improvements in pharmaceuticals, such as antibody targeted drugs as cancer therapeutics, treat as well as prevent chronic age-related illnesses, such as osteoporosis and arthritis. Improvements in treating dementia lessen the need for intensive long-term care of the elderly.

- *Let's Get Social.* According to researchers, mortality rates are dramatically lower with higher levels of social interaction. Also, good social connections help to improve mood and memory. People with poor social interactions are twice as likely to experience cognitive decline, as compared to people with five or more social bonds, according to one study. Sadly, many elders are isolated and alone. Twenty percent of the elderly are socially isolated to the point that their health is in danger, according to a General Social Survey.

Increasingly, the elderly are taking to the Internet to maintain their social interactions. Let's take a moment to look at older adults' online activity. According to a report published by Pew Internet and American Life Project, in 2012, 53 percent of American adults age 65 and older used the Internet. Seniors' most popular online activity is e-mailing. In 2011, 86 percent of Internet users age 65 and older used e-mail, and nearly half (48 percent) e-mailed daily. Moreover, cell phone ownership among seniors has grown. About 69 percent of adults age 65 and older said that they own a cell phone, an increase from 57 percent during 2010.

What are seniors' surfing activities? According to research done by Nielsen Norman Group, seniors mostly do the following online tasks:

- Look up health information
- Book travel arrangements
- Perform hobbies and interests
- Get the news
- Check financial information
- Socialize

Finally, let's glance at social media use among older adults, such as the use of blogs and online social networks like Facebook and Twitter. Take social networking. Among Internet users aged 65 and older, social networking site use grew by a whopping 150 percent, from 13 percent in 2009 to 33 percent in 2011, according to the Pew Internet and American Life Project. During early 2012, 34 percent of Internet users ages 65 and older visited social networking sites, such as Facebook, as compared to only 18 percent who logged on in 2009. Also, Twitter use is up among seniors. One in ten Internet users ages 65 and older uses Twitter or another microsite to share and check updates.

In the next chapter, we'll learn more about the Baby Boom Generation. We'll also focus on the complexities of Boomers' lives as they frequently juggle work and family, while also caring for their elderly parents or relatives. Finally, we'll peer behind the locked doors of the Lyon home.

CHAPTER 2

The Age of Aquarius

What do Michael Jordan, David Letterman, John Grisham, Meg Whitman, Steven Spielberg, Hillary Rodham Clinton, and Madonna have in common? They're all Baby Boomers—and they have lots of company. Baby Boomers are 84 million strong in the U.S. alone. The oldest Boomers are already senior citizens, and the youngest Boomers are or will soon be receiving their AARP applications in the mail. In fact, an American turns 50 every seven seconds!

Baby Boomers are redefining what it means to get old. Baby Boomers lead more active lifestyles, work longer, live longer, enjoy better health, and earn more than past generations of seniors. But refrain from calling Boomers "middle-aged." Rather, they see themselves as being in their "mid-youth," which partly explains their passion for youth-enhancing products and procedures. For example, the quest to find the fountain (or syringe) of youth has fueled face-freezing Botox's business. Botox injections are the top-ranked noninvasive cosmetic procedure, with 6.1 million Botox procedures performed in 2012 within the U.S., especially among older female Boomers. Thanks to Boomers' desire to stay young, industry growth is expected to plump up to $114 billion by 2015, a sales lift of roughly 50 percent.

In this chapter, we'll study Baby Boomers as a generational cohort. Also, we'll examine the aging of the Baby Boom generation by discussing key social and demographic trends. Finally, we'll talk about the future challenges that Boomers will face as they straddle the cusp of their Golden Years.

Meet the Boomers

If you came of age during the early 1950s through the late 1970s, you're a Baby Boomer. Let's travel down memory lane to see how far Boomers have come.

> *<u>The Fabulous Fifties</u>*. Do you remember the TV variety program *The Ed Sullivan Show*? If you're an older Boomer, you might remember Elvis's guest appearances on *The Ed Sullivan Show* in 1956 and 1957. During Elvis's first appearance, the network refused to shoot Elvis below the waist because of Elvis's famous pelvic gyrations. In a later broadcast, the cameras widened to show Elvis's moves, which by today's standards would be considered tame. In America, the 1950s was a period of unflagging optimism and economic robustness, following the dark days of the Great Depression and World War II. During this time, older Boomers were youngsters and tweeners, most of whom were raised with traditional family values "as American as apple pie" and lived in family suburban homes with the proverbial white picket fence. As kids, these Boomers frequently congregated at a local soda fountain often housed in a drugstore like Walgreens. Going to the drive-in theater was a popular family pastime. The admission price was about one dollar per car, and popcorn sold for only 25 cents. Moreover, Boomer kids were transfixed by popular television programs of the day, such as *Adventures of Superman, I Love Lucy, Leave It*

21

to Beaver, and *The Lone Ranger*, which they watched on black-and-white TVs.

The Cynical Sixties. You probably remember the 1967 movie *The Graduate* that captured Boomers' zeitgeist of the time. In it, Dustin Hoffman played Ben, a rudderless college graduate. At Ben's graduation party, Mr. McGuire, a buttoned-down, middle-aged family friend, advises Ben on his future. Mr. McGuire said, "I just want to say one word to you. Just one word. 'Plastics.'" "Plastics" was a trigger word for Ben and Boomers like him: it spoke to the "phoniness" in American society. Many Boomers felt the same way as Ben did. Moreover, "selling out" to the military-industrial complex, a broad term to include corporations and institutions that supported America's war machine, was not a future many Boomers could easily stomach. As teenagers and young adults, Boomers lived through such pivotal events as the Vietnam War and political protests against the war; John F. Kennedy's, Robert Kennedy's, and Martin Luther King's assassinations; the civil rights movement; and counterculture events like the Summer of Love and Woodstock.

The Swinging Seventies. As the "Me" generation, a term coined by author Tom Wolfe, Boomers wanted to make something of their lives and not just do something with them. So many Boomers set high expectations and strove to exploit their full potential. Rule-defying Boomers sought instant gratification through experimentation and exploration (think sex, drugs, rock & roll, and disco!). During this period, Boomer women burned their bras as a symbolic gesture in support for the women's liberation movement; the gay rights movement picked up steam; and a debate over women's reproductive rights ignited. Many Boomers shunned conventionality; as one author put it, "Individuality was lionized and conformity was eschewed."

The Aching Eighties. The combined effects of mass layoffs, a deep recession, high federal budget deficits, and a swelling of the national debt profoundly affected the economic well-being of Baby Boomers. By the mid-1980s, many struggling Boomers were cutting corners and economizing. At the same time affluent Boomers were driving the sales of luxury products and services. Moreover, the 1980s was a period of technological innovation as the first personal computer was introduced by IBM in 1981. Also, social and behavior change was afoot as a widespread response to the HIV/AIDS epidemic.

The Roaring Nineties. The economy started out wobbly but quickly picked up steam, resulting in the longest running economic expansion in American history. However, this was a jobless recovery, so not all Boomers were rejoicing and benefiting from the turnaround. By now, most Boomers had entered the workforce, and many Boomer households were led by dual-earner couples. With mounting demands on their time, many Boomers yearned for a better work-life balance. At the same time the effects of the Gulf War led to a war-induced spike in gas prices, as well as triggered or exacerbated the American recession.

The Terrible Two Thousands. Boomers were greatly affected by a globalization of the labor market, which led to diminished expectations as structural unemployment rose. In 2008 the foreclosure crisis and the financial market meltdown dealt Boomers a double whammy. During this time, more and more Baby Boomers embraced digital media, making the Internet their outpost for working, shopping, buying, dating, sharing, and learning. While the millennium is still being written, today's Baby Boomers are adjusting to an age of austerity and resetting their future priorities.

Next, let's look at demographic trends that are the shaping of things to come for this generation.

Boomer Demographics

If "demographics is destiny," Baby Boomers are certainly destined to bring about big demographic changes. Let's take a closer look at the size and composition of the Baby Boomer population.

- Baby Boomers compose 35 percent of the U.S. adult population, according to Scarborough Research.
- By 2015 people aged 50 and older will make up 45 percent of the U.S. population, according to the AARP.
- Boomers are the highest earners, with a median household income of $54,170, according to Harris Poll BoomerQuery. Baby Boomers' median household income was 55 percent greater than previous generations, with an average annual disposable income of $24,000, according to a U.S. Government Consumer Expenditure survey.
- By 2030 the population aged 65 and over will double to nearly 72.1 million, more than twice the number in 2000, according to the Administration on Aging.

- Baby Boomers control 67 percent of America's wealth, about $28 trillion, according to the U.S. Census Bureau and the Federal Reserve.
- Baby Boomers outspend the average consumer in almost every product category, including dining out, furniture, entertainment, personal care, and so on, according to a U.S. Government Consumer Expenditure survey. Baby Boomers outspent other generations by an annual $400 billion on consumer goods and services.
- Eighty percent of Boomers own their own homes, according to a Pew Research study.
- Boomers are the best educated of any group before it, with 28.5 percent holding a bachelor's degree or higher and 45 million boasting some college, according to ACNielsen.
- Sixty-five percent of elementary and high school students have Baby-Boom parents, according to ACNielsen.
- Forty percent of people age 50 and over control 79 percent of all financial assets, according to the AARP.

Next, let's take a look at key Baby Boomer trends.

Baby Boomer Trends

Keeping up with shifts in Baby Boomers' tastes and preferences is tricky, given the sheer size and diversity of this segment. Take Levi Strauss. The company has had Baby Boomers in its back pocket since the 1960s. When bell bottoms lost their appeal and traditional jeans became popular, Levi's innovated a slew of new styles. For example, Levi's launched the Dockers sub-brand, aimed directly at Boomer men's expanding waistlines. The Dockers slack was more structured than casual jeans but still relaxed enough to be comfortable. Let's take a glance at Baby Boomer buying trends.

- *Boomers are the darlings of consumer marketing.* In 2010 Baby Boomers accounted for roughly 38.5 percent of all dollars spent on nondurables like soap, toothpaste, and other consumer packaged goods, according to a Nielsen study. On the tech front, Boomers are wired: they represent 40 percent of customers paying for wireless services, 36 percent of smartphone ownership, and 41 percent of customers buying Apple computers. Also, many Baby Boomers are either reinvesting or investing for the first time in their education. One academic institution that caters to new and returning older students is the University of Phoenix. Its "Let's Get to Work" campaign addresses the educational needs of a growing number of older students who are retooling for the workforce, many of whom are Baby Boomers trying to launch new careers. In fact, the number of college students aged 40 to 64 has risen by roughly 20 percent to about two million over the past decade, according to a *U.S. News and World Report* survey.

- *Boomers just do it.* Boomers are a generation of doers. On average, Baby Boomers are 6 percent more likely to participate in a sports or fitness activity, as compared to other groups. People aged 55 and older now represent nearly 25 percent of all health club members, according to an International Health, Racquet & Sportsclub Association *(IHRSA)*. Many gym and health clubs are gearing up for this age group by adding service offerings that cater to its age-related needs, such as water aerobics and low-impact exercise classes, and by making their facilities senior-friendly.

- *Boomers are big on brands.* Boomers tend to be highly brand conscious. Boomer brands include Harley-Davidson, Volkswagen, Noxzema, the Beatles, Pepsi, Absolut Vodka, Saturday Night Live, Facebook, Coach, Levi's, Club Med, L'eggs, Frye Boots, and Clairol. Take Clairol, a Procter & Gamble beauty and grooming brand. The company introduced Clairol Revitalique, a hair care system targeted at Baby Boomer women. According to *AdWeek*, Revitalique is positioned as the "world's first anti-aging hair colorant."

- *Boomers want value.* Boomers want the most bang for their buck and go after value-added products and services that pile on the "extras" without costing extra. For example, fast-food restaurants have created value menus that include a cluster of inexpensive menu items. Consider Pizza Hut. Pizza Hut's clever "Price From the Past" commercial features a new "hand-tossed style" pizza pie for only $10.

- *Boomers are in the know.* Boomers crave information. They pay attention to ads about products and services and go online to find out more about those products and services. For example, 57 percent of Boomers searched online for an item they saw on television, according to Google. Also, Boomers were more likely to click on online ads than younger generations (76 percent versus 58 percent), according to Crowd Science.

- *Boomers take stock.* Many retiring Boomers prefer to handle their own money and investments, according to a *U.S. News and World Report*. To facilitate direct investing, money managers have created products and services, from annuities to asset management. For example, E*TRADE is an online discount stock brokerage service for self-directed investors. You've probably seen the cute E*TRADE baby ads, which trumpet the ease with which an average investor can manage his or her investment account by using E*TRADE; i.e., even a baby can master it.

- *Boomers are homebodies.* Many Boomers are upgrading their homes, downsizing, buying vacation homes, and purchasing investment properties, according to a Coldwell Banker Real Estate survey. To encourage Boomers to look for real estate online, the real estate website Zillow ran a commercial that showed how a home was a metaphor for a consumer's life: "You're not just looking for a house. You're looking for a place for your life to happen."

- *Boomers are nostalgic.* According to the *AdWeek* article "Seven Brands That Are Winning With Nostalgia: Living in the past isn't such a bad thing," big-brand marketers are using nostalgia marketing to grab Boomers' attention. Take Jack Daniel's. The whiskey became cool when the company launched its special edition to mark Frank Sinatra's 100th birthday. Jack Daniel's "Legend" campaign uses nostalgia to strike a chord with Boomers, with sales rising 27 percent during the campaign period.

- *Boomers do-it-for-me.* Today's Boomers buy products and services that make home life easier. For example, do-it-yourself (DIY) Boomers who once handled their own home repairs and renovations are now letting someone else do it, giving rise to the do-it-for-me market. Home improvement centers like Home Depot and Lowe's Home Improvement are offering services to cater to this new market. For instance, Atlanta-based Home Depot has added a range of installation and painting services to its repertoire.

- *Boomers are kings of the road.* While many Baby Boomers are or will be retiring soon, that doesn't mean that they plan to give up their car keys anytime soon. In fact, Baby Boomers purchase 62.5 percent of all new cars, according to Forrester Research. Auto industry experts expect that Baby Boomers will trade in their company sedans and commuter cars for a wide range of vehicles, from crossover utility vehicles to sports and muscle cars to hybrids. According to CNW Marketing Research, the bestsellers among Boomers include Jaguar, Mercedes-Benz, Cadillac, Acura, Toyota, Audi, Lexus, and Buick, but "not your grandfather's Buick!"

- *Boomers are travel buffs.* According to *Travel Marketing Decisions*, the official publication of the Association of Travel Marketing Executives, Boomers view travel as a necessity and not a luxury. Baby Boomers account for 80 percent of U.S. leisure travel spending, according to the Pew Internet and American Life Project. In the U.S., favorite Boomer destinations include Orlando, Las Vegas, San Francisco, New York, Los Angeles, Seattle, Honolulu, and San Diego. Internationally, Boomers' top luxury travel destinations include Italy, Japan, Turkey, Morocco, India, and Burma.

- *Boomers are what they eat.* While most Boomers will never give up their In-N-Out burgers, many Boomers are eating healthier and smarter, opting for foods that are good for the brain and the body. For example, cereal maker Kellogg Company has created new cereal varieties to cater to Boomers' growing health needs, such as Kashi Heart to Heart Nutty Chia Flax, Raisin Bran Omega-3, and Special K Multigrain. Moreover, several food manufacturers are making changes in food packaging to accommodate older Boomers. For instance, Diamond Foods engineered easy-to-open packaging for its Emerald snack nut line in response to aging Boomers reduced hand agility.

- *Boomers get personal.* Boomers spend money on many different personal care products, from cotton pads to deodorants, and from denture cleaners to adult diapers. Consider adult diapers. Kimberly-Clark Corporation makes the Depend diaper brand. You may have seen the Depend undergarment ad that shows "Dancing With the Stars" professional ballroom dancer Cheryl Burke and her partner spin and swirl around a dance floor. Beneath her sparkly dress, Cheryl discreetly wears a Depend diaper. The ad says, "Looks and fits like underwear. Protects like nothing else."

- *Boomers get back into the dating game.* About one third (31.3 percent) of adults aged 50 to 64 are widowed, divorced, or never married, according to U.S. Census data. As a result, Baby Boomers are a key target for the $2.1 billion dollar dating services industry. Online dating services are particularly popular among "silver surfers." For example, Our Time is the largest dating website catering to lonely heart Boomers, where "older singles connect for love and companionship."

- *Boomers shop online.* Baby Boomers have wholeheartedly embraced e-commerce. In fact, Boomers bought more products online than younger adults at a 2-to-1 per-capita ratio. According to Forrester Research, 72 percent of older Boomers shop online, while two thirds of Baby Boomers and other older adults bought from online businesses, representing $7 billion in sales, according to a Pew Research Center and SeniorNet. Several online businesses have Boomers on their radar. For example, powerhouse Amazon.com recently launched its 50+ Active and Healthy Living Store, a one-stop shop that offers hundreds of products aimed at seniors' "healthy living needs."

- *Boomers are sharers.* Boomers are big consumers of social media. According to a Pew Internet study, use of social networking sites among Baby Boomers grew 88 percent between 2009 and 2010 to 47 percent. According to the Pew Research Center's Internet & American Life Project, the number of people aged 65 and older who use social networking sites has nearly tripled, from 13 percent during 2009 to 43 percent during 2013. Interestingly, Boomers who care for their aging parents are the heaviest users of social media, as compared to other Boomers, according to comScore. These family caregivers use social media for 150 minutes per month and view 70 percent more pages than the average Internet user.

- *Boomers are entering their Golden Years.* Baby Boomers are reshaping retirement living. Many Baby Boomers don't see themselves living in assisted-living facilities but instead in high-end senior communities. Consequently, many developers are building independent living communities that are ultramodern and include the latest amenities and services, such as fitness centers, hair salons, and even grocery markets.

Next, let's find out why Baby Boomers are called the "Threshold Generation."

The Threshold Generation

If you're a Baby Boomer who feels as if you're stuck at the threshold of retirement but can't quite cross it, welcome to the "Threshold Generation," a term dubbed by The Pew Research Center. Let's learn more about thresholders.

- *Boomers delay their Sunset Years.* Baby Boomers are more worried than any other age group about retirement, according to an AARP poll. Over 70 percent of Boomers said that they must delay retirement, and half of them said that they won't be able to shed the 9-to-5 grind anytime soon. Six in ten Boomer women who work full-time said they must rethink when they plan to retire, as compared with slightly fewer than half of all men. Finally, according to a national survey by the Pew Research Center's Social & Demographic Trends Project, over half of all Boomers will likely delay their retirement, and another 16 percent said they never expect to stop working. Even the Boomers who plan to retire someday say that they expect to keep working until they reach age 66.
- *Boomers are watching their money.* Many Boomers don't think they'll have enough money to retire well, forcing some Boomers to downsize their lifestyles and curb their spending. According to a McKinsey Quarterly report, "The low savings rate and extensive liabilities of the Boomers have left about two thirds of them unprepared for retirement."
- *Boomers are checking their pulse.* "Nearly four times as many Boomers worry about health more than they worry about finances or outliving their money," according to the Center for a Secure Retirement Boomers. Moreover, most Boomers are worried about the runaway costs of health care and prescription drugs.
- *Boomers are pessimistic about entitlements.* About 70 percent of current retirees rely on Social Security for nearly half of their income. So it's no wonder that about 80 percent of Boomers

are concerned about the future of Social Security, with a third of Boomers believing that Social Security will be defunct in the next 20 years. In addition, 90 percent of Baby Boomers said that they were worried about Medicare, according to an eHealth Baby Boomer survey. Finally, about one third of Boomers said that "they don't know how they'll cover the cost of long-term care."

- *Boomers are workaholics.* Many Boomers don't want to retire but might not have a choice in the matter. According to global management consulting firm McKinsey & Company, a number of institutional and legal barriers, such as health care costs, labor laws, pension regulations, and corporate attitudes toward older workers, could prevent Boomers from prolonging their careers.

- *Boomers feel the economic pinch.* According to an AARP Public Policy Institute report titled "Boomers and the Great Recession: Struggling to Recover," a large percentage of Boomers have staggered through unemployment. Even Boomers who have jobs aren't doing as well as they have in the past. One expert says, "Trends such as decreased employer contributions to employees' 401(k) plans, frozen pensions, increases in health-insurance premiums, dipping home values, home foreclosures and increased college tuition for Boomers' children and/or retraining for Boomers themselves have altered the long-range view for many."

- *Boomers were rocked by the financial crisis of 2008-09.* According to the former Chairman of the Board of Governors of the Federal Reserve System Ben S. Bernanke, the financial crisis was caused by a complex interaction of "triggering events," including the subprime mortgage crisis; a "sudden stop" in syndicated lending to shaky corporate borrowers; and a reliance on volatile short-term funding. While no one was immune to the effects of the financial crisis, as a whole, Boomers were more deeply shaken by it, as compared to other investors. They lost 40 percent or more of their investment cache and were about twice as likely as other investors (who didn't suffer deep losses) to say they "have thought about delaying their eventual exit from the workforce." About three quarters of Boomers said they lost money in mutual funds, individual stocks, or retirement accounts such as a 401(k).

As a cohort, aging Boomers may rate higher on the misery index than other age groups. Still, don't underestimate Boomers' resolve to overcome the roadblocks that might stand in their way. Boomers are nothing if not resilient. Just check out any marathon starting line. Often you'll see Boomers standing poised for the race, wearing knee braces, smelling of Bengay, and brandishing a can-do attitude.

Visionary Ken Dychtwald, president and CEO of the consulting firm AgeWave, says, "Anyone who thinks [the Boomers] will turn 65 and be the same as the generation before are missing out on the last 60 years of sociology. The Boomers change every stage of life through which they migrate." Dychtwald believes that "a new model of life is emerging," where people aren't as much leading "linear" lives but instead are zigzagging along their life path. As an example, people are going back to school later in life to get an education.

Author Gail Sheehy, who wrote the popular book *Passages: Predictable Crises of Adult Life*, seems to agree with Dychtwald. She calls the mid-50s to the early 70s the Grand Tweens—"the pioneers and pathfinders among us." She believes that these trailblazers will reshape this life stage by infusing it with "a renewed sense of purpose."

The Sandwich Generation

Boomers wear many hats: they're parents, workers, activists, enthusiasts, community organizers, and so forth. These are roles that Boomers have chosen. But there's a new role that Boomers may not have banked on: that of a caregiver to an aging parent. Say hello to the "Sandwich Generation," people who are trying to juggle the competing demands of work, children, and aging parents—the Boomers' "new normal."

How many American mid-lifers are hustling to meet the needs of their aging parents and their growing children? A lot, according to a Pew Center study. In fact, one in eight Americans aged 40 to 60 is giving care and assistance to both a child and a parent. According to the AARP, 66 million Americans are taking care of their children, spouses, and parents, many of whom may be impaired or sick and in need of 24/7 care. For example, as mentioned earlier, Selma Lyon suffered from chronic illnesses, including diabetes, hypertension, stroke, advanced dementia, and cancer. She was wheelchair bound, diapered, crippled, lacked cognition, and progressively was unable to see, speak, and swallow. As a result, Selma depended on others for all of her basic needs. The party responsible for Selma's personal care hired professional caregivers to provide Selma with around-the-clock care and supervision.

With Americans living longer, the likelihood is strong that older Americans will be taking care of even older Americans, as multiple generations are living during the same time for the first time in history. For example, many Baby Boomers are caring for their grandchildren <u>and</u> helping out their Boomerang Kids, adult children who have moved back home for a variety of reasons. According to one expert:

> "People in their sixties who end up caring for an aging parent often feel they are getting a preview of what they may experience emotionally, physically and financially as they age—and at a time when they are confronting their own mortality more keenly than ever before."

Being a caregiver to an elderly parent or relative can lead to family problems. Oftentimes couples must make lifestyle adjustments in the way they spend their time and their money. As a result, family caregivers are at the highest risk for strained marriages or relationships for different reasons, such as the difficulty of holding down a job while caregiving; the stress of furnishing financial and physical assistance to an aging parent or relative; and the pressure of caring for an elderly parent or relative within the home. In fact, 89 percent of caregivers said that caring for an aging parent forced them to spend less time with their spouse, according to one survey. Moreover, 48 percent of caregivers said that they felt "less connected and attached to their partner."

In addition to the personal toll of being a family caregiver, the financial burden for family caregivers can be significant. According to a MetLife study of caregiving costs to working caregivers, adults who provide care for their aging parents lose an estimated $3 trillion dollars in wages, pension, and Social Security benefits due to time lost at work. The study further reported that average individual losses to female caregivers equaled $324,044, while male caregivers lost an average of $283,716.

If you're a family caregiver to a parent with dementia, you personally understand how difficult the situation can get. Startlingly, a Boomer becomes a dementia caregiver at a rate of almost one every minute. The majority of these family caregivers are caring for parents with Alzheimer's disease, which afflicts 50 percent of elders over 85. According to the National Institute on Aging (NIA), people with Alzheimer's can live up to 20 years after diagnosis, which means a dementia caregiver may be in it for the long haul. For instance, it was reported that Selma lived for many years with dementia, which was a contributing factor in her death.

In the next chapter, we'll address a silent crisis in America: that of elder neglect and abuse. The different types of and risk factors for elder abuse and neglect and the common characteristics of the victims and the perpetrators will be examined. We'll also explain how elder abuse and neglect are commonly detected and reported and by whom. Finally, we'll recount the real-life story about the Lyon family's struggle to save Selma, who became a victim of domestic abuse.

PART II
Elder Mistreatment

CHAPTER 3

Elder Neglect and Abuse

A disoriented, disheveled elderly woman shuffles down the street. She wanders into an apartment building. A crashing sound is heard. The local police are called to the scene. The police question the incoherent woman, her frail body poxed with cigarette burns. The police suspect elder abuse. Detectives are assigned to the case. A trail of evidence leads them to the elderly woman's neglectful, greedy son who has placed his mother, an Alzheimer's sufferer, in a nursing home. In this house of horrors, the patients are routinely tortured and victimized— and the director of the facility knows about the abuse and does nothing to stop it. This chilling story may sound too horrible to be real, and you'd be partly right in thinking that, because it's the premise for an episode titled "Vulnerable" that aired on the procedural police drama *Law & Order: Special Victims Unit*. But the ugly truth is that crimes against the elderly occur every five seconds all across America. It's no wonder, then, that elder mistreatment has been called America's "dirty little secret"—and it's only getting worse.

This chapter will discuss the disturbing social phenomenon of elder abuse and neglect in America. It will define and describe what elder abuse and neglect are, including the different types of and risk factors for elder abuse and neglect and the common characteristics of the victims and the perpetrators. It will relate how elder abuse and neglect are commonly detected and reported and by whom. Finally, it will recount the story of one family's struggle to stop predators from abusing and exploiting an elderly relative.

The Hidden Problem of Elder Abuse

If you're not a member of a profession that deals with or studies elder issues, it might seem that elder abuse and neglect are a relatively new social problem. The truth is that elder mistreatment is not a new social phenomenon. One of the first public reports on elder abuse was published in a 1975 *British Medical Journal* paper, which described the phenomenon of "granny battering" or "granny bashing."

By the mid-1970s, America had awakened to reports and articles on battered and abandoned elders that were documented in professional literature. At first, the response to these reports was disbelief and denial. However, once elder abuse stories hit the mainstream media, a huge public outcry was sounded—and the government listened.

In 1974 the federal government created the United States House Permanent Select Committee on Aging, which was responsible for conducting investigations and holding hearings on issues affecting older Americans, but not to form or pass legislation aimed at addressing the growing elder abuse issue. Through these early government efforts, elder abuse awareness grew, but funding for researching the problem did not. In 1992 the committee was disbanded, just as aging issues began to escalate further nationwide.

One contributing factor to the problem of elder abuse is *demographics*. As mentioned in Chapter 1, the U.S. population is aging. According to the U.S. Census Bureau, the number of seniors aged 65 and over will nearly double between 2010 and 2030, from 46 million in 2010 to 81 million in 2030. As a percentage of the U.S. population, seniors made up about 15 percent of the population in 2010. That figure is expected to rise to almost 22 percent by 2030. With the projected growth in the elderly population, then, the prevalence and incidence of elder abuse will likely increase.

Another demographic factor that plays a role in the well-being of the elderly is *life-cycle stage*, the shared life experiences within a cohort group that vary by chronological and cognitive age (or subjective age). Maintaining personal independence is important among the elderly. In many instances, older adults lose their independence because they're unable to fend for themselves (85% suffer from at least one chronic illness) or their families can no longer care for them. These functionally dependent elderly often require long-term care in nursing homes and other institutional settings. Still, the vast majority of older Americans do not live in institutional settings. In fact, only five percent of persons 60 years of age or older do. The rest live independently in the community, either in their own homes or in their relatives' homes. Given that, most elder abuse situations are happening in a domestic setting and not an institutional setting—and at the hands of the victim's family.

In addition to demographic forces, central to the elder abuse problem is *sociocultural attitudes toward aging*, especially in America. Unlike family-oriented cultures like Asian, Middle Eastern, and Indian societies that revere their elders, many Americans have negative attitudes toward aging. For example, elder adults are often stereotyped as "grumpy," "feeble," and "senile." According to a study published by the American Psychological Association (APA), negative stereotypes toward the elderly start as early as childhood and are then strengthened throughout adulthood. Paradoxically, the study also found that older adults held negative attitudes toward their own age group, just as their younger counterparts did. When a society has a negative view of aging, the presence of elder abuse and neglect can become all too real.

So how pervasive is the elder abuse problem? No one really knows for sure. In spite of the increase in elder abuse awareness, research on the problem isn't keeping pace with its escalation. In fact, only a few researchers and investigators produce research on elder mistreatment, and even they have difficulty accessing reliable sources like Adult Protective Services programs and other elder abuse services. These agencies are reluctant to cooperate with researchers for a variety of reasons, including protecting their clients' privacy, preventing a disruption to their clients' lives, apprehension toward evaluative research, and staffing shortages. One thing's for sure: the elder abuse problem isn't going away anytime soon—and it's growing into a national crisis.

What Is Elder Abuse?

Defining elder abuse would seem straightforward, but it's not. Because of the relative newness of this field of inquiry, sensitivity of the data collection, and widely varying state statutory laws, early researchers studying elder abuse found that a lack of "definitional consensus" existed. This is mainly because definitions and intent standards weren't generally uniform; they vary according to law, location, discipline, jurisdiction, parties, jurist, jury, and judiciary procedures. As a result, researchers and professionals have hatched a batch of definitions on what elder abuse is. Let's take a look at some.

First, the National Center on Elder Abuse (NCEA), a national resource center directed by the U.S. Administration on Aging (AoA), provides three broad categories of elder abuse: *domestic elder abuse*—mistreatment toward an elder by a person in a trust relationship with him or her in a home setting; *institutional elder abuse*—mistreatment toward an elder by a person who has a legal or contractual obligation to him or her in a residential setting; and *self-neglect* or *self-abuse*—when an elderly person fails to meet his or her basic needs such as physical and psychological needs. These categories are further broken down into types of elder abuse, which we'll examine later.

Next, each state has created statutory laws that address elder abuse, neglect, and exploitation. These statutes can vary greatly. For example, according to California state law, elder abuse is legally defined as follows: "**Abuse of an elder or dependent adult** includes physical abuse, neglect, financial abuse, abandonment, isolation, abduction, or other treatment with resulting physical harm or pain or mental suffering; the deprivation by a care custodian of goods or services that are necessary to avoid physical harm or mental suffering." Idaho state law simply states that elder abuse is "intentional or negligent infliction of physical pain, injury, or mental injury." Some elder abuse laws include provisions for psychological abuse, unreasonable confinement, or stipulations for institutional settings, while others don't. Several statutes include mocking, demeaning, cursing, and threatening an elder as emotional abuse, whereas other states require proof of extreme emotional duress. In addition, statutes differ in the language used to describe "whom" the laws protect. *Dependent adult, vulnerable adult, elderly person,* or *incapacitated person* are terms used to describe protected persons under the law. Custodial relationships are also called by different names, such as *caretaker, caregiver,* and *responsible person.* Even age parameters can differ significantly. For example, Massachusetts labels an "Elder "as "a person 60 years of age or older," whereas New Mexico defines an "Adult" as "a person 18 years of age or older."

Third, the American Medical Association (AMA) has developed its own definition of elder abuse. The AMA describes elder abuse in the following manner: "Abuse shall mean an act or omission which results in harm or threatened harm to the health or welfare of an elderly person. Abuse includes intentional infliction of physical or mental injury, sexual abuse, or withholding of necessary food, clothing and medical care to treat the physical and mental health needs of an elderly person by one having the care, custody or responsibility of an elder person." Similar to other elder abuse definitions, the AMA focuses on three things: the intent to do harm, the dependency of the elder, and the codependent relationship between a caretaker and a dependent elder.

Finally, in hunting for a conceptually balanced definition of elder abuse, one emerged. In a seminal report titled "Elder Mistreatment: Abuse, Neglect and Exploitation in Aging America" produced by the National Research Council (NRC), the authors define elder abuse as "intentional actions that cause harm or create a serious risk of harm, whether or not harm is intended, to a vulnerable elder by a caregiver or other person who stands in a trust relationship to the elder or failure by caregiver to satisfy the elder's basic needs or to protect elder from harm." Here, a distinction between abuse and neglect on the "basis of intent" is drawn by treating abuse as "an act of active commission" and neglect as "an act of omission."

For all the well-intentioned hair-splitting among lawmakers, researchers, and clinicians on what elder abuse is, plain language guidelines must be developed for the average person to recognize abuse, neglect, and financial exploitation and to do something about them. The fact is that actual abuse and neglect are rarely observed by clinicians or protective service professionals who have the legal authority to intervene with immediacy, but instead by people who interact with the elderly person routinely—and almost always away from prying eyes. So it would be helpful for us to understand what the observable markers of elder abuse and neglect are, especially since abuse and neglect often emerge under murky scenarios where what appears as small acts of neglect, such as not providing the elder with the proper doses of medication, can result in deadly consequences.

Elder Abuse by the Numbers

According to Adult Protective Services (APS), which is a first responder to reports of elder abuse, "the exact number of older Americans who are abused, neglected, or exploited each year is not known." Still, estimates on the prevalence and incidence of elder abuse are available. A reliable source for data on elder abuse is the National Center on Elder Abuse (NCEA). The NCEA has collected and distributed elder abuse data and information to professionals and the public since 1986. Though there are no official national statistics, the NCEA has collected statistical data that charts the spiraling rates of elder abuse being reported across the United States. Highlighted findings from the NCEA and elder abuse studies follow:

- An expert panel on the risk and prevalence of elder abuse and neglect estimated that between 1 and 2 million Americans age 65 or older have been mistreated by someone in a trust relationship with them.

- One survey placed the annual incidence of elder abuse and neglect in the broad range of 1 to 12 percent.
- Using a random sample, researchers found that only 1 in 14 incidents of elder abuse occurring in a home setting are ever reported to the authorities.
- Only 1 in 25 cases of financial exploitation of the elderly get reported to the authorities annually (about 5 million victims).
- For every one elder mistreatment case reported to the authorities, roughly five go unreported.
- A national study on the incidence of elder abuse reported that about 500,000 Americans aged 60 and over were victims of domestic abuse in 1996, and only 16 percent of these abuse situations got reported.
- A report found that 90 percent of elder abuse and neglect incidents were committed by known perpetrators, mostly spouses and adult children. Forty-two percent of murder victims over 60 were killed by their offspring, while 24 percent were killed by their spouses.
- Neglect is the most common type of abuse (58 percent), followed by physical abuse (15.7 percent), financial exploitation (12.3 percent), emotional abuse (7.3 percent), sexual abuse (less than 1 percent), and other types of abuse (5.1 percent), according to a national study on elder abuse.

You might wonder why it's so difficult to get agreement on the magnitude of the abuse problem. Oft-cited reasons are methodological and sampling differences, a general lack of uniformity in reporting and recording the problem, denied reports by the victim, and divergent professional views on what constitutes elder abuse. One thing all experts can agree on is that the elder abuse problem is far more persistent than the numbers reveal.

Types of Elder Abuse and Neglect

Just as experts disagree over elder abuse statistics, they often differ on what precisely constitutes elder abuse and neglect. Some experts say there's simply no gold standard—in other words, it (the abuse) is in the eye of the beholder. For starters, clinicians working with abused or neglected elderly victims typically identify forensic markers, which often overlap with disease markers, making it difficult to prove beyond a reasonable doubt that abuse occurred. Also, extreme cases of elder neglect—for example, where the caretaker intentionally denies the basic needs of the elder—would be considered elder abuse. Finally, experts disagree over which forms of abuse happen most often. For instance, the incidence of physical abuse was highest in one study, whereas psychological abuse was reported more frequently in another study. Other studies showed that passive neglect was the most common form, whereas another reported financial abuse, and yet another self-neglect.

Despite the haziness between abuse and neglect and the disagreement on the most common forms, common abuse categories have been developed. Using the NCEA's categorizations, the types of elder abuse are:

- *Physical Abuse*—the use of physical force that may cause pain or harm, including hitting, kicking, shoving, shaking, slapping, pinching, and burning.
- *Sexual Abuse*—unwanted sexual contact with an elderly person, such as forced sexual activity, suggestive talk, and sexual assault or battery.
- *Emotional or Psychological Abuse*—the infliction of mental anguish or emotional pain through verbal or nonverbal acts, like verbal aggression or threats, insults, intimidation, humiliation, harassment, and social isolation.
- *Neglect*—the intentional refusal or unintentional failure of a caregiver to meet the emotional and physical needs of an elder, such as failing to 1) provide life necessities (food,

water, clothing, shelter, medicine, comfort, etc.), 2) perform fiduciary responsibilities, and 3) furnish necessary care. Often a distinction between *active neglect* (the conscious and willful failure to cause physical or emotional distress) and *passive neglect* (the nonwillful failure to fulfill a caregiving obligation or duty) is made.

- *Self-Neglect*—the conduct of an elderly person that threatens his or her own health or safety. Here, the elder may refuse or fail to provide for his or her basic needs, which in turn may result in a collapse in his or her health, domestic squalor, dangerous hoarding, or social withdrawal.
- *Abandonment*—the desertion of an elderly person by an individual in a caregiver relationship with an elder or by a person with physical custody of an elder.
- *Financial or Material Exploitation*—the misappropriation of an elder's funds, property, or assets, including the theft of checks or money, the use of coercion or deception to get an older person to sign important documents (e.g., contracts, trusts, wills), the embezzlement of an elder's funds, and the improper use of a conservatorship, a guardianship, or a power of attorney.

On the face of it, financial exploitation may not seem to carry the same weight or severity as other forms of abuse. Not true—financial abuse can be just as devastating to the elderly victim as other forms of abuse. Moreover, financial abuse can be difficult to detect, pursue, and prove, especially when monetary giving is common in many families where financial exploitation most often occurs. Strange though it may seem, financial abuse frequently happens with the tacit authorization of the elder person.

Risk Factors of Elder Abuse and Neglect

You might be wondering why seniors are targeted for abuse. In a 1990 hearing before the Subcommittee on Health and Long-Term

Care of the Select Committee on Aging, members of Congress and senior citizen advocates addressed what the committee chairman, Joseph P. Kennedy, II, called an "ugly problem" of elder mistreatment. The select committee issued a report that identified elder-specific risk factors for elder mistreatment, including:

- *Retaliation*—an adult child may exact revenge against the elderly parent for childhood mistreatment—in other words, the abused becomes the abuser.
- *Transgenerational violence*—a family history of violence or an acceptance of violence is a way of resolving problems.
- *Parent-child conflict*—an unresolved conflict between the parent and the adult child may result in the adult child withholding care or being less willing to provide for the needs of the elderly dependent parent.
- *Broken family ties*—the estranged adult child thrown into the role of caregiver to the emotionally distant parent may harbor resentment or contempt toward the dependent parent.
- *Lack of financial resources*—the adult child dependent on the elder for money, or vice versa, may become resentful or abusive.
- *Demands on caregiver*—an overwhelmed caregiver unable to keep up with the care and demands of a chronically ill or an impaired elder may develop feelings of anger, frustration, and resentment.
- *Longer life spans*—elders are living longer and, as they age, may become frail and infirm and thus require more care for many more years.
- *History of mental illness*—when an adult child caregiver has a mental problem or the elder does, the elder may become a target when the caregiver lashes out.
- *Unemployment*—if the breadwinner of the family is/becomes unemployed, intrafamily conflict can lead to violence toward family members, including the dependent elder.

- *History of substance abuse*—caregivers who abuse mind-altering substances like alcohol and drugs can become more abusive or more apt to exploit others, including elders.
- *Greed*—opportunistic family and nonfamily may unduly influence a pliable elder out of a sense of entitlement or naked temptation.
- *Environmental conditions*—external stressors or social problems like living in crowded housing or other poor living conditions can set the backdrop for elder abuse.

Above all, the number one risk factor for elder abuse is *vulnerability*. Vulnerable older people are susceptible to the abusive behaviors of people who hold negative views toward elders. This is especially true of North American cultures where older people are generally perceived as impaired, infirm, dependent, and of no social value. Next, let's discuss victimology, specifically elder- and caregiver-specific risk factors.

The Victims

In the calculus of elder abuse, *gender* matters. If you're a female reading this book, know that you're at greater risk to become an elder abuse victim during your lifetime. Based on elder abuse studies, the characteristics of a typical elder abuse victim in a domestic setting are:

- Unmarried or widowed white female aged 75 or older
- Shared living arrangement with family or relative
- Dependent on a caregiver
- Cognitively impaired
- Socially isolated with minimal social support
- Poor health and functional impairment
- Unable to report abuse because of memory or communication problems

In contrast, other studies have shown that married men were targeted more often than married women mainly because married men are older and more infirm than their female counterparts. Abuse against an older man often amounts to "payback" for the man's past abuse toward his children or his spouse. Putting gender aside, a spouse has been identified as the abuser in over half of elder abuse cases, followed by other relatives (18%) and offspring (16%), according to one urban study. Ultimately, gender may be less relevant in determining risk assessment as was once believed.

Another elder-specific risk factor is *psychological factors*. Psychological factors include depression; denial and avoidance; personality traits such as stoicism; self-blame; excessive loyalty to family members; and hostility or aggression resulting from Alzheimer's disease. For example, an elderly victim may feel powerless to do anything about the abuse or may not wish to "betray" abusive family members by disclosing the abuse to outsiders, which emerged as a feature in the Lyon elder abuse case highlighted in this book.

In addition to psychological factors, *cultural factors* are persistent risk factors. Cultural mores may make it difficult to assess elder abuse in situations where the markers of abuse are present. For instance, abusive relationships tend to be accepted by elderly Asian Americans who are less likely to seek aid.

Finally, one of the biggest elder-specific risk factors is the presence of *dementia*, a brain illness that affects a person's cognitive functioning over time. Because dementia is frequently used as an objective yardstick against which to assess a person's legal competence and also enters into the elder abuse equation, let's take a few moments to discuss it.

Dementia

Several recent reports surfaced about Margaret Thatcher's struggle with dementia. As the former British prime minister and the subject of the acclaimed film *The Iron Lady*, Thatcher had developed stroke-related dementia. Her daughter said that she first realized her mother's decline when Thatcher couldn't tell the difference between the 1982 Falklands War, which Thatcher was instrumental in winning, and the Bosnian conflict. Thatcher's charted decline started in 2000 and escalated until her death in 2013, demonstrating that people can live with dementia for many years after its diagnosis. What is dementia, and should you be worried about it? Let's find out.

The World Health Organization (WHO) defines dementia as "a syndrome, usually of a chronic or progressive nature, caused by a variety of brain illnesses that affect memory, thinking, behavior and ability to perform everyday activities." Dementia afflicts about 35.6 million people worldwide. The number of people with dementia is projected to double in the next 20 years, from 65.7 million in 2030 to 115.4 million in 2050. In the U.S. alone, about 4 to 5 million people live with some degree of dementia. A startling fact is that a new case of dementia is reported every four seconds.

As we age, dementia can cast a dark shadow on our lives. In fact, roughly 5 to 10 percent of those aged 65 and older and 30 to 39 percent of those aged 85 and older are likely to face the debilitating effects of dementia. The reality is that dementia will somehow touch us all: you've probably met someone with dementia or have a family member who may be a dementia sufferer. A loved one may start having difficulty with short-term memory, losing things, forgetting to pay bills, refusing to bathe, forgetting to eat, getting easily agitated or confused, or developing faulty perceptions, all of which are common signs of dementia. In short, the dementia victim will become unable to handle everyday activities known as *activities of daily living*, or *ADLs*.

Bear in mind that dementia is not a specific disease. According to the National Institute of Health (NIH), dementia is "a word for a group of symptoms caused by disorders that affect the brain." Various diseases, infections, strokes, head injuries, drugs, and nutritional deficiencies are frequently cited as primary causes of dementia. Alzheimer's Disease (AD) accounts for 60 to 80 percent of dementia cases, with vascular dementia ranking as the second most common type of dementia, according to the Alzheimer's Association. All dementias exhibit dysfunction in the cerebral cortex—in lay terms, our gray matter—which explains why dementia impairs people's sensory and cognitive functions. As a degenerative disease, most types of dementia are irreversible, although prescription drugs on the market can slow its progression or minimize its symptoms.

Given that dementia is a late-life disease, you might be worried about getting dementia and, in turn, becoming dependent on others for your care in the future. This is especially true if you have a family member who suffers from dementia. So the question becomes, *Is dementia inherited?* Yes, it can be. But most cases of dementia are <u>not</u> inherited. According to the Alzheimer's Society, the two forms of dementia are *sporadic dementia*—where an individual family member gets dementia (noninherited)—and *genetic or familial dementia*—where dementia runs in families and results from a genetic fault (inherited). So if you inherit the gene and if you live long enough, the likelihood of your getting dementia increases.

In the context of elder mistreatment, Alzheimer's disease and related dementias are huge risk factors. According to the authors of the National Research Council (NRC) report "Elder Mistreatment: Abuse, Neglect, and Exploitation in an Aging America," studies have shown that the prevalence rates of elder mistreatment in samples of dementia caregivers were highest, as compared with rates in other general population surveys. One author found the risk of mistreatment of Alzheimer's disease patients by caregivers was greatest when the sufferer resided with immediate family members other than the spouse, as the distressing effects of dementia can impact not only the loved one stricken with dementia but also the family caregiver, who may lack a full awareness and grasp of the syndrome or who may be unable to cope with the stress of caring for the loved one with dementia. In fact, research has found that caregivers who have displayed violent feelings, or actually have become violent, frequently care for seriously impaired elders such as a demented adult. Other research on dementia caregivers examined caregiver characteristics, and found that "anxious and depressed caregivers engaged in more abuse than other caregivers of individuals with dementia."

In the Lyon family, several elderly family members on one side of the family had developed dementia. Mason, a doctor and Selma's nephew, revealed that after Selma's first stroke, she developed vascular dementia (VaD), with a progressive worsening of her memory and cognitive functions. At first, the mental changes were subtle, like short-term memory loss and uncharacteristic emotional breakdowns, which appeared to reach a plateau state for several years. Then a series of mini-strokes caused a more rapid decline in her memory and brain function, referred to as *multi-infarct dementia.*

During the first few years of the conservatorship, family members observed that Selma retained some awareness and alertness, but these began to progressively wane to the point at which she could no longer recognize family members. Selma could make small utterances, like grunts or moans, but her ability to speak continued to fail her until she could speak no more, hear no more, swallow no more, and see no more. She eventually lapsed into a *persistent vegetative state (PVS),* where Selma experienced sleep-wake cycles but lacked cognitive functioning. More about Selma's condition and its impact on her care management will be presented in a later chapter.

The Perpetrators

A mother and her daughter walk into a house. The mother enters a living room, and her daughter trails behind her. The mother trips over something. The daughter screams and bolts out of the room. The mother verbally lashes out at someone. A slap is heard. An elderly person is seen, touching her face while grimacing. The mother continues to screech at the elderly person. This public service announcement (PSA) ends with a message on elder abuse awareness. As the PSA demonstrates, the most common face of an elder abuse perpetrator is that of a family member. Let's learn more about the perpetrators of elder abuse.

A family household can be a dangerous place, as elder abuse frequently happens behind closed doors in a domestic setting while committed by someone closest to the elder. Profiles of abusers usually focus on the pathological characteristics of the caregiver or the "psychopathology of the abuser" in addition to situational factors. Put all together, a snapshot of a typical abuser in a domestic setting is:

- Family caregiver
- Financial dependence on the elderly victim
- Low self-esteem
- History of mental or physical illness
- History of substance abuse
- Living with elderly victim
- Poor sense of self-control
- Inadequate set of coping skills
- History of family violence
- Life stressors such as unemployment, caregiver burden, and relationship conflicts

One study found that abusers were usually women who worked in stressful, low-paying jobs and who were the family caregivers for a dependent elder. The caregiver burden can impact all manner of the caregiver's life. In fact, clinicians estimated that 46 to 83 percent of caregivers suffered from depression, while their physical and financial health were disrupted.

In contrast, most elder mistreatment was perpetrated by someone other than an immediate family member, according to a study produced by the National Opinion Research and the Department of Sociology at University of Chicago, Illinois. Fifty-seven percent of respondents who reported verbal abuse said that a nonfamily member was responsible, followed by a spouse or romantic partner (26%) and a child (15%). "Other" abusers included distant family members, many of whom are unrelated, such as in-laws, ex-spouses, and siblings. An interesting finding was siblings were the second most commonly cited perpetrators of financial exploitation after children. In the Lyon case, the alleged abusers included a blood relative, his family, and their attorney.

Elder Abuse and the Law

The law has finally caught up with elder abusers, but the punishment hasn't always fit the crime. On a federal level, only a few laws have been passed. In 1965 the first federal initiative passed by Congress was the *Older Americans Act (OAA)*. This law provided state grants to furnish comprehensive social services to the elderly as well as to fund community planning, research projects, and personnel training in the field of aging. To administer this federally funded program, the law also established the *National Aging Network*. The network is housed in the Administration on Aging (AoA), a federal clearinghouse for issues affecting elders.

Yet the government has been woefully slow in creating a federal law to stamp out elder abuse and bring the perpetrators to justice. A comprehensive federal elder abuse law was passed for the first time in 2010. Called the *Elder Justice Act (EJA)*, this piece of legislation was part of President Barack Obama's health reform bill, the *Patient Protection and Affordable Care Act (PPACA)*. The EJA was designed to commit federal resources "to prevent, detect, treat, understand, intervene in and, where appropriate, prosecute elder abuse, neglect and exploitation."

In spite of these government efforts, the feds couldn't deliver on the full promise to prevent elder victimization. In 2011 the *Elder Abuse Victims Act*, a bill that would establish an Office of Elder Justice within the Department of Justice (DOJ) to address elder abuse issues, was squashed by Congress. The act would have advanced the rights of elderly victims and boosted the justice system's capacity to pursue and to prosecute elder abuse cases.

On the state level, a set of elder abuse laws has been created. These laws include the *Adult Protective Services Laws* allowing for and regulating the provision of services in elder abuse cases; *Long-Term*

Care Ombudsman Program (LTCOP) advocating for the rights and safety of elders residing in institutional settings; and *Institutional Abuse Laws* covering elder abuse and neglect committed in long-term care facilities and other such settings. In addition, several states, including California, Missouri, Nevada, and Florida, have passed criminal laws authorizing prosecution for elder abuse as one or more separate crimes.

The Lyon Case: Cries of Silence

The circumstances surrounding the Lyon case will help illustrate the difficulties and obstacles faced by families in which elder abuse and neglect become known. Based on court records, legal documents, and personal accounts, several forms of suspected elder abuse and neglect emerged in the Lyon case, including emotional and possible physical abuse, abandonment, neglect, and financial exploitation, the latter of which will be discussed in a later chapter.

For nearly a half century, Selma Lyon shared her home with her son Zachary. According to court documents, Zachary never left home and had never been gainfully employed, even though he was highly educated. Zachary was financially dependent on Selma and his aunt, Minerva, who died quite tragically around the time that the Lyon family began to suspect elder neglect was occurring in the home.

Shortly after Minerva's death, Zachary married Minerva's home health aide, Sybil. Following Zachary and Sybil's civil ceremony, Sybil, together with her family comprised of another adult and a minor, lived away from Zachary for some months. But when the Lyon family started circling the wagons by asking questions about Sybil— where she fit into Zachary's life and how his relationship with her and her family were adversely impacting Selma's well-being—Zachary's new family responded by moving into Selma's home against Selma's wishes. In no time, Sybil took control of the household.

Prior to Zachary's new family's encroachment on Selma's home, one of Selma's sisters witnessed that Selma was being medically neglected by Zachary, and that Selma's home was no longer livable. She then sounded the alarm by asking other relatives to assess Selma's situation. The first family member on the scene was Selma's niece Agatha.

In an interview, Agatha said that when she entered Selma's home, she was horrified by what she found. The home, usually kept pristinely clean, was in shambles. Agatha said, "When I entered my aunt's house, the wall of stench was nauseating. Her home had been turned into a litter box. Cat feces speckled the house. Cat urine marinated in pools. Even worse, my aunt was grossly ill-kempt. She had not bathed for some time, had no clean clothing and undergarments, and hadn't even a pair of shoes that matched!" Selma, a former academician who had been fastidious in her cleanliness, was reduced to an unwashed indigent, even though she was well-off.

Because Selma was under Zachary's care, the family implored him to better provide for Selma's basic needs. If he wasn't willing to do that, then another relative would. For months, Selma's family begged Zachary to get Selma to a doctor, hire a housecleaner, and retain a caregiver for Selma. Zachary would agree to these requests but never follow through with them. The situation got so bad that a family member finally blew the whistle by contacting Adult Protective Services (APS). The agency was unhelpful, leaving Selma increasingly vulnerable.

Livingston, a lawyer and Selma's nephew, confronted Zachary about his neglect and disregard for Selma, as well as his lack of accountability on how Selma's money was being spent by him. Selma wasn't sure who paid her bills, how much was being spent, and where her money was going. Furthermore, witnesses saw Zachary place documents in front of Selma and instructed her to sign them. Selma never questioned what she was signing—she did whatever Zachary told her to do.

Selma's relatives became increasingly convinced that Selma was entrapped in a bad situation. Her diabetes wasn't being managed, nor were her other chronic health issues being addressed. Noah, a medical specialist and Selma's nephew, approached Zachary about his neglect of Selma, urging him to get Selma appropriate medical treatment. Zachary was dismissive. He commented that Selma would "probably die in a few years and that it didn't matter."

When relatives asked Selma about Sybil, Selma would frequently reply, "Who's Sybil?" In spite of her forgetfulness, she knew that Sybil was exploiting her son. "He gives her [Sybil] money. She takes advantage of him," Selma told her sister.

Selma thoroughly disliked Sybil and her family, and wanted them to vacate her home. "My sister [Selma] told my nephew's wife and her family to leave," said one of Selma's sisters. But Zachary's new family wouldn't go. As revealed in court documents, "Selma repeatedly told others that she does not want them [Zachary's family] in her house [...] She calls them 'insects.' Selma no longer has the mental and physical ability to remove them from her home."

Sybil called the shots. One observer described her as "cunning and practiced at control."

After months of Zachary's inertia, Selma's family placed more pressure on Zachary to properly care for Selma and to account for how he was spending her money. Instead of addressing the family's appeal, Zachary and Sybil responded by imprisoning Selma and closing her off from the outside world. Zachary and his new family hid the phone from Selma so that she could not take or make calls. Moreover, they persuaded a doctor that they were attending to Selma's health care needs, yet continued to overlook them, according to one family source.

Selma was often abandoned. She was left idle and home alone, with no means to reach out. "Selma is unable to call out. The phone has been moved from where it has been the last 40 years. Because of her short and long-term memory loss and general confusion, Selma cannot find it. She is often left alone, unable to call out in the event of an emergency and unable to answer the phone if others wish to check on her," according to court documents.

For weeks on end, no family members could get through to Selma. Whenever a relative would call Selma's home, someone would pick up, and then he or she would slam the phone down. Or the phone would ring and ring and ring, with no answer. Or an automated answering machine message would kick in. Later, the family found out that all their numbers had been blocked.

Selma was isolated from everyone but Zachary and his new family. When family members tried to visit Selma, they were told that Selma wasn't home or to go way. "When visitors appear, Zachary and Sybil call an attorney who says he represents Selma. The attorney threatens to call the police if the visitors refuse to leave. The attorney has told visitors he will come over himself to throw them out," according to court documents.

In addition to the isolation, Selma's medications weren't being monitored properly, and her diet was poor. According to one caregiver, Selma had been fed sweets and pizza daily, even though she was a diabetic. The caregiver said, "They [Zachary and Sybil] joked about feeding Selma sugar."

The more family members tried reasoning with Zachary, the more he dug in his heels. Zachary told Noah that he did not want "financial controls placed on how he could spend Selma's money." In fact, household spending patterns were a legitimate concern. Based on account statements, large sums of money disappeared from Selma's bank accounts during the months that Zachary's new family occupied Selma's household. Over that five-month period, over $90,000 of Selma's money was used up. Whereas Selma's monthly expenses rarely climbed above $2,500, now monthly costs had gone up to $7,000.

The family had had enough of Zachary's stonewalling. Noah warned, "Selma is being emotionally neglected. If something isn't done soon, Zachary will dry up Selma's estate inside of six months." Selma's family living overseas also worried about Selma's safety. They said Zachary had hung up on them when they wanted to speak to Selma. They believed that Selma's family in the States should act aggressively, as they felt that Zachary was trying to usurp Selma's money for himself and "the girl [Sybil]," which could leave Selma broke, homeless, and debilitated.

To get the ball rolling, Attorney Young, Agatha's lawyer, corresponded with Attorney Gilroy, the attorney whom Zachary hired for Selma. Young stated, "The family as a whole has become very concerned about Selma's welfare, particularly since the recent marriage of Zachary and the consequences of having Zachary's new wife in the household [...] I believe that Zachary is 'attorney shopping' until he finds someone who will allow him to unduly influence Selma's estate planning documents in a way that services his own interests."

Young wasn't alone in her belief that Zachary was disregarding Selma's needs and wishes. "His [Zachary's] statements and actions indicate that he would not use trust assets to hire caregivers for Selma, seeming to prefer to preserve assets for his inheritance," as provided by an attorney working on Selma's case.

Gilroy's response to Young's correspondence was tepid. Instead of heeding Young's warning, Gilroy implemented changes to Selma's estate plan by putting Zachary in charge of Selma's finances and him and his wife in charge of Selma's health care. Gilroy included language that prevented family members from seeing Selma and getting involved in Selma's affairs.

An inescapable impasse between Zachary and Selma's relatives had been reached. As a result, the family decided to explore legal remedies to protect Selma. To this end, Livingston consulted several attorneys, including Attorney Forte, an elder law attorney who was eventually retained to represent the family member and who would go on to petition the court for a conservatorship.

During an initial consultation with Livingston, Forte illustrated what would be at stake if the family didn't act quickly and decisively. She indicated that a typical elder abuser finds professionals who will satisfy his or her requirements and not the elder's. One ploy used by elder abusers is to isolate the elder, have all the elder's assets placed under the abuser's name, take the elder from doctor to doctor for medication, and eventually overmedicate the elder until death. No autopsy would be done because the death of an elder with health problems is rarely regarded as suspicious. The elder would then be buried, and the elder's assets would disappear, without the knowledge of the family. Due to the elder's age, no one would be the wiser as to the fact that the elder was actually a victim.

To begin with, an expert evaluation was needed to assess Selma and Selma's household. To accomplish this, a psychologist was sent to Selma's home. The psychologist observed that the house was filthy. She also noted that Sybil and Zachary had hidden the home phone from Selma. According to court documents: "A psychologist who evaluated and observed Selma in her home, with Zachary and his new family present, believes Selma suffers from severe depression, emotional abuse and possible physical abuse."

Now that Selma's family had expert evidence that proved that Selma was being mistreated, doing nothing was no longer an option. The family weighed their legal alternatives. In the end, they felt that they were left with no other solution than to seek the most restrictive legal remedy to protect Selma: a conservatorship.

In the next chapter, we'll explore the nature and prevalence of elder exploitation. Also, we'll examine elder fraud as well as cover different types of influence. Finally, we'll revisit the Lyon case, where exploitation was one of its main features.

CHAPTER 4

Elder Exploitation

You've probably heard the sensational story of fallen Wall Street money manager Bernie Madoff, who literally "made off" with some $65 billion of his clients' money by means of an elaborate Ponzi scheme. The news reports mostly featured Madoff's celebrity and wealthy victims, such as Hollywood titan Steven Spielberg; actor Kevin Bacon and his actress wife, Kyra Sedgwick; Europe's richest woman, Liliane Bettencourt; baseball great Sandy Koufax; and Livingston Gottesman, a board member of Berkshire Hathaway whose CEO is investment guru Warren Buffett.

If you dig deeper into the tales of loss, you'll discover that many of Madoff's victims were ordinary and elderly Americans, who entrusted Madoff with their life savings and who lost everything. In one case, an 80-year-old man in ill health and his wife were financially ruined by Madoff. As a result of Madoff's malfeasance, the couple were forced to sell every asset they owned just to survive. The elderly husband remarked, "I cannot begin to describe to you the toll that Madoff's actions have taken on us financially, physically and emotionally."

In the end, Madoff was given a heavy sentence of 150 years behind bars at a federal correctional complex, where he has kept company with other crime kings—a small consolation to Madoff's victims who may never be whole again.

In this chapter, we'll define elder exploitation, explore the nature and prevalence of the problem, and discuss financial exploitation in a domestic setting. Also, we'll examine elder fraud as well as cover different types of influence. Finally, we'll revisit the Lyon case where exploitation was one of its main features.

Throughout this chapter, "elder exploitation" may be variously referred to as *financial abuse, financial exploitation, material financial abuse, fiduciary abuse, economic exploitation,* or *material exploitation,* because this type of abuse covers a wide gamut of exploitation.

What Is Elder Exploitation?

Called the "Crime of the 21st Century," elder exploitation has ignited "a time bomb with the older generation growing proportionately larger," according to one expert. One study called elder exploitation "a many-headed Hydra for both elders and their families, as the tentacles of exploitation reach far beyond a single event reported or a single elderly victim." What exactly is elder exploitation, and why should you be concerned about it? Let's find out.

Most definitions of elder mistreatment mention "exploitation." Like other forms of elder abuse, professionals haven't arrived at a definitional consensus. For example, the American Medical Association (AMA) defines financial exploitation as "the inappropriate use of an elderly person's resources for personal gain," whereas the National Center on Elder Abuse (NCEA) describes financial or material exploitation as "the illegal or improper use of an elder's funds, property, or assets." The National Academy of Elder Law Attorneys (NAELA) states that "*Exploitation* is usually defined as taking financial advantage of a disabled or elderly victim." Finally, in a study done by the MetLife Mature Market Institute (MMI), the National Committee for the Prevention of Elder Abuse (NCPEA), and the Center for Gerontology at Virginia Polytechnic Institute and State University, elder financial abuse is described as "the unauthorized use or illegal taking of funds or property of people aged 60 and older...perpetrated by those who gain, and then violate, the trust of an older person."

In the book *Abuse, Neglect, and Exploitation of Older Persons*, elder exploitation is grouped into two categories: *violation of personal rights* and *material financial abuse*. First, *violation of personal rights* occurs when someone prevents an older person from freely making common decisions, such as prohibiting an elder from marrying or divorcing, forcing an elder to change his or her residence against his or her will, preventing an elder from making financial decisions, and so on.

Next, *material financial abuse* occurs when someone benefits or gains from the use of an older person's financial resources or property without the elderly person's permission, such as through theft or misuse of the elder's money or property. By and large, material financial abuse happens when an older or a dependent adult can no longer manage his or her financial affairs due to an impairment. As a result, the elderly person may voluntarily rely on others for help. If the helper is untrustworthy or unscrupulous, he or she could coerce or trick the elder into doing something that could jeopardize his or her financial well-being, such as signing away home ownership or real property.

As described in the last chapter, each state has crafted elder abuse laws, which usually include elder exploitation. For example, the New York statute reads: "Financial Exploitation means improper use of an adult's funds, property, or resources by another individual, including but not limited to, fraud, false pretenses, embezzlement, conspiracy, forgery, falsifying records, coerced property transfers, or denial of access to assets." In California, the statute says: "Financial abuse" [...] occurs when a person or entity does any of the following: (1) takes, secretes, appropriates, or retains real or personal property of an elder or dependent adult to a wrongful use or with intent to defraud, or both; (2) assists in taking, secreting, appropriating, or retaining real or personal property of an elder or dependent adult to a wrongful use or with the intent to defraud, or both." The parameters of these laws can vary according to the person's age, psychological health, the perpetrator's intent, the victim's disadvantage, and the nature of the relationship between the perpetrator and the victim, among other things.

The Nature and Prevalence of Elder Exploitation

The headlines read as follows: "Financial abuse costs elderly billions"; "Financial advisor defrauded elderly victims of $580,000, prosecutors say"; "Elder financial abuse hurts the economy"; and "Scam artists targeting elderly victims." These stories spotlight incidents of elder exploitation, which is the fastest growing form of elder abuse. Let's see how big the problem is.

The Federal Bureau of Investigation's Uniform Crime Report (UCR) and the Justice Department's National Crime Victimization Survey furnish annual crime statistics. Neither source, however, provides data on victimization by fraud or by age. An obstacle to quantifying the rate of financial crimes against elderly is *underreporting*. Researchers point to several problems when exploitation goes unreported. First, underreporting makes it tough to stop the abuse or mobilize a community or family intervention. Next, underreporting makes it difficult to develop problem-oriented solutions due to insufficient information on the intended targets, the most common modus operandi, and the perpetrator's etiology. Finally, underreporting may encourage revictimization or the victimization of others.

What prevents elderly victims from reporting exploitation? First, a victim may feel ashamed that he or she was duped or may feel partially to blame for the situation. Second, a victim may fear that his or her family members will believe that the victim is unable to take care of his or her own affairs. Third, a victim may not know that support services are available to him or her. Fourth, a victim may have close attachments to the perpetrator and not want to get him or her into trouble, particularly if the perpetrator is a family member. For instance, Selma Lyon was extremely attached to her son who perpetrated the alleged financial abuse. Selma would have rather suffered under the abuse before doing anything that might bring any harm to him, according to a family representative. Finally, even if a victim reports a loss due to financial exploitation, an investigation may be difficult to conduct if the victim is cognitively impaired and can't remember the details of the incident, or if the victim isn't even aware that he or she had been victimized.

But it's not just the victims who fail to report exploitation. Professionals such as bankers, attorneys, accountants, and doctors— who are the first defense against elder exploitation—are often slow to report suspected abuse. This is largely because professionals usually have brief and periodic interactions with the elderly, lack or have a limited understanding of "undue influence," or are unwilling to get involved when the exploitation has occurred in a domestic setting. For instance, two relatives contacted Selma's regular doctor about the alleged neglect toward Selma by family members within Selma's household. The doctor ignored their warnings. Finally, even seasoned professionals say it's hard to determine whether a misguided but legitimate financial transaction is really an exploitative one.

Now that we've established the difficulty in gathering accurate prevalence data on elder exploitation, let's look at what we do know.

- According to the National Center on Elder Abuse Bureau of Justice Statistics, financial exploitation represented 12.3 percent of reported elder abuse cases in 2012.
- One in four seniors living in the U.S. was a victim of elder financial exploitation at a total annual cost of more than $3 billion annually, according to the Professional Fiduciary Association of California.
- The U.S. House of Representatives Select Committee on Aging compiled data from 24 states in 1990. Among the Americans who were victims of elder abuse, 20 percent were victims of financial exploitation.
- Prevalence rates of financial exploitation are higher in some states than in others. For example, in Illinois and in Oregon, financial exploitation was reported as the most frequent form

of elder abuse, according to researchers and government statistics. Financial exploitation occurred in half of all abuse cases in New York. In California, fiduciary abuse was found to be the most common type of exploitation (41.5 percent of abuse cases), according to welfare statistics.

- Minority populations experienced greater financial abuse, as compared to other populations. For example, financial exploitation was most frequently reported among Korean immigrants and black elders.
- Financial abuse is often accompanied by other types of elder mistreatment, according to researchers. In one study, 33.7 percent of reported elder abuse included financial exploitation in conjunction with another form of abuse, whereas 37.6 percent involved only financial abuse.
- One out of every five citizens over the age of 65 (over 7.3 million older Americans) has fallen prey to a financial swindle, according to one survey.

An excellent source of incidence data on elder financial abuse is the 2011 MetLife study. Several key findings are worth highlighting.

- Over half of reported cases of elder financial exploitation were perpetrated by strangers (51 percent), followed by family, friends, and neighbors (34 percent), businesses (12 percent), and Medicare and Medicaid fraud (4 percent). Other findings showed that financial exploitation perpetrated by a family member was as high as 90 percent.
- Family, friends, and neighbors accounted for the highest average loss to victims ($145,768), followed by fraud by strangers ($95,156), Medicare and Medicaid fraud ($38,263,136), and business and industry fraud ($6,219,496).
- Women were nearly twice as likely to be targeted for elder financial abuse, as compared to men. Most victims were aged 80 to 89, lived alone, and depended on others for medical or financial assistance.

On a practical level, elder exploitation is often difficult to assess, as compared to other types of abuse. For example, determining at which point a simple task like helping an elder pay bills becomes abusive can be ambiguous. In Selma's situation, for instance, Selma's son helped her with bill paying after Selma's first stroke, according to a family source. That informal arrangement became abusive when the son felt that he was entitled to Selma's assets and then methodically created joint accounts that benefited him. Selma's situation is a classic example of financial abuse in a domestic setting, in which exploitation is a pattern of behavior as opposed to a single incident. It also illustrates the difficulty in determining the precise moment when the abuse begins.

Another complicating factor in assessing elder exploitation is *culture*. Experts say that cultural considerations should be factored into the assessment of financial abuse. For instance, Selma was foreign born. In her culture, kinship ties are strong, and family members customarily help each other based on need.

Why are seniors prime targets for financial crimes? In the case of financial fraud, the Federal Bureau of Investigation (FBI) cites several reasons. First, seniors usually have a "nest egg" and excellent credit, which attract scammers. Second, older Americans, especially the "Silent Generation" (people born from 1925-1942), were raised to be courteous and trusting, which are qualities scam artists play on. Third, elderly victims are less inclined to report a fraud, as they don't always know where to go to report it. Fourth, elderly victims feel ashamed that they've been scammed and thus hide the incident from family members and others. Fifth, elderly victims often make poor witnesses—scammers actually count on this. For instance, it might take an elder several weeks or months to realize that he or she was scammed, making it difficult for the elder to remember what happened.

Types of Financial Elder Abuse: Strangers

A Palm Beach newspaper ran a story about a "boiler room" scam that bilked $2.6 million from timeshare owners, many of whom were elderly victims. According to the complaint filed in a federal court, the shady telemarketing operation convinced timeshare owners to shell out closing fees for the impending sale of their timeshares. The telemarketing scheme used "openers or fronters" to cajole a victim (an owner) into selling his or her timeshare. If the victim expressed an interest, he or she would be forwarded to a "closer" who negotiated the sale and closed the deal. The victim was then instructed to mail or transfer "upfront fees" to the telemarketer, who assured the victim that the closing would happen in a few weeks, which was a lie. Financial crimes against the elderly like this one can happen in a fraction of minutes, yet the devastating effects can last a lifetime. Let's examine crimes against the elderly that are committed by strangers.

According to the MetLife study, elder financial abuse can be grouped into three major categories: *crimes of occasion (or opportunity), crimes of desperation,* and *crimes of predation (or occupation).* First, *crimes of occasion* happen when the victim stands in the way of what the offender wants. Second, *crimes of desperation* are usually committed by a family member or a friend who is desperate for money and will do almost anything to get his or her hands on it. Finally, *crimes of predation* occur when a person builds trust through a personal or a professional relationship with the elder, with the purpose of eventually exploiting him or her.

The U.S. Department of Justice's (DOJ's) Office of Community Oriented Policing Services has also established a classification system for elder financial abuse. In its Problem-Specific Guides Series, a special report on "Financial Crimes Against the Elderly," financial crimes against the elderly are grouped into two general categories: *fraud committed by strangers* and *financial exploitation by relatives and caregivers.* These categories can overlap on the bases of target selection and the means used to commit the crime.

Since seniors are often victims of *fraud*, let's look at it more closely. The DOJ report defines fraud in the following manner: "Fraud generally involves deliberately deceiving the victim with the promise of goods, services, or other benefits that are nonexistent, unnecessary, never intended to be provided, or grossly misrepresented." To win your cooperation, fraudsters manipulate your emotions by using different ruses, such as making you feel as if you're part of an exclusive group, creating a sense of urgency, and convincing you to look no further into the transaction. Additionally, the fraudster won't take "no" for an answer, will fire back with a blizzard of objection-handling techniques, and will use hardball selling techniques to get you to comply. According to the DOJ report, these slam-dunk techniques are core components of fraud and are particularly effective in appealing to people's desire "to feel special, to find a bargain, and to please."

The number of different types of fraud is limited only by the perpetrators' imagination to concoct them. Let's look at the most common forms of elder fraud committed by strangers.

- *Ponzi Schemes*—To bilk his victims, many of whom were elderly, out of billions of dollars, Bernie Madoff used a Ponzi scheme. Here, the schemer promises you higher returns or dividends over traditional investments. The kicker is that instead of investing your funds, the scammer pays dividends to initial investors by using the funds of subsequent investors. As a result, you might end up getting nothing and instead lose everything.

- *Pyramid Schemes*—Also known as "franchise fraud" or "chain fraud," these schemes were particularly popular during the 1980s. Today, many people think of them whenever they hear the term "multi-level marketing," which is a marketing practice used by legitimate businesses like Amway, Avon, and Mary Kay Cosmetics. Like Ponzi schemes, in pyramid schemes the perpetrator collects money from you, which in turn is paid to earlier victims to give the fraud "a veneer of legitimacy." The main difference between a Ponzi scheme and a pyramid scheme is that you, as a victim, are encouraged to recruit more folks (victims) in exchange for a recruitment commission. But what the perpetrator doesn't tell you is that only a few people recoup their investments, as it's "mathematically impossible" for everyone to make money due to the high dropout rate.

- *Market Manipulation Fraud*—Also called "pump and dump fraud," market manipulation fraud builds "artificial buying pressure for a targeted security," which is controlled by the fraudsters. Here's how it works: In "the pump," trading volume for the targeted security is artificially increased, which in turn artificially increases the price of the targeted security. In "the dump," the perpetrator quickly sells off the targeted security in the inflated market, which generates illegal gains to the fraudsters and losses to you.

- *Medical Equipment Fraud*—You see a direct-response TV ad for medical equipment on TV or read about it in a magazine. You become interested when you learn you can get the product for free during a trial period. Before you share any personal information with the direct marketer of these products, know that these offers may be fraudulent. Your insurance company might get charged for the product, or you might never receive it.

- *Rolling Lab Schemes*—Be wary of tests offered to you at health clubs, retirement homes, or shopping malls, which are billed to your insurance company or Medicare. Many of these tests are fake!

- *Medicare Fraud*—This fraud is often committed by medical equipment manufacturers that offer you free medical equipment or products in exchange for your Medicare number. To bill Medicare for the merchandise, a physician's signature on a special form is needed. Either the con artist fakes a signature, or the con artist might bribe a corrupt doctor for it. Then the con artist bills Medicare for the merchandise, which may be unnecessary or was never ordered.

- *Telemarketing Fraud*—If a telemarketer calls you with an offer and says, "You must act now or the offer won't be good"; "You've won a free gift vacation or prize, but you have to pay for postage and handling or other charges"; or "You must send money, give a credit card or bank account number, or have a check picked by up by courier," hang up! Using telephone or e-mail, a perpetrator may solicit money for fraudulent investments, insurance policies, charities, sweepstakes, and so on. Typical bogus products and services sold through telemarketing scams are offers of free prizes, vitamins, health care products, and inexpensive vacations.

- *Internet Fraud*—The Internet is awash with scammers who use a variety of schemes to get you to part with your money. For example, lottery scammers frequently use the Internet to hunt down their victims. According to experts, the Jamaican lottery scammers make about 300,000 calls each day to the U.S., with American citizens losing $300 million each year to this scam. In fact, in Jamaica, lottery scam gangs kill each other over "sucker lists" of elderly people who fall for these scams. Scarily, if a victim stops sending money, the scammer may use Google Earth maps to pinpoint the victim's home. The scammer then threatens the victim that the scammer is just down the street to pay the victim a visit if the victim doesn't pay up.

- *Social Media Scams*—Over half of all seniors use the Internet, and over a third of them use social media, according to the Pew Research Center. Scammers are increasingly using social media, such as Facebook and Twitter, to exploit seniors. For example, in the "granny scam," a scammer poses as a grandchild who claims that he or she needs money to take care of an emergency. To be convincing, the scammer gathers information about the grandparent by visiting his or her social media profile pages. To legitimize the relationship, the scammer also obtains the names of surviving spouses and grandchildren as well as photos of them. Another popular online scam is the "romance scam" on dating sites. Here, the scammer mines personal information about the "mark" through his or her profile pages. Then the scammer makes initial contact with the mark and strikes a friendship or a romance with him or her. Weaving a sob story, the scammer manipulates the mark to send the scammer money to resolve an issue.

- *Prizes and Sweepstakes Fraud*—The commercial voiceover says that you can win an attractive cash or gift prize by sending money to cover things like taxes, shipping, or processing fees. Let's say you send the money. One of two things happens next: the prize never arrives, or the prize does arrive and is a piece of junk. In the case of cash sweepstakes, there's a next-to-zero chance of seeing a dime.

- *Advanced Fee Fraud*—You've probably heard of the "Nigerian 419 scam," which is a form of an advanced fee scheme. Using snail mail or e-mail, the author, usually impersonating a government official, offers you an opportunity to share in a percentage of millions of dollars that the author/self-proclaimed official (the scammer) is attempting to legally transfer out of Nigeria. The scammer encourages you to send information, such as the name of your bank, bank account numbers, and other identifying information, to a fax number provided in the letter or e-mail, which opens a door to the scammer to empty your bank accounts.

- *Charity Contributions Scams*—The perpetrator gets you to donate to a nonexistent charity or a religious organization. This type of scam is even more prevalent following a natural disaster such as Hurricane Sandy.

- *Home and Automobile Repairs Scams*—The perpetrator persuades you to approve emergency home repairs, often requiring a deposit before performing the work. The work may never be performed, get only half finished, or be shoddily done.

- *Loan and Mortgage Scams*—We all remember the foreclosure crisis of 2008 that was partly fueled by predatory lending practices. Predatory lenders offer loans with astronomical interest rates, hidden fees, and punishing repayment schedules, making it difficult for many elderly to pay. Worse still, the elder's home may be at risk if it is used as collateral to secure the loan. In the "reverse mortgage scam," shady realtors or financial advisors steal the equity from the property of unsuspecting victims.

- *Heath, Funeral, and Life Insurance Scams*—Shifty salespeople take advantage of elders' end-of-life concerns by convincing them to buy policies that duplicate existing coverage, don't provide the coverage promised, or are phony.

- *Health Remedies Scam*—The perpetrator preys on elders' health concerns by selling them useless remedies or guaranteeing miracle cures.

- *Travel Scams*—Hawkers sell low-cost travel packages to seniors. These packages may be inflated in price, offer inferior accommodations, or not include the promised services.

- *Mail Fraud*—Mass mailings of fraudulent offers are often sent to homes and businesses. The unsuspecting homeowner or the business owner may "self-select" by returning the postcard or by calling to inquire about the offer, which may be a sham. You've probably seen these direct mail pieces in your mailbox, which often look official, use personalization, and employ credibility enhancers like the titles and signatures of company officers.

- *Door-to-Door Sales Scams*—A perpetrator sells products or services door-to-door to homeowners or business owners. In one version, the perpetrator poses as a utility worker to gain access to your home. While he or she is distracting you, the perpetrator's accomplice burglarizes your home.

- *Identity Fraud*—According to the U.S. Department of Justice (DOJ), 8.6 million Americans were victims of identity theft at a cost of $13.2 billion in 2010. Identity fraud occurs when someone assumes your identity for his or her financial gain. Criminals get your information by stealing your wallet, dumpster diving, or compromising your creditor's bank account information.

None of us want to believe that we can fall for these gimmicks, but it can happen to the best of us because scammers are really good at what they do. Scammers are tricksters who win your trust and confidence through charisma. They establish credibility by comparing their businesses to those of established organizations. They give you the impression that you've been "chosen" or are "lucky" to receive an exclusive offer and then pressure you to make a snap decision. In the case of the elderly, scammers communicate caring compassion for elders' well-being, while also convincing them to keep the "special offer" secret, which reduces the chance of exposure.

Now let's take a look at financial elder abuse committed not by strangers, but by family members and caregivers.

Types of Financial Elder Abuse: Family Members and Caregivers

You've probably heard of a durable power of attorney (DPA), which is a simple, easy legal tool to help you with financial assistance if you need it. However, the DPA is just as easy for people to obtain and misuse, which is why it's been called "an invisible epidemic," "license to steal," and "the Crime of the 1990s."

Consider the *Business Week* article "License to Steal From Seniors: How to Protect the Elderly from the People They've Chosen to Trust," about an 87-year-old woman whose son abused a durable power of attorney. The elderly woman became a victim of financial abuse at the hands of her own son soon after she had given him durable power of attorney to make financial decisions for her. She knew that something wasn't right when her son told her that she couldn't afford to move into an assisted-living facility. She had the money, but her son told her that she didn't. The elderly woman's friend contacted Adult Protective Services (APS). The agency discovered that the son had transferred $225,000 from his mother's account to his own without her permission, which is a clear case of elder exploitation and a breach of trust.

Unlike strangers who commit financial crimes, relatives and caregivers who perpetrate financial crimes against the elderly are involved in an ongoing trust relationship with the victim. Oftentimes the family perpetrator will misappropriate or misuse the elderly victim's money, property, or valuables for personal gain and to the disadvantage of the victim. Common methods employed by family perpetrators include:

- Stealing money, property, or valuables
- Borrowing the elder's money without paying it back
- Withholding needed services for the elder, such as medical care, to conserve funds
- Giving away or selling the elder's possessions without permission
- Cashing the elder's pension or Social Security checks without permission
- Misusing the elder's ATM or credit cards or using them without permission
- Shelling out the elder's money to others without permission
- Manipulating the elder into parting with resources or signing away property
- Setting up joint bank accounts under the pretext of assisting the elder with finances
- Forcing or coercing the elder into deeding property to the perpetrator

- Convincing the elder to sign a durable power of attorney that gives the perpetrator the legal authority to manage the elder's financial and/or medical affairs
- Using nefarious means such as undue influence, duress, fraud, or lack of informed consent to get the elder to create or change a living trust or a will that makes the perpetrator the elder's sole beneficiary

To get the elder to cooperate, the perpetrator will often coerce, intimidate, threaten, or even abuse the elder. Or the perpetrator may make empty promises of lifelong care to the elder. To ensure that no one comes to the elder's aid, the perpetrator will isolate the elder from family members, friends, and other concerned parties. The perpetrator may even convince the elder that no one else cares about him or her, except for the perpetrator.

The Roles of Mental Capacity, Consent, and Undue Influence

One of the pillars of American life is the freedom of self-determination. We treasure our right to choose where we want to live, to do what we want with our lives, and to acquire and bequeath our wealth and assets to whomever we want to receive them. Our legal system can, however, place limits on these decisions if we suffer from diminished decision-making capacity. In the context of elder exploitation, it's important for us to determine if an older person understands or understood what he or she was doing when he or she engaged in a transaction, and whether she or he was coerced, tricked, or under undue influence by someone when the transaction took place. To do this, we must become familiar with the concepts of *mental capacity, consent,* and *undue influence.*

First, *mental capacity* refers to a person's functional skills used in his or her everyday life, such as memory, calculation, information processing, and so on. As we age, these skills may naturally diminish, but the decline may be faster if we suffer from things like certain physical and psychological illnesses, nutritional deficiencies, and so on. Determining when an elder lacks sufficient decision-making capacity is seldom black and white. For instance, an elder may not be able to make financial decisions, but he or she may still retain the capacity to make medical decisions for him- or herself. Finally, diminished decision-making capacity can be sporadic and gradual. For example, elderly people with mild cognitive impairment have good days and bad ones.

Second, *consent* occurs when you "accept or agree" to someone's proposal, according to the National Committee for the Prevention of Elder Abuse (NCPEA). You need to have sufficient mental capacity to comprehend the consequences and implications of your actions for consent to be legally binding. For example, one of the attorneys involved in Selma's case remarked that due to Selma's cognitive changes, she was probably unaware of the implications of her agreeing to allow her son to remove substantial assets from her trust and then creating joint accounts. Given that her son was newly married, issues of exposure and common property were palpable, let alone the potential for misuse of these assets.

Third, *"undue influence* refers to a person's free will being usurped by the will of another," according to an American Bar Association publication titled "Psychological Aspects of Undue Influence." P. Mark Accettura, the author of *Blood & Money: Why Families Fight over Inheritance and What to Do About It*, defines undue influence as follows:

> "Undue influence is the theft of free choice by a person of trust. It is a deliberate act of usurpation. The influencer attempts to replace his victim's thoughts with the influencer's own in furtherance of the influencer's agenda. Undue influence is a form of elder abuse that begins with the trusted influencer gaining the confidence of his vulnerable victim. The influencer then violates that trust by coercing his victim either to gift or bequeath assets to the influencer."

State laws on undue influence vary, but most states require proof that the victim was subjugated or controlled by the perpetrator—in other words, the victim's free will was dismantled by the perpetrator. The courts determine whether undue influence was employed by assessing the appropriateness of a transaction, the exertion of pressure on the elder to make the transaction or dissuade him or her from seeking advice, the nature of the relationship between parties (for example, a confidential fiduciary relationship), the "fairness of the transaction," and the mental and physical condition of the victim at the time of the transaction.

In a domestic setting, the mixed bag of tricks used to unduly influence an elderly victim are both creative and cunning, according to P. Mark Accettura. He states that most influencers depend on a recipe of isolation, timing, and indoctrination to implement their schemes against dependent or impaired elders. According to Accettura, common situations and signs of undue influence include the following:

- You live alone and have no children.
- Your mental and physical health starts to fail and you lose cognition.
- An estranged child or a distant family member suddenly wants to be your caretaker, or a nonfamily caretaker takes over your finances.
- Your professional advisors, such as your accountant or attorney, are replaced for no justifiable reason.
- A new caretaker is identified as your agent under a power of attorney or a joint owner on your bank accounts for bill-paying purposes.
- Checks that are drawn on your accounts are written to cash, to the caretaker, or to the caretaker's family.
- You're denied access to family members or visitors, with bogus reasons given for your unavailability.
- A caretaker always accompanies you and speaks for you.

- You become convinced that you can't get by without the caretaker and that other family members only want your money.
- Your will is prepared and executed by the influencer, often in secrecy.

As an illustration, a typical modus operandi used by an influencer is to overmedicate the elder to the point that he or she becomes acquiescent or disoriented. The influencer then isolates the declining elder and poisons the relationships between the elder and his or her family members or friends. By manipulating and brainwashing the elder into thinking that the influencer is the only person who cares about the elder, the influencer convinces the elder that family members and others are plotting to steal the elder's money and are also conspiring to throw the elder into a nursing home. Along the way, the influencer promotes him- or herself as the elder's rescuer. In Selma's situation, her son and his new family isolated Selma in her home, and brainwashed Selma into believing that Selma's relatives had abandoned her and were trying to cheat her, according to one family source. The relative commented, "They [Zachary and his new family] promoted themselves as Selma's saviors and her relatives as the bad guys."

Perpetrator Characteristics

A typical exploiter is a son, a daughter, a spouse, or another relative. An Adult Protective Services (APS) study found that roughly 40 percent of perpetrators of financial abuse were the victim's son or daughter, 20 percent were other relatives, 1.5 percent were spouses, and 4 percent were nonrelatives. According to another report, a victim's children or grandchildren were most frequently identified as perpetrators, regardless of the victim's gender. These relatives often depended on the elderly victim for their housing or other assistance or had substance abuse problems. Finally, a national survey revealed that perpetrators were significantly younger than their victims, with 40 percent age 40 or younger and another 40 percent age 41 to 59.

In addition to the exploiter's relationship to the elder and the age of the exploiter, the *gender* of the exploiter is also significant, according to an article titled "Exploitation of the Elderly: Undue Influence as a Form of Elder Abuse." For example, a typical male perpetrator is a relative caregiver who is sociopathic or antisocial and suffers from a history of mental illness, substance abuse, or health problems. Also, the male perpetrator may be financially dependent on the elder. In contrast, a typical female perpetrator assumes a caregiving relationship with the elder, in which the female perpetrator encourages dependency and helplessness and thus intensifies the elder's vulnerability. By isolating the elder, the female perpetrator commonly presents herself as the elder's protector. Also, the female perpetrator may fake credentials; exaggerate her position; or be opportunistic, predatory, dysfunctional, controlling, deceitful, intimidating, and abusive, several characteristics of which were displayed by Sybil, according to family observers and the court-appointed psychologist.

Finally, P. Mark Accettura profiles the influencer as a predator in the following way:

> "Influencers, whether due to resentment, repressed anger, or other rationalization, come to believe that they are entitled to the victim's assets. The most pernicious predators are those with long-term controlling relationships with their elderly victims... They do not feel remorse for their actions, and when confronted, frequently respond with more aggression and anger toward the victim."

The author adds that adult children who don't have much going for them are often the most available to care for the elder and, thus, the most likely to manipulate the elderly parent. In fact, statistics showed that an unemployed, dependent adult child was the most likely to steal from a parent and influence him or her "to disinherit more successful beneficiaries."

Next, let's examine *execution variables*, or *vulnerability enhancements*, which set the stage for elder exploitation in a domestic setting. These include the following conditions:

- *Capitalizing on a Certain Mental State.* A perpetrator times the right moment to strike, such as when an elder is less alert or more confused.

- *Escalating an Elder's Distress.* One ploy is to play head games with an elder by increasing his or her fear, discomfort, pain, and so on. For example, an elder may complain about something, such as that he or she is unable to get around the house easily. Instead of remedying the problem, a manipulator will exacerbate it, say, by locating the elder at the farthest room of the house. The manipulator will then offer a solution, such as buying a mobility scooter for the elder, but only if the elder agrees to sign certain documents, which may be described as purchase orders but in reality are something else, such as bank signature cards that are used to create joint accounts with the manipulator.

- *Pressuring an Elder.* One trick is to bully an elder into doing something that the perpetrator wants him or her to do by claiming that the elder wanted it done. For example, a perpetrator may convince an elder that it was his or her idea to change his or her will.

- *Mimicking the Perpetrator.* A dependent, submissive elder may be trained by a perpetrator to follow the perpetrator's lead. For example, Selma's attorney observed that Zachary "coached" Selma on what to say and do.

- *Enhancing Dependency Needs.* Creating greater dependency in an elder makes it easier to manipulate him or her. For example, overmedicating an elder or putting him or her on a poor diet can result in fatigue, which can make the elder more malleable.

- *Relationship Poisoning.* This occurs when someone unjustifiably damages a person's relationship with someone else, according to professor and psychologist Ira Daniel Turkat. "Damaging the relationship between a vulnerable individual and an intended beneficiary can facilitate a manipulative person's drive to divert the vulnerable person's assets," says Turkat. For example, in an attempt to manipulate Selma into disavowing her relatives, Zachary pounded in the idea that Selma's family members were "crooks" who were only after her money, according to one of Selma's nephews. "Zachary was poisoning Selma as to the rest of the family," according to an attorney working on Selma's conservatorship case.

- *Spin Doctoring.* A manipulator will exert influence by making him- or herself indispensable to an elder by doing tasks that the elder can't perform alone, such as bill paying, grocery shopping, and so on. The manipulator will then repeatedly tell the elder how lucky he or she is to have the manipulator do all those things.

- *Isolating an Elder.* This is a central feature of exploitation. By isolating a vulnerable elder and restricting others' access to him or her, a manipulator can more easily influence the elder. In Selma's situation, Zachary, his new family, and their attorney went to extreme lengths to isolate Selma. Zachary and his new family hid the phone from Selma. They refused to allow visitors to see Selma. They even tried to deny access to professionals who were sent by the court and other agencies to help Selma. Their attorney, for example, threatened the psychologist, who was sent to do an evaluation of Selma's situation. The attorney said that the psychologist was trespassing, and he threatened to call the police and get a restraining order against her.

- *Playing the Savior.* One ruse is to modify information or events to manipulate an elder's perceptions. For example, a manipulative caregiver will reenact an event, such as an unscrupulous telemarketer running a scam, and convince an elder that had it not been for the manipulator, the elder would have been exploited, which paints the real exploiter as the elder's savior. A manipulator may also reinterpret events to manipulate a vulnerable person's emotions and increase his or her paranoia that others are out to get him or her.

- *Idle Family Members.* You'd think that family members and relatives are the best defense to elder exploitation, and they are IF they're actively involved in an elder's life. But relatives will often sit on the sidelines instead of coming to the elder's aid mainly because they don't want to interfere, aren't aware of the exploitation, or are aware of the exploitation but don't know what to do about it. For instance, Selma's siblings, whom Selma had helped when they were in need, were not actively involved in preventing and remedying Selma's abusive situation. Instead, the family members who came to Selma's direct aid were a niece, a few nephews, and an in-law.

Another way to look at vulnerability enhancers is by *perpetrator types.* According to an article titled "Probate Psychological Aspects of Undue Influence," four sets of manipulators exist:

- The *con artist* schemes to get someone else to part with his or her resources. The con artist is a professional liar who has a history of exploiting others.
- The *sociopath* gets a thrill out of exploiting others and is driven by the need to feel power and control over others as well as to abuse them. One of Selma's caregivers observed that Zachary and his new family showed little or no empathy toward Selma's visible frailty and fragility. Instead, they seemed to exploit her weakened state to get what they wanted from Selma.
- The *opportunist* doesn't plan to exploit the vulnerable person but soon finds "the fruits of temptation too great to resist." The opportunist rationalizes or justifies his or her manipulations; i.e., "I deserve this for all I have done." Likewise, Noah said

that Zachary was unabashed about claiming that he deserved "everything because he had lived with Selma."

- The *career criminal* makes an occupation of ripping people off, specifically the elderly, and is generally a nonrelative perpetrator. Most states don't require criminal background checks or don't forbid offenders of particular crimes from working with elders. As a result, many ex-convicts become caregivers for vulnerable elders.

Victim Characteristics

According to an article titled "Exploitation of the Elderly: Undue Influence as a Form of Elder Abuse," *risk factors*, or *victim vulnerabilities*, that make an individual more susceptible to exploitation are as follows:

- Age (over 75 years of age)
- Gender (female)
- Ethnicity (white)
- Income (middle to high income)
- Home ownership and visible assets
- Brain illness, such as organic brain damage or cognitive impairment
- Physical, emotional, and mental state, such as frailty or depression
- Recent loss of a spouse or a divorce
- Living with the abuser, often a family member who suffers from mental illness or substance abuse or who is unemployed
- Social isolation
- Estrangement from children and other relatives
- Fear of changing living circumstances
- Taking several medications
- Lack of familiarity with finances
- Easily influenced, deceived, or intimidated

As a whole, older white women are targets for elder exploitation more often than men. According to the National Elder Abuse Incidence Study (NEAIS) published in 1998, a comprehensive elder abuse study conducted by the National Center on Elder Abuse (NCEA) and the American Public Human Services Association, 91.8 percent of financial abuse victims were older women (80 years or older). The NEAIS report also found that the majority of financial abuse victims were white (83 percent), according to substantiated Adult Protective Services reports.

Why are women mostly targeted for financial exploitation? First, according to an Institute for Health Metrics and Evaluation (IHME) report, women live longer than men, on average, 81.3 years for women versus 76.2 years for men. Second, women are perceived as "weak and vulnerable" by offenders. Third, when the male spouse dies or loses capacity, the wife may be left to handle finances, with which she may be unfamiliar. In seeking help, then, she may become a target for exploitation.

Selma Lyon fits the profile of a typical victim of elder exploitation. At the time of the documented victimization, Selma was a well-to-do elderly widow. She suffered from chronic illnesses and cognitive impairment, as well as from depression following the death of her closest sister. Selma's son lived with her and depended on her financially. Over time he isolated Selma from her relatives and also took over Selma's finances. Selma wanted to remain living in her home and would never accede to moving into an assisted-living facility or to living with another family member. Because of Selma's dementia and frailty, she became easily confused and disoriented, which made her more easily influenced, deceived, and intimidated by others.

Let's take a moment to examine the risk factors of elder fraud. According to a U.S. Department of Justice (DOJ) Office of Community Oriented Policing Services Problem-Specific Guides Series report, the notion that elderly fraud victims are uninformed, socially isolated, and impaired is outdated, even though cognitive impairment can be a predisposing factor. In fact, most elderly fraud victims are characterized as educated, informed, and socially active, according to an AARP survey. The same survey reported that over two thirds of elderly fraud victims said they had trouble distinguishing between fraudulent and legitimate pitches, even though 90 percent of the respondents knew about telemarketing fraud. In addition to these findings, researchers have identified several personal characteristics that may predispose a person to victimization, including homeownership; an unlikelihood of seeking advice before making a purchase; an unfamiliarity with consumer information and rights; financial risk-taking behavior; an openness to marketing appeals; and an unawareness of scams and deceptive selling practices.

In contrast to financial abuse perpetrated by family members, fraud committed by strangers contains "victim compliance" to some degree, according to the Department of Justice (DOJ). At one end of the continuum, you've got a victim who has no idea that he or she has been victimized, such as when someone steals a victim's identity or credit card. At the other end, you've got a victim who becomes revictimized. For example, you've probably heard of "mooch" or "sucker" lists that are populated with susceptible elders' names. These lists are kept by fraudulent operations and sold to other operators. Somewhere in the middle you've got a victim who makes poorly informed or researched transactions. On top of it all, people's positive traits, such as generosity, kindness, empathy, and trusting others, can work against them in the context of fraud scenarios. Likewise, people who are careless, easily manipulated, and susceptible to flattery are at risk too.

Above all, "the strongest predictor of future victimization is past victimization," say researchers. For example, past victims can get sucked in by fraudsters who promise to get their money back from earlier frauds. These scammers run "recovery rooms," where they get in touch with past victims, offer to investigate previous frauds, and promise to recoup victims' losses—for fees, of course. As you might guess, after a victim pays a recovery fee, the second scammer becomes unreachable. Revictimization is also a central feature in financial exploitation perpetrated by relatives and caregivers. These perpetrators frequently escalate from small transactions like bank withdrawals to bigger ones such as raiding an elder's entire estate.

The Lyon Case: The Love of Money Is the Root of All Evil

By all accounts, the Lyon household was in disrepair. Selma was completely disoriented due to the onset of dementia, and she was being neglected by Zachary. Minerva was hospitalized for a heart attack that proved fatal. Zachary appeared overwhelmed and was being uncooperative toward family members who wanted to help both him and Selma. He simply shut everyone out, except for one person, Sybil.

During this difficult time, family members had grown concerned that Selma's personal and medical needs were being ignored. They urged Selma to stay with one of her siblings, at least temporarily. But Selma didn't want to leave Zachary living on his own, nor did she want to leave her home.

Livingston knew that if Selma had set up durable powers of attorney (DPAs) for health care and for finances, these instruments would provide instructions on what to do and who should do it in the event of incapacity. Only Zachary would know if these legal documents existed—and he wasn't talking.

Livingston finally got fed up with Zachary's foot-dragging, and threatened to take legal steps if Zachary continued to dodge the DPA question. Zachary finally produced the documents. In the DPAs, both Zachary and Selma's brother were named as coagents—and they were listed as coagents on Minerva's too.

But the news came too late: Minerva tragically died.

Minerva was barely cold in her grave when Zachary made a run on her assets. Unbeknownst to Selma's family, Zachary had set up joint accounts with Minerva for bill-paying purposes. Shortly after Minerva died, Livingston discovered that Zachary removed Minerva's name from all the accounts and took possession of the assets, even though they were supposed to be shared with other family members.

Out of the blue, Zachary married Sybil in a civil ceremony. Afterward, Zachary and Sybil lived apart. Sybil and her family lived somewhere in the area, while Zachary remained in Selma's home.

After a few months, Sybil and her family unexpectedly moved into Selma's house, which triggered an unusually large hike in household expenses. Noah said, "I suspect that Zachary is using Selma's money for his and his family's needs and not Aunt Selma's." Based on Selma's bank statements (which were obtained by court order), regular ATM withdrawals were being made. So tracking how Selma's money was being spent was next to impossible.

Livingston and other family members grew increasingly concerned over Selma's situation. Livingston said, "We knew Zachary was unable to care for her. We also felt that Selma's resources weren't being used to satisfy her needs." Zachary interpreted the family's concern as interference—Sybil saw Selma's family as a threat to whatever plans she had for Zachary and Selma.

Livingston was taken aback when he learned that Zachary wanted to dispose of Selma's real property. Zachary used the rationale that Selma needed the money for her health care, even though Selma had plenty of money in the bank and enjoyed excellent health care coverage.

Once Livingston caught wind that Zachary had removed Selma's bank accounts from her trust and created joint tenancy accounts, Livingston grew increasingly uneasy. When Selma was asked about the joint accounts, she said she wasn't aware of their existence and didn't want this arrangement. "I told Zachary in no uncertain terms that he *must* return Selma's assets to her trust," Livingston said. But Zachary ignored him.

When Zachary told Noah that Sybil would not be happy unless she had "a million dollars in the bank," Noah knew that there was an imminent danger. Other relatives felt strongly that Zachary, with the help of Sybil, would siphon off all of Selma's assets inside of a few months. The relatives agreed that they needed to act quickly and decisively. Since Livingston was the go-to person in the family, the relatives trusted him to do what was best for Selma. So Livingston agreed to act as the initiator if the family chose to do an intervention.

"The first thing we had to consider was Selma's capacity," recalled Livingston. "A troubling trend was occurring in which Selma's wishes, as stated in her original trust that was drafted when Selma had capacity, were changing. In other words, her original wishes were being altered under Zachary's undue influence. Frankly, in Selma's present state of mind, anyone could take undue advantage of her and put her assets in jeopardy," added Livingston.

To get started, Livingston contacted Attorney Wright, Selma's estate planning attorney. Livingston raised several concerns regarding Selma's unmet health needs and Zachary's manipulation of Selma's assets. Wright did not know about the joint accounts, nor did he know that Zachary was in charge of Selma's spending.

In Selma's durable power of attorney for finances, Selma named more than one agent; Zachary and Selma's brother were appointed coagents. To complicate matters, Zachary and Selma's brother were at odds. The brother wanted Zachary to retitle Selma's assets to the trust, but Zachary refused.

"Selma's attorney instructed Zachary to take his name off of all Selma's accounts and place the assets back into her trust. He said that if they [Zachary and Selma's brother] are unable to work together, then an institutional trustee should be considered. We knew Selma would not want a nonfamily member handling her estate matters," Livingston said. Certainly the likely wish was that "Selma preferred a family member and would not have wished to incur the cost of a faceless corporate trustee," Livingston's attorney provided.

Before doing any work on Selma's estate plan, Wright wanted to have Selma seen by a specialist to address her capacity. Otherwise, any changes to Selma's estate plan would be contestable if Selma lacked capacity when they were made.

Wright recognized that the air of distrust between Zachary and Selma's brother was thickening. He proposed that Selma, Zachary, and Selma's brother, along with Livingston, meet to iron things out.

Livingston agreed to meet, but felt that they'd get nowhere with Zachary. Livingston suggested that a third party, such as another family member or a close family friend, should take over the task of managing Selma's assets, as Livingston felt that Zachary was manipulating and coercing Selma—and nothing and no one could stop him because he was living with her. Wright had also witnessed Zachary's manipulations: "He [Zachary] invites her [Selma] to speak when he's confident that she'll give the response he wishes and not to speak when she seems uncomfortable."

At this point, referring Selma's matter to the appropriate agency seemed almost inescapable. Livingston researched "where" reports of elder abuse should be made, such as Adult Protective Services (APS), local law enforcement, or the district attorney's office. Along the way, he was met with conflicting information. On the one hand, APS said that its agency investigates these complaints. "They [APS] told me that each investigator determines the scope of investigation and individually (subjectively) evaluates whether an abuse has taken place. Whether they will investigate beyond a visit, the depth or extent of the investigation, or whether another party can halt the investigation through intervention or legal action, seem to be questions that APS will not answer until after a complaint has been received and an investigator has been assigned," Livingston discovered. On the other hand, the local police department told Livingston something entirely different. "Every complaint of elder abuse must be handled by the police—no exception," according to the police department. The person Livingston spoke with at the police department said that any calls made to APS would be referred to the local police department for investigation. An APS representative rebutted by stating that APS would do the investigation.

Meanwhile, Selma's situation grew more dangerous when Zachary and Sybil isolated Selma from the world. As a result, Livingston chose to call APS on Zachary and Sybil. APS sent a case worker out to assess Selma's home situation. The APS report was inconclusive, and the file was closed.

Livingston spoke to Wright about Selma's worsening situation. Wright told Livingston that Zachary became "agitated" when they discussed the specifics of handling Selma's affairs. Wright said he was going to ask Selma to resign as trustee. Wright asked Livingston if he would be willing to replace Selma. Livingston agreed. Presciently, Livingston told Wright that Zachary would probably have him fired if this change was made, which was the fate of other attorneys who would not do what Zachary wanted. Livingston told a family member, "If Zachary manipulates Selma to fire her attorney, I *will* call APS again."

Wright said he had wanted to do an accountancy for Selma, but he needed the bank statements to do that. Zachary had these records in his possession but refused to share them. "I grew suspicious of how Selma's money was being spent. If Zachary jumped ship or continued to drag his feet, I was going to file for a conservatorship, requesting that her nephew Livingston be made Selma's temporary or permanent conservator," Wright commented.

As a last-ditch effort, Wright sent Zachary a certified letter that outlined the actions that Zachary must take in order to make Selma's trust whole again. Zachary never responded. Instead, he fired Wright and hired a new attorney for Selma, Attorney Gilroy.

On behalf of the family, Attorney Young contacted Attorney Gilroy to furnish him with information about Selma's situation. Young said, "The attorney [Gilroy] didn't know that Zachary was transferring Selma's money in and out of trust accounts, nor did he know that large sums of money sat outside of Selma's trust." Young advised Gilroy that Selma was being unduly influenced by Zachary, who was trying to implement changes to Selma's estate plan. Young warned Gilroy, "Plenty of people are aware of Selma's situation and APS has been called. If this situation continues, the family will seek a conservatorship."

Agatha also spoke with Gilroy. He told Agatha that he was representing Selma and Zachary to perform changes to Selma's trust. Agatha recalled, "Gilroy said he planned to represent Zachary *and*

Selma to work with the family to arrive at a settlement. I told him I wasn't aware that there was a dispute that needed settling!"

After Agatha's conversation with Gilroy, she felt sure that he was overreaching and being just as controlling as Sybil and Zachary. Agatha also felt that Selma had absolutely no say in her own affairs. Agatha remarked, "Zachary and Sybil are the master and the mistress whom Gilroy was really serving."

Selma's relatives agreed that seeking a conservatorship for Selma was the only way of protecting her. Livingston became the petitioner, the person presenting the formal application for the appointment of a conservator to the court.

In the Petition for Conservatorship, Attorney Forte laid out the allegation of undue influence. Forte provided: "The son [Zachary] has convinced the mother [Selma] to move significant sums from her trust to joint tenancy accounts with him. One bank refused, questioning her capacity. He took her to a series of attorneys to get the bank to comply. Two attorneys told him to return the money to the trust. He refused, going to a third attorney."

The petition for a temporary conservatorship was granted by the court. The judge appointed Livingston to be Selma's temporary conservator and instructed Zachary to provide Livingston with any changes made to Selma's trust by Attorney Gilroy along with Selma's bank statements. At that time, Zachary furnished the trust changes but still refused to provide the bank statements.

Livingston discovered that the changes to Selma's trust were sweeping. They made Zachary Selma's sole trustee and gave him full powers over Selma's medical and property management decisions. Zachary would be given a monthly salary to live with Selma, plus room and board for him and his family. All of Selma's title deeds were included in the trust changes.

Later on, in the presence of Zachary, a family member asked Selma whether she approved the trust revisions. Selma said she didn't remember. She said that she couldn't read because she couldn't see. According to Selma, the "mean attorney" put papers in front of her and said, "Sign here." "With a few barely legible signatures from

Selma, Zachary and Sybil were made Selma's keepers," said the family member.

After the conservatorship hearing, Agatha called to check on Selma, who was very upset. Selma said, "I know everything that the relatives are doing to me. They're crooked." Agatha assured Selma that the relatives loved her and that they were honest people. In the background, Agatha could hear Zachary and Sybil coaching and prodding Selma. When Livingston called to check on Selma, he got the worst of it, with Selma accusing him of being a "thief."

Livingston reported this phone episode to Attorney Forte, stating that Selma had become very agitated when he and his cousin called Selma, and that Zachary and Sybil were distressing Selma. In response, Forte shot off a letter to Zachary that contained a firm warning: "Emotional abuse is as much a crime as financial abuse [...] It is against the law. There are civil and criminal sanctions if it occurs."

Yet Selma's torment and exploitation did not end there.

In the next chapter, we'll introduce "who" does "what" in conservatorships, describe how conservatorships are formed, and identify the advantages and disadvantages of conservatorships. Also, we'll share the truth about conservatorships: where they succeed and where they fail. Finally, the details of the Lyon conservatorship case will be disclosed.

PART III

Conservatorship System

CHAPTER 5

The Paper Chase

You may have heard the term "conservatorship" in the context of entertainment news. Older celebrities like the late Mickey Rooney, the star of such film classics as *The Adventures of Huckleberry Finn* and *The Black Stallion*, and the late Peter Falk, who played the disheveled, shrewd police lieutenant on *Columbo*, were placed under conservatorships. But conservatorships aren't just reserved for eldsters. American pop princess Britney Spears and the late British soul singer Amy Winehouse were conserved for running amok and posing a danger to themselves.

In this chapter, we'll introduce "who" does "what" in conservatorships, describe how conservatorships are formed, discuss the pros and cons of conservatorships, and expose the dark side of conservatorships. Finally, we'll revisit the Lyon family to learn how they came to the difficult decision to seek a conservatorship to protect Selma.

For the purposes of this discussion, the terms "guardianship" and "conservatorship" will be used interchangeably, although they're often used differently in elder law and in state law. In California, where the Lyon case took place, the term *conservatorship* means guardianship of person and/or property, whereas the term *guardianship* relates to minors.

What Is a Guardianship?

Let's begin with a little history on the origin of the guardianship concept. It dates back to Roman times. Marcus Tullius Cicero (106-43 B.C.), a Roman philosopher, lawyer, and statesman, codified the guardianship concept into Roman law, with an eye toward managing an incompetent's property. In England during the early 1300s, guardianships appeared in common law with the passage of *De Praerogativa Regis*, a statute that allowed kings to take ownership of the property of mentally disturbed individuals.

During the medieval period, a legal process was established to determine a person's mental competency. Known as a writ *de idiota inquirendo*, this old common law instructed a sheriff to determine whether a person was an incompetent. Once the writ was issued, the alleged incompetent was tried by jury, and if deemed incompetent, the chancellor placed the incompetent in the care of a friend who received compensation for all of his or her trouble. In addition, the incompetent's heir was put in charge of the estate. The heir reported on the status of the incompetent's estate to the court of Chancery, a court of equity in England and Wales that included trusts, land law, and the administration of estates.

During the early 1600s, an heir's guardian obligations were codified and crossed the Big Pond to the United States. In the aftermath of the American Revolution, the states employed *parens patriae* (Latin for "parent of the nation"). The law allowed the state to exercise jurisdiction over persons with disabilities or incapacities by appointing officials, usually guardians, to care for these persons if they were unable to care for themselves, from children to the developmentally disabled, from alcoholics to the mentally incapacitated—and ever increasingly the elderly.

A good working definition of the term *guardianship* appears in "Public Guardianship After 25 Years: In the Best Interest of Incapacitated People?," an interdisciplinary report funded by The

Retirement Research Foundation. In it, *guardianship* is defined as follows:

> "... a relationship created by state law in which a court gives one person or entity (the guardian) the duty and power to make personal and/or professional decisions for another person (the ward or incapacitated person). [...] Guardianship can "unperson" individuals and make them 'legally dead.' Guardianship can be a double-edged sword, 'half Santa and half ogre.'"

The report further described a public guardianship as "the appointment and responsibility of a public official or publicly-funded organization to serve as legal guardian in the absence of willing and responsible family members or friends to serve as, or in the absence of resources to employ, a private guardian." Public guardianship, then, constitutes a set of state and local mechanisms invented to deal with an "unbefriended" group by serving as a "guardian of last resort."

Because of a guardianship's far-reaching power to strip people of their fundamental rights, you'd probably think that guardianships would be legislated, regulated, and controlled at the federal level. Not so—adult guardianships are a state-based legal function. The foundation of the public guardianship system is established by general guardianship code, while legal proceedings can vary by state.

In the past two decades, a tidal wave of change in guardianship laws has occurred, specifically on procedural protections, court oversight, and capacity determination. In 2007, 44 states provided statutory provisions on public guardianship, according to one study. Roughly 15 states passed 18 adult guardianship bills in 2008, according to the American Bar Association (ABA) Commission on Law and Aging. For example, in an effort to boost fiduciary accountability (a *fiduciary* is "a person who is invested with the rights and powers to be exercised for the benefit of another person"), Colorado enacted a new statute coined the "judicial toolbox" to enlarge and standardize judicial rules governing court-supervised fiduciaries.

Guardianships by the Numbers

You might be wondering how many people's lives are managed under a guardianship. The answer is that no one knows for sure. According to a report published by the House Select Committee on Aging, more than 500,000 older Americans are under a guardianship at any given time, which is probably an underestimate. One barrier to collecting hard data on adult guardianships is the states. Remember that each state establishes its own guardianship laws, nomenclature, procedures, determination of incapacity, and powers and authority of conservators, which can widely differ from state to state. For instance, conservatorships are called adult guardianships in some states, such as in California and in Maine. Another stumbling block is a lack of uniformity and consistency in state and local court data collection systems within all areas of the guardianship process. In some jurisdictions, for example, probate categories for case types are often lumped together. For instance, instead of creating separate categories for each type, such as "conservatorship/trusteeship" and "elder abuse," some jurisdictions create broad categories like "guardianship/conservatorship/trusteeship."

To address the dearth in guardianship data, the American Bar Association (ABA) Commission on Law and Aging collected general adult guardianship data together with information on the extent to which guardianship abuse occurs and the extent to which guardianships protect individuals from such abuse. The report concluded that state court administrative offices kept few guardianship statistics; that state-level data in a majority of reporting states were completely lacking; that reported data were restricted to filings and depositions; and that *nearly no data were available on elder abuse cases.*

Finally, a U.S. Government Accountability Office (GAO) study found a serious gap in the availability and reliability of statistical data to address and fill the cracks in the guardianship system. The study concluded: "Without better statistical data concerning the size of the incapacitated population or how effectively it is being served, it will be difficult to determine precisely what kinds of efforts may be appropriate to better protect incapacitated elderly people from exploitation, abuse and neglect."

Models of Public Guardianships

Guardianship laws are established by the state, but that doesn't necessarily mean they're determined by the state. In a working paper prepared for the U.S. Senate Special Committee on Aging, the authors drew four distinct models of public guardianship—*court model, independent state offices, social service agency,* and *county level*—to describe guardianships in statutory and administrative terms. Each model works differently.

> *Court Model*—Here, rulemaking power rests in the hands of the chief administrative judge of the state. The chief judge of the court appoints a *public guardian,* an official of the court. In 2007 five states adopted this model: Georgia, Mississippi, Washington, Delaware, and Hawaii.

> *Independent State Office*—Similar to the public defender model, the public guardian is appointed by the governor. In 2007 four states followed this model: Alaska, Illinois, New Mexico, and Kansas.

> *Social Services Agency Model*—The public guardian office is embedded in a social service agency. Some call this the "conflict of interest model" because the

agency furnishing the services is also the guardian. In 2007 about 22 states used this model, including Connecticut, Florida, New Hampshire, Vermont, Virginia, North Dakota, Indiana, and Montana.

County Model—A public guardian is a local official within the county. The county government appoints the public guardian, while the state attorney general regulates the county offices. In 2007 about 13 states employed this model, including Arizona, Missouri, and California.

Because the Lyon case featured in this book originated in California, specifically Los Angeles County, let's talk about the conservatorship system in California. As mentioned earlier, California has adopted the county model of public guardianship. Here, public guardians are named in each county. Each county differs in its interpretation of government and probate code. No state office of the public guardian exists. Instead, a state association exists, the California Association of Public Administrators, Public Guardians and Public Conservators, of which most county public guardians are members. Older or dependent persons and people whom the court deems "gravely disabled" are two populations served by these public guardians.

The public guardian is a long-established legal entity in L.A. County. The Los Angeles County Public Guardian (LAPG) was founded in 1945. By 1987 the LAPG was placed under the auspices of L.A. County's Department of Mental Health. The LAPG obtains referrals through community members, hospitals, and agencies that request an investigation to determine if an alleged incapacitated person qualifies for a conservatorship. In Los Angeles and other California counties, however, the public guardian is usually reluctant to get involved if an incapacitated person's family can more effectively intervene on behalf of the incapacitated person.

Using California as a backdrop, let's look at how a public guardian can enter into the guardianship picture. Say a public guardian determines that a situation, such as a functionally impaired elder living in squalor or an elder unable to take care of his or her basic needs, warrants an intervention through the placement of the elder in a conservatorship, and no family member is willing to step up to assist the elder. (Note that under normal circumstances, a public guardian does not have priority over family members when somebody needs a conservator.) To do that, the public guardian files a *petition* (a formal written application requesting a court to perform a particular judicial action) with the probate court. The petition must demonstrate that the proposed conservatorship is the "least restrictive alternative" to address the particular situation. A superior court investigator will then review the petition to determine whether the impaired elder agrees or opposes the conservatorship. Following that, the impaired elder is served with a copy of the petition by mail or by a process server 10 to 15 days later.

By now, the impaired elderly gets sucked up into a legal maze, where he or she will be at the mercy of the court. If the impaired elder doesn't object to the conservatorship, a public guardian will be appointed. If the impaired elder does object, a court-appointed attorney, known as *PVP* (*Probate Volunteer Panel*) *counsel*, will be assigned to the impaired elder (the client). In some counties, the courts don't so easily and instantly name a PVP, such as in Orange County, California; whereas in others they do, such as Los Angeles County. Three things can happen next: the client will consent to the appointment, the matter will be set for a court trial, or the matter will be set for a jury trial. More about a typical legal proceeding later.

In a nutshell, a conservatorship is a court case where a judge appoints a "reasonable person or organization," a "conservator" or guardian, to make medical and/or financial decisions for an incapable adult, a "conservatee" or ward. In the above illustration, the impaired elder would be the conservatee, and the public guardian would be the conservator, *the guardian of last resort*. However, some critics of the Office of the Public Guardian debunk the notion that the public guardian is still acting as the guardian of last resort. These detractors claim that nowadays the public guardian is "eager" to pursue conservatorships for individuals with large estates.

The scary thing is that any of us could become a ward of the state. Growing old and forgetful, getting ill, becoming unable to take care of ourselves or our affairs, getting into a crippling accident, or depending on others for our care could happen to any of us. Losing capacity doesn't distinguish between the genius or the average, the rich or the poor, or the healthy or the unhealthy.

Types of Conservatorships

As indicated earlier, guardianships are defined by state law and vary from state to state. Consider California. In "The Golden State," conservatorships come in four forms: *general conservatorships, limited conservatorships, temporary conservatorships*, and *Lanterman-Petris-Short conservatorships (LPSs)*. The first three forms are considered *probate conservatorships* based on California Probate Code, while the fourth form is designed to care for individuals suffering with serious mental illness and who need special care. For the intended purpose of this book, let's confine our discussion to probate conservatorships. Now let's describe each.

First, *general conservatorships* are ordinarily used for adults who are unable to take care of themselves or their finances. Under a general conservatorship, the judge would choose a person or an organization, the "conservator," to make some or all life decisions for the protected person, the "conservatee." Things like medical and housing decisions would be made by the "conservator of the person." The conservator of the person might also make property decisions, or someone else might be appointed to do that, the "conservator of the estate." For example, in the Lyon case, the conservatee, Selma, was permanently ushered into a general conservatorship. Three court-appointed fiduciaries—a conservator of the person, a conservator of the estate, and a trustee—were nominated and given the "exclusive authority," or the ultimate legal control, over every single aspect of Selma's life.

Second, adults with developmental disabilities who are unable to fully care for themselves or their finances may be placed under a *limited conservatorship*. These conservatees don't usually need a high level of care or assistance, as compared to conservatees in general conservatorships. They often suffer from long-term developmental disabilities, such as mental retardation, cerebral palsy, autism, and other impairments, that started before they turned 18.

Finally, when a conservatorship is required urgently, the judge may grant a *temporary conservatorship* by appointing a temporary conservator of person and/or property for a stated period of time. Generally speaking, a temporary conservatorship will often last up to 60 days, but the term can be extended if the Court finds good reason to lengthen it. A temporary conservatorship is a "Band-Aid" over a potentially festering situation and is usually granted if the matter is urgent. The request for a temporary conservatorship is generally filed as part of a general conservatorship case. In this instance, a temporary conservator may be appointed until a general conservator is found. The temporary conservator's duties may include arranging for immediate care and support for the conservatee and also protecting his or her property from damage or loss. For example, in celebrity legal news, the ailing 95-year-old actress Zsa Zsa Gabor was placed under a temporary conservatorship when her stepdaughter and Gabor's ninth husband feuded over Gabor's finances and care. In Gabor's case, her husband was made temporary conservator, and was required to allow the daughter access to her mother and receive financial information from him.

Next, let's learn who can become a conservator.

Conservators and the Roles They Play

Given the extreme levels of intrusiveness and control over people's lives, you'd think a conservator would need special qualifications or specialized knowledge in accounting, law, or social work to become a probate conservator. Not true—pretty much anybody may qualify to become a conservator. In most states, the one prerequisite is that you're mentally competent. In fact, only about 18 states place some restrictions on who can become a guardian, and just a handful of states prohibit convicted felons from being appointed as guardians.

Under a probate conservatorship, two types of probate conservators can be appointed: a *conservator of the person*, responsible for handling the conservatee's health care and other basic needs, and/or a *conservator of the estate*, responsible for handling the conservatee's financial matters. If a person wishes to assume dual roles, he or she must petition the court for both. Ultimately, the needs of the conservatee will determine if both a conservator of the person and a conservator of the estate are needed.

So who can file for a conservatorship? Typically, the people who can file for a conservatorship are:

- Proposed conservatee
- Spouse, domestic partner, or relative
- Interested state or local public entity or agency
- Interested friend or person

Around 95 percent of conservators play dual roles of conservator of the person and conservator of the estate, while about 5 percent are different people or private or professional conservators, according to one conservatorship attorney. In addition, several co-conservators can be named, which can make things much more complicated and costly whenever a petition is filed by any one of the co-conservators.

Whoever is chosen, the proposed conservator must be bondable, which means he or she must hire an attorney. In other words, a surety agency (think bail bondsman) must be willing to issue a bond. If for any reason the proposed conservator is unbondable, such as if he or she has any liens or judgments against him or her or is a felon or convict, then he or she is ruled out as a candidate.

If the proposed conservatee isn't in a position to nominate a person, the court will follow a list of preferences established by law (in order of preference from first to last): a spouse or domestic partner, an adult child, a parent, a sibling, a public guardian, or others the law approves. Let's say the first person in the order of preference, the spouse, doesn't wish to be the conservator. He or she can nominate another person or entity, such as a family member, friend, or relative. If none of them wishes to be the conservator, a professional conservator who charges fees for services (which can be quite high) can be hired.

If no one files a petition, the public guardian will typically act as conservator and be legally responsible for making all decisions for the incapacitated person. In most counties, the public guardian will be appointed only if the proposed conservatee has sufficient assets to pay for services. In such cases, the public guardian will take custody of the elder's funds and deposit or invest them and thus assume the elder's personal and financial responsibilities.

It's worth spending a few moments to discuss professional, or private, fiduciaries in a conservatorship context by taking a look at California's thriving fiduciary industry. In California about 500 professional conservators oversee roughly $1.5 billion in assets. Until recently, a person with a clean felony record and $385 dollars in his or her pocket for the state registration fee could become a conservator. In some states, a person with a poor credit history or a criminal using a fake identity was allowed to become a conservator. No requirements or special knowledge in relevant areas like social work, law, or accounting are necessary.

For years, California conservators were subject to fewer state regulations than hairdressers or guide-dog trainers. No agency licensed conservators or investigated complaints. Courts were too backlogged to supervise their work, oversight was erratic or cursory at best, and questionable conduct was rarely sanctioned. The result: conservatees were victimized by the very conservators whom the court appointed to protect them.

Years later in 1999, California law established a statewide registry of private conservators, guardians, and trustees. In turn, the California Department of Justice gave judges access to centralized information about professional conservators. Judges were required to check the information in the statewide registry before making appointments. Also, judges were supposed to report complaints to the registry that were filed against a conservator or a guardian. Finally, the public was given access to information on professional trustees, conservators, and professional guardians through the State of California's Office of the Attorney General website.

In addition to the statewide registry, in 2006 California created a new state agency charged with licensing and regulating professional fiduciaries, including conservators, guardians, and trustees, called the Professional Fiduciaries Bureau. As of 2009, professional fiduciaries must be licensed to receive court appointment. However, the law applies only to private conservators or guardians with two or more conservatees at the same time and who aren't related by blood to the conservator. Public guardians or public officers acting for a public agency, attorneys, CPAs, brokers and investment advisors, IRS agencies, and employees of trust companies, among others, are exempted from licensing. Those who wish to be licensed as a California professional fiduciary must apply and take and pass an exam for licensure. Private fiduciaries with five or more years of experience automatically meet the education/experience qualification, but those individuals with less experience must meet a higher bar by having a BA or BS degree and at least three years of experience to get licensed. So California has gotten tougher on private conservators, which provides added protection if you find you must hire one.

The Conservatorship Court Process

Whenever you see court and process in the same sentence, you know you've gotten yourself into a situation that could be lengthy, costly, and possibly ugly. Let's describe the conservatorship process by walking through a typical case in the California courts.

Step 1: Assess the Situation. Let's assume that someone wants to conserve you for certain reasons. Say your adult son feels you're unable to take care of yourself and fears for your personal health and welfare. In this scenario, your son will play the role of the proposed conservator, and you will be the proposed conservatee. If your son wishes to be conservator over your person, he must prove to the court that you're unable to properly provide for your basic needs, such as food, clothing, and shelter. If he wishes to be conservator over your estate, he must prove that you're "substantially" unable to manage your financial affairs or "resist fraud or undue influence." To accomplish this, your son would have to provide "clear and convincing evidence" (the "legal burden" or a "burden of persuasion"), such as unpaid bills or self-neglect, as proof to the court that you're unable to manage your affairs.

Step 2: Gather the Information. Nowadays, if your son is like most people, he'll learn about the conservatorship process by doing his research. Perhaps he'll visit court and legal websites that address the conservatorship process and download the information packets and forms. After reviewing the materials, he might file the paperwork, or he might prefer hiring an attorney who specializes in elder law or conservatorships to file the paperwork with the court on his behalf.

Step 3: Prepare the Petition. As the *petitioner* (the person who puts forward the formal, written request to a court that requests an action to a particular situation), your son will file the case in court by completing the *Petition of Conservatorship*, the proposal to the court to appoint him as your conservator. Information included in the petition are the justification for the conservatorship; the proposed conservatee's inabilities; the proposed conservator's qualifications; where the proposed conservatee will live; what services the proposed conservator will provide the proposed conservatee; and the explanations for why alternatives, such as general power of attorney, durable power of attorney for health care or estate management, and so on, aren't doable. The proposed conservator must show that a conservatorship is needed because the proposed conservatee is incompetent, which is known as the *burden of proof.* The burden of proof that must be met is that the conservatorship is "the least restrictive alternative or the least intrusive option."

Step 4: File the Petition. Your son, or his attorney, must file the petition and any other legal documents with the court clerk in the Probate Department of the Superior Court of California. He must also pay the filing and court investigator fees. The clerk will then schedule a court date. Where a danger to your health or assets is apparent, your son's attorney might prepare and file a request for a temporary conservatorship until the hearing date for the Petition for Conservatorship. Here, *Letters of Temporary Conservatorship*, or *Letters*, are issued to the temporary conservator until permanent Letters are available.

Step 5: Inform the Proposed Conservatee. Your son, as the petitioner, must have you served with the citation and a copy of the petition at least 15 days prior to the hearing. This "notice" must include the basis for the petition, the type of conservatorship being sought, and the ramifications of the conservatorship on your life—in effect, what rights will be denied either partially or wholly to you. If you're physically or mentally unable to attend the hearing on the petition, you'll be required to obtain a physician's declaration as proof.

Step 6: Inform Your Relatives. Your son, as the petitioner, must mail a written notice of hearing on the conservatorship matter to your spouse or domestic partner and also "second-degree" relatives, such as siblings and other immediate family members. In the case of an emergency conservatorship, your son can ask the court for an *ex parte* order to hold a hearing within a shortened time. In this instance, your son just needs to give relatives a 24-hour notice.

Step 7: Interview with the Court Investigator. After the petition is filed, a court investigator will be assigned to the case, and court investigator fees will be paid. The court investigator acts as the judge's eyes and ears by furnishing "neutral information" about the case. The court is concerned with your proper care and treatment, which the court investigator must first assess. The court investigator tries to do an "unannounced visit" so that he or she can assess your situation as it really is and not how it might be staged by others. In addition to explaining your rights and disclosing the effect of the court proceeding, the court investigator will interview you; inform you of the petition, review the allegations contained in it, and determine if you oppose it; find out if you'd prefer another conservator; and assess whether you have the ability to vote. The investigator will also interview your family members. Finally, the court investigator will file a confidential report for the court, send copies of it to all parties, and make final recommendations to the judge.

Step 8: Attend the Hearing. The court will set a hearing date. You must attend the hearing unless you're excused from it due to illness. At the hearing, the judge will determine if all parties have been notified, whether the conservatorship is warranted, and what types of "special powers" may be granted to your son if the judge approves the conservatorship. The judge may also appoint you an attorney, called a *PVP* (*Probate Volunteer Panel*), or you can request the court to appoint a PVP. If you oppose the conservatorship, you can explain why at the hearing. You can also request a jury trial. If the court grants these requests, then nothing else will happen at that time. If not, the judge will either grant or deny the conservatorship.

Let's say the judge grants the petition. An order appointing your son as your conservator for the conservatorship of your person and/or estate will be filed, and *Letters of Conservatorship* will be issued to him. The Letters will prove that your son has been appointed as your conservator, show that your son has the authority to act as your conservator, and spell out the permitted actions your son is authorized to take that affect your life. If you have an estate, a surety bond must be filed unless the court has frozen your assets.

By the judge granting the conservatorship, your son will assume all the powers allowed under the law. He will be able to:

- Change your mailing address to his
- Decide where you will live
- Open bank accounts in his name funded with your money
- Take over all your assets and decide how to invest or sell them
- Collect your income and pay your bills

- Open a new safe deposit box in his name
- Make all medical decisions for you and consent to your medical treatment
- Enter into agreements such as leases and home care contracts
- Get the court's permission to revoke your trust, durable power of attorney (DPA), and other legal documents
- Request information about all your affairs from government agencies, pension plans, private businesses, and so on
- Apply for government and other benefits on your behalf
- Probe into every aspect of your life and make life decisions for you

Frighteningly, your life may no longer be your own to determine or manage, although that all depends on the rights and powers the judge will allow you to retain. For example, although you might not be able to manage your finances, you might still retain the legal capacity to make medical decisions for yourself. Also, you may keep other rights, such as the right to marry or vote, receive personal mail, accept visits from family and friends, and so on, but that all depends on the limitations the judge places on your rights. In California, for instance, once a conservator is appointed by the Court, he or she will serve the conservatee with the *Notice of Conservatee's Rights*, which will identify the rights that the conservatee may still retain.

Now that your son has been made your conservator, by what standard will he (or should he) make decisions for you? Through "substituted judgment"—in other words, your son should make surrogate decisions by determining what you would do in a particular situation if you were competent. To do this, your son will need to determine your "best interests," a decision-making standard that considers what your prior wishes would be, or current wishes are, if you had capacity. If your wishes are unknown, then you son decides what's in your best interests.

As your conservator, your son must do certain things to prepare himself for the task as well as regularly follow up with the courts. To learn about his responsibilities as a conservator, he should purchase or download a copy of the *Handbook for Conservators*, a massive how-to guide on being a conservator. Your son can also get training for conservators offered by the court. In addition to educating himself on what it takes to be a conservator, your son must report to the court with regular reviews as well as meet with the court investigator, who will stay involved.

To ensure that your son is meeting his responsibilities as your conservator and upholding your rights as a conservatee, the investigator will review the case, usually six months after appointment, then again in six months, and then every 12 months thereafter. As long as your son is acting in your best interests, it's very likely he'll remain as your conservator. But if your son shirks his responsibilities, then the investigator may ask the judge to intervene. At that point, the judge may sanction or remove your son as your conservator, appoint a successor conservator, or end the conservatorship.

What happens if you oppose the conservatorship, aren't happy with something your son is doing, or want your son removed as your conservator? First, you can oppose the conservatorship by getting the Letters of Conservatorship revoked.

Second, if you oppose an action taken by your son, you can appeal it. Let's say your son removes you from your home, moves you to a nursing home, and then obtains an order authorizing the sale of your home, an occurrence that happens all too often. In response, you can appeal the order authorizing the home sale.

Third, if you're unhappy with your son as conservator and you'd like someone else to take his place, any interested person can petition the court to have your son removed. The petition must present facts showing cause for your son's removal. If the judge agrees with your son's removal, the judge can appoint a relative, friend, public guardian, state or local entity, or even you as successor conservator.

From start to finish, the costs of conservatorship are substantial. Your son, as the proposed conservator, pays the initial expenses of the petition and the hearing, although he can request the court to approve reimbursement through your estate. All ongoing expenses must be paid through your estate unless someone else is willing to pay them. In addition to the initial legal fees, other conservatorship expenses include:

- Ongoing legal expenses for preparing and filing petitions and regular accountings with the court, court filing fees, investigator fees, appraisal fees, and other related expenses
- Conservator's fees, ranging from $50 (an hourly fee usually received by family members) to $135 an hour and even higher, to handle or delegate health and personal care and/or financial duties
- Trustee and other professional asset manager fees for high-value estates, typically running from 1-1.5 percent of the asset value annually

Now let's look at the pros and cons of conservatorships, the shelf life of a conservatorship, and alternatives to conservatorships.

Pros and Cons of Conservatorships

In a world of do-it-yourself law, you might be tempted to handle the legal process on your own if you decide to pursue a conservatorship. However, it would be advisable to consult an attorney specializing in this legal terrain beforehand, such as an elder law attorney or a conservatorship attorney. He or she can advise you on whether or not a conservatorship might solve a particular problem, describe the obstacles you could face, and provide the pros and cons of seeking a conservatorship. Let's look at them here.

Conservatorship Pros	Conservatorship Cons
• Subject to court supervision as a safeguard	• Leaves a paper trail and is time-intensive and costly to set up
• Often requires the conservator to gain permission prior to making major decisions	• Often removes decision-making control from family and gives it to third-party surrogates

Conservatorship Pros, cont. | Conservatorship Cons, cont.

Conservatorship Pros, cont.	Conservatorship Cons, cont.
• Often requires the conservator to post a bond	• Can create an even bigger problem
• Requires court filings and accountings on a regular basis	• Requires the ongoing assistance of an attorney
• Requires the maintenance of detailed records	• Requires court hearings where a physician's evaluation can overly influence the adjudication process
• Monitored by the court	• Almost automatically granted at the adjudication stage, i.e., "rubber stamping"
	• Hearings are typically nonadversarial and brief, often lasting only 2 to 5 minutes
	• Requires court filings on a regular basis (for conservator)
	• Requires keeping detailed records (for conservator)
	• Proceedings and documents are a matter of public record
	• Courts don't have the resources to monitor conservators properly; abuses often go unnoticed
	• Can be very costly, especially if a professional conservator is used
	• Can chew up estates and deny beneficiaries their inheritance
	• Court decisions tend to be "absolute"; no or limited consideration is given to alternatives
	• Rarely takes into account "the principle of the least restrictive alternative," e.g., consideration given to partial or limited conservatorships

Conservatorship Pros, cont.	**Conservatorship Cons, cont.**
	• Court-appointed attorneys represent the court's <u>and</u> client's interests and thus create an inherent conflict of interest
	• Usually permanent

Clearly, the disadvantages of a conservatorship outweigh the advantages, which is not to say that conservatorships are entirely a bad thing. But as a solution to family disputes over how an incapacitated elder's life should be managed, *conservatorships should be a last resort.* Not only is a conservatee legally required to relinquish decision-making power over his or her life to someone else, possibly a faceless third party, but the conservatee is also rendered powerless to do something about it. Like a train wreck waiting to happen, loved ones are helpless in preventing a conserved family member from having his or her estate bled dry and in stopping him or her from being subjected to unwanted medical treatments. If someone dares to file an objection, he or she will quickly find out that the deck is stacked against him or her.

As mentioned, a conservatorship tends to be permanent. Still, it may be terminated for these reasons:

- You die.
- You run out of money.
- You no longer need assistance.
- The conservator resigns.
- The conservator dies.
- The court removes the conservator.

In the last three situations, the conservatorship doesn't usually end. Instead, the court will appoint a new conservator to take over the conservator's duties.

In a later chapter, we'll discuss alternatives to a conservatorship, such as durable power of attorney, living trusts (also known as "inter vivos" trusts) court authorizations for medical care, and other options. But even if you've created these legal instruments, you still can be conserved. The conservatee in the Lyon case had long established a living trust, durable powers of attorney for health care and for finances, and even named conservators in the event a conservatorship was required. None of these contingencies prevented the conservatorship from happening.

The key take-away is that *a conservatorship is the most restrictive form of court intervention that may deny you all, or some, of your freedoms indefinitely.* It can reduce you to the status of an infant with as few rights as a felon.

Who Is Guarding the Guardians?

By now, you've probably determined that a relatively unrestricted guardianship system with few checks and balances is an open invitation to potential abuse—and you'd be right for several reasons. First, few restrictions protect an elderly ward from an abusive guardian, according to a report titled "Abuses in Guardianship of the Elderly and Infirm: A National Disgrace" produced by the U.S. House Permanent Select Committee on Aging. The report revealed that only half of the states require guardians to supply annual reports on their wards, with little or no auditing. Other findings showed that the procedure by which guardians were named lacked due process; the courts were too overstrained to monitor guardianship arrangements; and a swift and final abrogation of an elder's freedoms gave elders fewer rights than a typical prisoner.

Second, woeful inadequacies have been discovered in judicial court monitoring. Because of "lax" reporting standards by the courts, many seniors have become victims of exploitation and abuse, according to a 90-plus-page report released by the Government Accountability Office (GAO). Likewise, the court's guardianship monitoring efforts were found to be "generally inadequate," according to adult guardianship court data.

Third, gross oversights and accountability issues within guardianship programs continue to persist. University of Kentucky researchers, the American Bar Association (ABA) Commission on Law and Aging, and Washington State University produced a comprehensive report on the state of public guardianships titled "Public Guardianship After 25 Years: In the Best Interest of Incapacitated People?" Using site visitations in Arizona, California, Delaware, Maryland, and Wyoming, the authors concluded that "public guardianship programs are frequently understaffed and underfunded." Also, they found that oversight and accountability were uneven. Finally, they discovered that the states had significant unmet needs for public guardianships and other surrogate decision-making services, yet they frequently couldn't quantify these needs.

Fourth, the guardianship industry is underregulated. A *Boston Globe* report exposed the "virtually unregulated" guardianship industry in Massachusetts. The report raised a large cause for concern to the point at which an issue of *New England Psychologist* warned: "The state currently has no procedure for licensing guardians. There is no minimum or standardized training requirement or assessment required to act as guardian, and the courts have no way of tracking how many wards a guardian has... To compound matters, no one is really watching."

Fifth, as guardianship abuse has gained national attention, the public wants to know "Who's guarding the guardians?" To find out, the AARP Public Policy Institute partnered with the American Bar Association (ABA) Commission on Aging to conduct a two-year study on guardianship monitoring practices by interviewing 400 experts, including elder law attorneys, judges, court managers, and guardians. In their published report titled "Guarding the Guardians: Promising Practices for Court Monitoring," the following conclusions were drawn:

- Guardianship monitoring practices appeared "lax" in several areas and "vary widely."

- Guardian report and account verification was "frequently lacking." Only 16 percent of respondents said that every report was verified, opening the door to guardian malfeasance.
- Guardian training was "seriously lacking."
- Staff and resources were insufficient in many jurisdictions.
- Only a few courts routinely monitored the ward's condition.
- Some courts failed to set bonds or acquire "proof of bond," resulting in the theft of wards' assets.

Sixth, the courts have used an inadequate screening process in the appointment of guardians. The U.S. Government Accountability Office (GAO) issued a report titled "Guardianships: Cases of Financial Exploitation, Neglect, and Abuse of Seniors" that explored the widespread allegations of elder mistreatment by guardians. The study reviewed hundreds of elder abuse allegations and cases across the country over a ten-year period. The study found that:

- State courts "failed" to adequately screen guardians prior to their appointments, assigning people with criminal convictions and/or financial troubles to manage wards' substantial estates.
- State courts "failed" to properly oversee guardians after their appointments, permitting vulnerable elders to be abused and their assets to be misused.
- State courts "failed" to report known abusive guardians to federal agencies, allowing these guardians to continue to receive their wards' federal benefits (e.g., Social Security benefits).

The full report cited a number of tragic guardianship abuse cases that would make your hair stand on end. A few follow.

- A guardian embezzled over $640,000 from an 87-year-old Alzheimer's patient. The guardian, a former taxi cab driver, spent the stolen funds on things like a Hummer and exotic dancers. When county employees caught wind of the guardian's misdeeds, they discovered that the victim, who was wearing nothing more than an old knit shirt and a diaper, was living in the filthy basement of the guardian's home.

- A guardian and his wife, one a licensed social worker and one a registered nurse, sexually and physically abused 20 residents with mental incapacities living in their unlicensed group home. The couple billed Medicare for what they coined "therapy." The victims lived in a house that was described as "dirty and bug-infested." The "therapy" (forced sex) was videotaped by the couple.
- A court-appointed lawyer/guardian stole over $4 million from 23 wards under his supervision, including seniors with mental and physical impairments.
- A probate judge was appointed as guardian to a 91-year-old ward with senility. She was persuaded to bequeath $250,000 to the judge/guardian who colluded with his accountant and the court-appointed attorney.

Finally, the press has been more vigorous in its reporting of guardianship abuses. Consider these stories.

- 1987: The *Associated Press* conducted a year-long series titled "Guardians of the Elderly: An Ailing System" that uncovered the growing problem of guardianship abuse on a national scale. The investigation condemned the guardianship system for declaring elders "legally dead." The probe found that the guardianship system is "a dangerously burdened and troubled system that regularly puts elderly lives in the hands of others with little or no evidence of necessity, then fails to guard against abuse, theft, and neglect."
- 2003: *Washington Post* published a number of articles that exposed neglect and exploitation committed by court-appointed attorneys and guardians in the District of Columbia.

- 2004 and 2005: *The Dallas Morning News* published a series focusing on guardianship neglect in Texas.
- 2005: *Los Angeles Times* examined over 2,400 conservatorship cases and chronicled the findings in a series titled "A Broken System." Situations were brought to light in which "judges frequently overlooked neglect and outright theft" committed by conservators. Instances of predatory practices by professional conservators—who exploited the elderly and stripped them of their possessions by manipulating the legal system—surfaced. It was found that many conservators abused their authority over frail elders by "ignoring their needs and isolating them from loved ones." Other shady conservators drained elders' estates or chewed up seniors' estates by charging outrageous fees.

But it's not all bad news: some states are attempting to clean up their act. For example, California is among a few states that has implemented reforms to its conservatorship system through the Omnibus Conservatorship and Guardianship Reform Act (2006). The act widened oversight and stiffened requirements for conservators, attorneys, and judicial officers. Three years later, researchers from the Goldman School of Public Policy at the University of California at Berkeley examined the extent to which progress had been made in safeguarding the rights and welfare of the elderly since the passage of the act. Key findings revealed that California's conservatorship system was still busted. The published report concluded that court oversight of conservatorships was still inadequate, due process rights weren't sufficiently protected, and less-restrictive forms of conservatorship were insufficiently emphasized.

Finally, in a paper titled "Conservatorship in Crisis: Civil Rights Violations & Abuses of Power" authored by Linda Kincaid, MPH, who runs the California elder advocacy group the Coalition for Elder and Dependent Adult Rights (CEDAR), the future outlook for conservatorships remains stark and suppressive. Kincaid warns:

> "Oversight of conservators is inadequate. With little accountability for abusive actions, conservators exercise

nearly absolute power over their conservatees. History has shown repeatedly that absolute power of one group over another leads to abuses of rights and abuses of persons."

The Lyon Case: War of Words

Selma's family continued to campaign on her behalf to ensure that she was well-taken care of physically, emotionally, and financially. They grew deeply concerned when Zachary went "attorney shopping" to find an attorney who would make the changes he wanted on Selma's estate planning. Among the attorneys who were hired and fired was Attorney Wright.

According to court documents, Wright came into the picture when an immigration attorney referred his client Zachary to Wright for estate planning. Wright met Zachary, Selma, and Zachary's wife Sybil at the immigration attorney's office. During this meeting, Zachary told Wright that "he and his aunt, Selma, were being 'harassed' by a bank that refused to transfer accounts out of Selma's revocable living trust and into joint name between Zachary and Selma." Wright advised Zachary that there was a "clear conflict of interest." It was then agreed that Wright would represent Selma's interests.

It was later discovered that Zachary hit a roadblock when the bank in question wouldn't allow him to make changes to Selma's accounts because they deemed her incapable to make them. Up to this point, Zachary had successfully moved and manipulated Selma's assets in and out of accounts and placed his name on them. Later on, Livingston had uncovered proof that Zachary had done the same asset shuffling with Minerva's assets.

Selma didn't comprehend the potential danger in her assets sitting outside of her trust. "It became apparent that she [Selma] didn't fully understand the ramifications of taking bank accounts out of the trust. Once I explained the purpose of the trust and purpose of placing assets in the trust, Selma agreed that assets should be reregistered," indicated Wright. So Wright insisted that Zachary take his name off of all Selma's assets and accounts and place them back in the trust.

"Over the ensuing months, I had many conversations with Zachary, always lengthy and sometimes heated. Zachary advised me that he was against placing the assets in trust," said Wright. Zachary rationalized that he was living with Selma and thus he should control her assets. Wright held firm, and followed through with Zachary to determine whether he had put Selma's money back into her trust accounts. Zachary hadn't.

For nearly three months, Wright requested month-end bank statements showing that the assets had been placed in trust. They never came.

Wright tried reaching Selma by telephone and left many messages. No one called him back. "I became so concerned about not being able to contact Selma that I visited her house. I was met by, I believe, Sybil. The door was not completely opened. I was told that Selma was not there. While driving away, I received a call on my cellular phone from someone who described himself as an attorney. He advised me that 'Selma and Zachary' had retained him. I questioned how both could retain him," Wright indicated. In fact, it never became perfectly clear "who" Gilroy's client was (i.e., Selma or Zachary), as he refused to give a firm or straight answer when he was queried about representation.

With the appearance of another lawyer, Attorney Gilroy, the family had to retell their side of Selma's story. Since Attorney Young had a good command of the facts, she contacted Attorney Gilroy on behalf of the family. In a letter, Young conveyed Selma's family's extreme concern over Selma's health and welfare as well as Zachary's unwillingness to account for Selma's assets. She cautioned Gilroy, "Several family members are taking steps to begin an emergency conservatorship. As a result, any changes made to Selma's estate plan will be challenged by the family as having been drafted under Zachary's undue influence."

Gilroy never replied to Young's letter. Gilroy's nonresponse gave the family the answer they were looking for: they had no other choice but to seriously consider an emergency conservatorship to protect Selma.

Livingston polled each family member to determine where he or she stood on the conservatorship decision. Doctor relatives were very concerned that Selma was badly in need of proper geriatric care due to Selma's history of stroke, onset of dementia, and poorly managed diabetes. Under Zachary's care, they knew Selma wouldn't get the treatment she needed, and so they were pro-conservatorship. Other close family members were fed up with Zachary's uncooperativeness, and felt that his intransigence would continue, regardless of how much or how long they tried mediating with him, and so they were pro-conservatorship. In the end, all family members, except for a sister who joined forces temporarily with Zachary and Sybil, agreed to seek a conservatorship to protect Selma.

Livingston began a search for an attorney who could represent the family. He interviewed several before he found an attorney who was a specialist in elder law and accepted conservatorship cases, Attorney Forte, a vigorous elder advocate.

Livingston did a phone consultation with Forte, who said she'd consider the case. She said effective solutions for situations like Selma's weren't always available and pointed out several overriding concerns. First, a title search would need to be done to find Selma's assets, noting that nothing prevented Zachary from taking money in and out of Selma's trust because of his physical proximity to her. Second, if Attorney Gilroy was in actuality Zachary's attorney and not Selma's, then Gilroy wouldn't have a fiduciary obligation to Selma, and so he could milk Selma's estate. Third, nothing stopped Selma from signing documents to give away her assets to Zachary if Attorney Gilroy stuck them in front of her face. Finally, timing was always difficult. Wright also stressed the timing issue: "You either jump in too soon or too late when everything's raided."

After speaking with Livingston, Forte accepted the family's conservatorship case. She filed the Petition for Appointment of Probate Conservator of Person and Estate with the Superior Court of California in Los Angeles County, where probate cases are heard.

Livingston was named as the petitioner and the proposed conservator for Selma. In the petition, Forte laid out the facts of the case. She explained that Selma suffered from short- and long-term memory loss and mental confusion from a series of strokes over time, and that Selma depended on others for her care and for bill paying. A brief history of Selma's background, Zachary's background, and the general facts of the elder abuse case against Zachary and his new family were also detailed. In that regard, Forte used the psychologist's evaluation as compelling evidence of the abuse.

In addition to filing the petition for conservatorship, Forte petitioned the court for Temporary Restraining Orders (TROs) against Zachary, his family members, and Attorney Gilroy to stop them from isolating Selma. In the Petition for Protective Orders, Forte expressly requested that "Zachary may not personally, or through agents, cause or encourage others to isolate Selma from persons seeking her out at her residence or by phone" and also that "Gilroy may not state he is Selma's attorney and may not prevent others from having access to her by threats of restraining orders, calling the policy, or in any other way."

A preliminary hearing for the emergency conservatorship was held. The judge didn't grant the TROs, but he did grant the emergency conservatorship. Livingston was made temporary conservator over finances, which put him in charge of day-to-day accounts. A temporary conservator of the person wasn't granted at that time. In addition, the judge assigned a court-appointed attorney, Attorney Hall, for Selma. That meant Gilroy was removed as Selma's (presumed) legal representative. The judge denied Gilroy's fees.

"The judge ordered Zachary to turn over the amendments to Selma's trust that he had Gilroy draft. Based on the trust amendments, Zachary was made Selma's sole trustee. He was to receive a monthly salary for him and his family to live with Selma. The deeds to Selma's properties were also included in the changes to Selma's estate plan. Zachary was given complete control over Selma's person and property," Livingston explained. Also, the judge issued a standing agreement for Zachary not to isolate Selma. Zachary agreed to this in court but later reneged. The judge also ordered Zachary to provide Livingston with Selma's bank statements, which he failed to do.

Following the hearing, it was decided that in lieu of a jury trial, which Attorney Hall was inclined to pursue when evidence of alleged financial elder abuse became known, Attorney Forte posed the idea of striking a settlement agreement, which she felt was in everyone's best interests. Forte pressed the importance of acting soon because of Selma's age and her health problems. To represent them in the settlement talks, Zachary and Sybil hired a new lawyer, Attorney Walker. It was agreed by all parties that Walker would draft the original settlement agreement.

Eventually, petitions to roll back Selma's trust to its original status were filed and approved by the court. The court granted a permanent conservatorship and approved the settlement agreement and its stipulations. Instead of making Livingston Selma's conservator for her person and her property, he was made Selma's conservator of the estate; he waived his fees. They also named a conservator of the person, Mr. Gaines, who had a background in the health care industry, and also a trustee, Mr. Powell, a partner in a fiduciary service. Both fiduciaries charged professional fees for their services and were generally held in good standing by the court and by the attorneys working on Selma's case.

A senior care network was assigned to assess Selma's health care needs, but their services were terminated, as Mr. Gaines, who had an extensive background in health care, preferred not to defer medical care management to them. Mr. Gaines ordered 24/7 caregiving to handle Selma's care needs. For now, Selma was allowed to remain living in her home.

A neurological exam was conducted to test Selma's capacity. The neurologist's report stated that Selma met the "criteria for a diagnosis of dementia." The report further said that Selma showed "significant severe losses in cognitive function... and is no longer able to make decisions for herself or care for herself adequately." If there was ever a doubt about Selma's capacity, it was gone.

To get Zachary to cooperate during the settlement talks, the parties agreed to Walker and his client's cherry-picking amendments, which had been drafted prior to Gilroy's changes to Selma's estate plan. These amendments favored Zachary financially at the time of Selma's death.

According to the settlement agreement, Zachary and his new family were allowed to live with Selma for a designated period of time. When they moved out, they took furniture and cars owned by Selma, which were stipulated in the agreement. In the wake of their move, Zachary and Sybil kept tabs on Selma and her home by doing drive-bys, according to Selma's neighbors and Selma's caregivers. Zachary was allowed "free, unfettered" access to visit his mother. Other than a few visits early in his mother's conservatorship, he never saw her again.

The court approved thousands in legal fees and other disbursements for a few months of casework, which were solely paid by Selma's estate.

There was no jury trial.

In the next chapter, we'll describe the duties and responsibilities of the conservator of the person. Also, we'll take a close look at end-of-life decision making for patients by surrogates and use the Lyon case as a vivid illustration.

CHAPTER 6

The Death Dealers

End-of-life decisions are the most difficult, complex, emotional, and sensitive decisions we'll ever have to make for ourselves and for our loved ones. In legal and medical circles, the Terri Schiavo case offers anecdotal evidence of the bioethical and family struggle in making surrogate decisions for a loved one who becomes incapacitated.

Terri Schiavo was only 27 years old when she suffered a cardiac arrest, resulting from a potassium imbalance probably due to her bulimia. She fell into a persistent vegetative state (PVS), "a wakeful unconscious state," due to heart failure and oxygen deprivation. Terri was "locked in," with no possibility of improvement, for 15 years.

Terri's husband and Terri's parents were at loggerheads on what decision Terri would have made if she were aware of her condition, which was irreversibly bleak. They also disagreed on the nature of Terri's condition, even though court-appointed doctors confirmed that Terri would never regain normal brain function. At the heart of the debate, which took place on the national stage, were whether to prolong Terri's life through artificial life support and whether Terri had any hope of rehabilitation.

For several years Terri's doctors made every attempt to bring Terri back to a state of awareness through different therapies. None worked. In spite of Terri's dismal prognosis, Terri's parents believed she was conscious.

Eight years after Terri had collapsed, Terri's husband petitioned a Florida court to remove Terri's feeding tube. He claimed that Terri told him that she would not wish to remain in a vegetative state with no hope of recovery. However, Terri's parents objected to the withdrawal of her feeding tube. They said that they'd keep Terri alive no matter what, even if it meant "the amputation of [Terri's] limbs."

A drawn-out court battle between Terri's parents and Terri's husband ensued. The Schiavo case was heard over 20 times in Florida courts. The original court decision resulted in the feeding tube being removed, only to be reinserted a few days later. Several court appeals followed, and even the federal government got involved when President George W. Bush signed legislation designed to keep Terri alive. A federal court upheld the original decision, and Terri's feeding tube was finally withdrawn.

Had Terri Schiavo made her wishes known in an advance health care directive, the daunting and heart-wrenching task of determining what Terri would have wanted could have been avoided. Then again, a court-appointed guardian for Schiavo said: "... even if Theresa had told them [her parents] of her intention to have artificial nutrition withdrawn, they would not do it." The Schiavo case illustrates the painful challenge that families face when they must make end-of-life decisions for a loved one.

In this chapter, we'll describe the duties and responsibilities of a conservator of the person. Also, we'll discuss the standards of decision making, which should be instituted by all fiduciaries. Finally, we'll take a close look at the critical role of surrogate decision-making at the end of life by using the Lyon case as a vivid illustration.

Throughout this chapter, the terms *conservatee* and *ward* and *conservator* and *guardian* are used interchangeably. The use of these terms is predicated on elder law and state laws.

What Is a Conservator of the Person?

As presented earlier, a *conservator* is a court-appointed person or an organization that handles the affairs for a person, a *conservatee*, who can no longer manage them for him- or herself. The conservator can be your spouse, domestic partner, relative, interested state or local public entity or agency (such as a public guardian), or an interested friend or person.

The *conservator of the person* helps the conservatee with his or her physical and personal needs. For example, if you're unable to take care of your *activities of daily living* (*ADLs*), specifically your daily self-care, or make medical decisions for yourself, a conservator of the person would help you with these. Ultimately, the conservator's aim is to maintain the "best quality of life" possible for you as well as to make choices that promote your self-esteem and preserve your dignity.

Being a conservator of the person is a huge responsibility—the court is entrusting the conservator with the incapacitated person's complete well-being. Legally, if you're selected as a conservator of the person, you must abide by the law and be prepared to justify to the court that the decisions you're making for the conservatee are warranted. Practically, you must think like the conservatee by making choices that he or she would have made for him- or herself had he or she been capable.

In granting a conservatorship, specifically a court-appointed conservator of the person, the courts tread very carefully, especially in instances where the proposed conservator of the person attempts to place the proposed conservatee in a "lockdown," such as secured-perimeter residential care facility. To support the proposed conservator's request for appointment and his or her request for specific powers (e.g., "dementia powers"), then, a doctor's declaration must fully explain the proposed conservatee's disabilities. For example, if the proposed conservatee suffers from mental illness or decline, such as dementia, a physician or a licensed psychologist must supply a *Capacity Declaration*, which is filed as an attachment to the petition.

The proposed conservator must therefore meet a higher burden to be granted dementia powers, as well as to obtain a special order to place the proposed conservatee on psychotropic drugs.

In the Lyon case, Selma was appointed a conservator of the person, Mr. Gaines. At the outset, Mr. Gaines assessed Selma's emotional and physical needs. He selected a geriatric specialist to oversee Selma's care and ordered 24/7 home care for Selma. Mr. Gaines also had Selma routinely seen by his assistant as well as a home health nurse. Selma's outward health and well-being improved under Mr. Gaines's care management, which was one of the family's central goals in pursuing the conservatorship path. Still, there were bumps in the road for Selma and her family, according to a family source. At times, family members stood at a crossroads between what Mr. Gaines believed was best for Selma and what they felt was best for Selma.

What Are the Duties and Responsibilities of a Conservator of the Person?

The National Guardianship Association (NGA), an organization that sets standards and guidelines for guardianships, has produced a useful manual that contains the standards of practice to be followed by court-appointed guardians. The guardian's relationships with the court and the ward/conservatee, the standards for decision making, the duties and responsibilities of guardians, and other obligations discharged to guardians are spelled out in the NGA manual. Bear in mind that each state sets guidelines for conservators to follow, as well as special requirements to meet, so always check with your local probate court or your attorney.

Let's look at what a conservator of the person must do to properly serve the personal and physical needs of his or her conservatee. For illustrative purposes, let's say the court has appointed you as your elderly father's conservator of the person because he can no longer fend for himself. First things first, obtain your *Letters of Conservatorship* from the court clerk's office. The Letters supply proof to doctors, health insurers, and others that you've been appointed as your father's conservator of the person and thus can act on his behalf.

Prior to making important decisions for your father, determine his basic needs by considering his personal preferences, such as your father's beliefs, cultural and religious values, and ethnic identity, if you don't already know them. If there's a conservator of the estate or a trustee in the picture, then you'll need to work alongside him or her. That way, you'll know what your father can afford for his care, since the conservator of the estate or the trustee will need to approve these expenses. In addition, develop a care plan for your father. Some courts might even require that you file a formal written plan. The plan will address your father's medical, mental health, social, and recreational needs, among other things. Finally, visit your father at least monthly to ensure that his basic needs are being properly met.

Now let's look at your conservator of the person to-do list, which is mostly derived from the *Handbook for Conservators*, an excellent source for new and soon-to-be conservators.

Living Arrangements

You'll need to decide where your father should live. If your father is like most elderly, he'll want to remain in his own home. In fact, 90 percent of seniors said that they wanted to stay in their own homes as they age, according to an AARP survey. If your father has certain mental and physical challenges that require the assistance of a professional, consider hiring a home health aide (HHA) or a Certified Nursing Aide (CNA) to help him with activities of daily living (ADLs), such as eating, bathing, and dressing, and instrumental activities of daily living (IADLs), such as meal preparation, bill paying, and grocery shopping.

In the event you choose to move your father from his primary residence, you should bear a few things in mind. One, if you live out of state and want to move your father to your home or to a location closer to you, a judge can prevent you from doing that unless the judge gives you permission. Two, some state laws will require that you select the "least restrictive, appropriate" environment that would meet your father's needs and be in his best interests. Three, if your father has dementia and you're unable to line up an aide to provide him with the most optimal home care, you might have to move him to a dementia care unit, known as a *secured-perimeter residential care facility*, or another institutional setting, such as an assisted-living facility, a board-and-care facility, or a skilled-nursing facility. Choose a facility that will minimize the risk of harm to him and maximize his quality of life.

In Selma Lyon's case, after a hip surgery, Mr. Gaines sent Selma to a locked Alzheimer's and dementia care unit during her recovery and then for permanent placement, where reportedly many of his other conservatees and clients resided. During family visitations, relatives became worried when they found Selma to be in a terribly depressed state. She was placed in "chemical restraints" (overmedication) and, for hours on end, sat slumped in a wheelchair, head and face drooping downward, and unattended to by the staff. Observing that Selma was miserable and fearing that she was losing her desire to live, both Agatha and Livingston campaigned to return Selma to her home, with the help of Livingston's attorney. In the end, they succeeded in persuading Mr. Gaines to return Selma to her home.

Health Care and Medical Treatment

In addition to providing adequate living conditions, you have a duty to keep your father healthy and to maintain and monitor his *medical needs*. If your father already has a primary care physician (PCP), health care providers, a druggist, and other support services, determine if these should be continued or modified in some way. If you need help in making these decisions, disease-specific support groups and organizations can provide information and assistance.

If your father doesn't have *health insurance*, such as a health maintenance organization (HMO) like Kaiser Permanente or a preferred provider organization (PPO) like Blue Shield of California, obtain it for him. Getting dental insurance is advisable too. Know that your father is eligible for Medicare benefits if he's 65 or older. Other types of health coverage include Medigap, Medi-Cal (if you live in California), retiree health benefits, Obamacare (the Affordable Care Act), and so on. Again, if you're not managing your father's money, speak with the conservator of the estate or the trustee to see what your father can afford for health insurance. In addition, determine who will manage the paperwork and payments, such as filing insurance claims, paying insurance premiums, and so forth.

In addition to arranging your father's health coverage, secure appropriate *medical care* for your father. Remember that you will be authorizing any necessary medical treatments for your father. That said, your father has the right to refuse any medical treatment unless the court has taken away this right and granted it to you. At that point, the judge would have given you "exclusive authority" to make medical decisions for your father, and your Letters of Conservatorship would specify that. Still, you may not approve "extraordinary procedures," such as sterilization, electroshock therapy, and psychosurgery, without prior authorization from the court, or if such a procedure is indicated in your father's living will or durable power of attorney.

If your father had executed any *advance directives*, such as a durable power of attorney for health care, or other written or oral declaration of intent, such as a declaration as to medical or surgical treatment, respect your father's wishes as spelled out in these documents. Also, share these documents with the court and with other interested parties.

In Selma's case, Selma had executed a durable power of attorney for health care, as well as named who she wanted to serve as her conservators, in her living will before she lost capacity. However, Selma was vague in her instructions on artificial life-sustaining procedures, which is all too common in these types of documents. When Selma became terminally ill with cancer and when her dementia progressed to the point that she lost all her faculties, she was fitted with a gastrostomy tube, or G-tube, that delivered artificial nutrition and hydration (ANH). Yet Selma had signed a declaration that directed her agents to withdraw or withhold artificial life support. But the declaration was deemed invalid by the court because it was determined that Selma had signed the form when she lacked capacity to make such decisions for herself. It was argued by one of the attorneys involved in Selma's case, however, that even though Selma was unable to make appropriate financial decisions, that didn't mean that she was incapable of making medical decisions at the time of the signing.

In making an informed medical decision for your father, always get a second medical opinion for "any medical treatment or intervention that would cause a reasonable person to do so or in circumstances where any medical intervention poses a significant risk to the ward," according to the NGA. If you aren't sure about a recommended procedure or treatment, think carefully before giving your consent; the same goes for medications and their dosages. Oftentimes medications are administered to elders to make them "easier to manage," which is patently wrong. So watch for any symptoms that could indicate improper dosage of or a reaction to a medication. In Selma's instance, Mr. Gaines and his physicians placed Selma on several new medications. Whereas she was formerly taking only a couple of drugs, now she was taking almost a dozen of them. In fact, Mr. Gaines had to petition the court to get approval to place Selma on dementia and psychotropic drugs, which was approved.

In addition to medical care, arrange regular *dental care* for your father. Healthy teeth, or well-fitting dentures, are essential to your father's overall health. For example, Selma may have developed *bruxism*, teeth grinding, as a side effect of certain medications she was given, according to one of the family doctors. Probably for this reason, her teeth started fracturing. A concern was that she could develop a tooth infection. So Mr. Gaines and his oral surgeon elected to remove all of Selma's teeth, which seemed extreme to Selma's relatives. She was then placed on a pureed diet.

Lastly, provide any *medical devices*, such as walkers, hearing aids, eyeglasses, wheelchairs, and so forth, on which your father relies. Also, if your father is a diabetic, as Selma was, *foot care* is extremely important. Finally, your father's *general personal hygiene and grooming* must be maintained. If your father is impaired and needs help with bathing and grooming, bring in an aide to help with these.

Basic Needs

Putting your father on a good nutritional *diet* is exceedingly important to his overall health. Oftentimes elderly people don't get enough food or stop eating because of a psychological issue, such as depression, the death of a loved one, or loneliness. Or elders forget to eat due to an impairment like dementia. Also, elders may need to be on a special diet due to certain medical conditions, such as heart disease or diabetes. For example, Selma was a diabetic. According to Mr. Gaines, her diabetes was poorly managed and controlled prior to the conservatorship. He placed Selma on a diabetic diet, which was managed by Selma's caregivers who prepared Selma's meals. Finally, meal services and websites are a source to tap into if you or someone else can't do meal preparation for your father. For example, Meals on Wheels is a community-based service that provides home-delivered meals to the elderly who are unable to prepare meals for themselves and who are homebound.

In addition to attending to dietary needs, acquire basic items like appropriate *clothing* for your father. Don't forget that your father's *social and recreational needs* are important too. For example, obtain large-print magazines and books if your father's vision is poor. If your father enjoys surfing the Internet or using social media, provide him with the right equipment. Also, arrange trips and outings for your father if he's able to travel. If not, visiting nearby destinations will provide outside stimulation, such as going to senior centers and adult social day care programs. If you're unable to drive your father here and there, senior transportation services are available in many communities.

DO encourage family members and your father's friends to visit him as often as they can and as often as he's comfortable. DO NOT isolate your father! In Selma's case, Selma was isolated from her relatives by her son, his new family, and the attorney whom the son hired to act as Selma's enforcer. *Intentionally isolating an elder is a form of elder abuse.*

Finally, if you aren't sure what types of assistance your father needs, consult *a case management service* to help you prepare a care plan. For instance, a geriatric case manager had originally been retained to assess and manage Selma's care needs. In addition, you can contact a caregiving agency to arrange for a trained aide to provide home care for your father if he needs help with grocery shopping, personal care, and so on. For example, Selma received 24/7 supervision from first a live-in caregiver and then from 12-hour shift caregivers. Be forewarned that caregivers can be very costly if you go through an agency and if the agency does shift billing. For Selma, her caregiving costs alone ran in excess of $150,000 per year.

Conflict of Interest and Service Providers

As a cautionary note, never give the hint of "a conflict of interest or impropriety" when securing ancillary and support services. According to the NGA, "Impropriety or conflict of interest arises when the guardian has some personal or agency interest that can be perceived as self-serving or adverse to the position or best interest of the ward." As a simple illustration, let's say you have a friend who is a caregiver or a cousin who is an accountant, both of which are services you need for your father. You may not hire your caregiver/ friend or accountant/cousin "for profit or a fee unless no alternative is available" or you get court approval. In Selma's case, speculation swirled around the primary care physician (PCP) selected for Selma by Mr. Gaines. According to Livingston's attorney, the PCP was the medical director of the dementia care unit where Selma was placed and where reportedly many of Mr. Gaines's conservatees and clients resided. The PCP was believed to have a financial interest in the unit. In addition, Selma's home nurse was the son of the owner of the dementia care unit, according to Selma's caregivers. Whether the alleged impropriety existed, the appearance of it was enough to raise the question.

What Standards for Decision Making Does a Conservator of the Person Use?

As your father's conservator of the person, you should follow certain decision-making principles, specifically *informed consent, substituted judgment, best interests,* and *least restrictive alternative.* Let's discuss each.

First, the principle of *informed consent* constitutes "a person's agreement to a particular course of action based on a full disclosure of facts needed to make the decision intelligently," according to the NGA. In simple terms, it means that you're basing your decisions on complete information. As your father's conservator, you're allowed access to the same information and freedom of choice as your father would have if he were able to make decisions for himself. It's really important that you fully understand the issue for which you're giving informed consent, and that you know your father's preferences with respect to the issue. In addition, you should assess the risks versus the benefits of each alternative that could resolve the issue as well as identify the least restrictive alternative for each. For instance, Mr. Gaines gave informed consent for all of Selma's medical treatments and procedures. Occasionally Mr. Gaines elicited family input on critical medical issues that Selma faced. Still, Mr. Gaines had the final say even when family members opposed his decisions.

Second, in addition to making decisions on the basis of informed consent, you should follow the principle of *substituted judgment,* a standard of decision making that "substitutes" or guides surrogate decision making. In other words, you must make decisions on behalf of your father as he would have made them for himself if he were competent. Here again, you must determine your father's prior wishes, which may be contained in his living trust or will if he has one. Several situations arose in which Selma's family members objected to decisions that were made by Mr. Gaines based on their knowledge of Selma's prior wishes. As an example, Livingston and Agatha were opposed to Selma's being overmedicated as well as her placement in an institutional setting. They knew that Selma needed certain drugs for specific chronic conditions, but they were very opposed to the controversial administration of psychotropic drugs, which Selma would never take on her own. Agatha said, "Our aunt [Selma] did not need to be narcotized into submission." Also, they knew that Selma wanted to live in her home and that she had the financial means to remain there.

Third, *best interest* is a standard of decision making used when the conservator doesn't know the wishes of the conservatee. Using the best interest standard, you should "consider the least intrusive, most normalizing, and the least restrictive course of action possible to provide for the needs of the ward," according to the NGA.

To demonstrate the slippery slope debate of the best interest standard, let's look at Selma's situation. When Selma could no longer swallow, Mr. Gaines and his doctors approved the use of a nasogastric tube to provide nourishment and hydration. Later, Selma's doctors opted to surgically implant a gastrostomy tube, or G-tube, in Selma's abdomen to furnish artificial nutrition and hydration (ANH). Selma, who suffered from untreated cancer, was pretzelized (her entire body was contracted), unable to speak or swallow, blind, deaf, cognitively absent, and stuck in a vegetative quagmire. Livingston asked his sister-in-law Harper, a clinical nurse and palliative care expert and educator, to informally assess Selma. Harper compared Selma to a "corpse with a feeding tube—the only thing keeping her alive is the tube." As a result, several family members felt that it was no longer in Selma's "best interests" to allow her to suffer in this manner, nor would Selma wish to live like this on the basis of her personal preferences, cultural values, and ethnic background. Mr. Gaines put the matter before two specialists. Harper and her husband Mason reviewed the specialists' reports. Neither specialist agreed to tube removal. Harper said, "They [the specialists] argued that Selma had a 'biological existence'—in other words, her heart was beating and her lungs were working."

Fourth, using the *least restrictive alternative*, the conservator of the person should evaluate each alternative in making a decision and choose the option that meets the conservatee's needs, while also putting the fewest restrictions on the conservatee's freedom, rights, and independence. As always, you should know your father's preferences in evaluating each alternative. For example, if your father's preference is to live at home and you can maintain his protection and safety there, then consider this option as a living arrangement for him.

Working With the Conservatee: Do No Harm

At some point, the conservator of the person might be faced with circumstances in which he or she must decide whether to authorize or withhold medical treatment, possibly a life-saving or -sustaining procedure. According to the NGA, the general rule of thumb is that it is "legally and ethically justifiable to consent to the withholding or withdrawal of medical treatment, including artificially provided nutrition and hydration, on behalf of the ward." However, the NGA also states that the default position is in favor of continuing treatment. For example, Selma had many hospitalizations for a variety of medical issues. When she was diagnosed with cancer, Mr. Gaines determined that it would not be appropriate for Selma to undergo cancer surgery or treatment (Selma's family members agreed with him) given Selma's advanced age, physical frailty, and severe dementia. Furthermore, it was believed that Selma might not survive the surgery. Given these factors, Selma's cancer was left untreated.

One of the most complex and controversial health care decisions that both families and medical professionals must make is whether to consent, withdraw, or withhold medical treatment. The position that the NGA takes is that if the ward (conservatee) had expressed his or her preference concerning the withholding or withdrawal of medical treatment, then the guardian (conservator of the person) must follow the ward's (conservatee's) wishes.

In Selma's case, the majority of her family members opposed artificial life support, stating that she would not wish it. Mr. Gaines retained two doctors to assess Selma regarding the appropriateness of withdrawing the feeding tube. One doctor believed that discontinuing artificial nutrition was an "ethical" issue. To this, Harper rebutted:

> "One could argue that it is unethical to allow Ms. Lyon to suffer any longer. It is clear that artificial nutrition is the only thing preventing her from dying with dignity. I encounter these ethical issues in my job every day of the week and we [the medical team] always allow the family to make decisions in the best interest of their loved one."

Let's segue into a discussion of end-of-life health care decisions by first examining ethical issues and then legal considerations.

End-of-Life Decisions: An Ethical Dilemma

Virtually all of us will be making end-of-life health care decisions for ourselves and for our loved ones. For our discussion, let's look at the ethical and legal implications of withholding or withdrawing nutrition or hydration, with a focus on the use of feeding tubes in elderly dementia patients.

According to an article titled "Withholding or Withdrawing Nutrition or Hydration" published by the National Reference Center for Bioethics Literature (NRCBL), the patient's physician and family members ordinarily make end-of-life medical decisions in the absence of an advanced care directive, with the physician usually prevailing. To make your wishes known on life-sustaining procedures, you can draw up *a living will*, which includes a signed declaration of medical treatment preferences, and/or you can set up *a durable power of attorney for health care (DPAHC)*, which appoints an agent (a representative) to make medical decisions based on an understanding of your wishes.

Know that a DPAHC does not guarantee that your agent will carry out your wishes. Rather, it means that you'll have a representative when the time comes to make health care decisions if you're unable to make them. As a surrogate decision maker, the agent's goal should be to make the choice that the patient would have made if he or she were able to make an informed decision. Too often, however, surrogate medical decisions are based on what the patient's surrogate believes is appropriate.

Several studies have explored the opinions of seniors about life-sustaining treatments. In one study, researchers asked 84 cognitively intact American men and women over 65 years of age whether they would want life-sustaining treatments, specifically artificial feeding, if they suffered with dementia. Ninety-four percent of the respondents said that they wouldn't want artificial feeding if they couldn't express their wishes or care for themselves. Moreover, the majority of physicians were not in favor of administering artificial feeding in dementia patients. In an attitudinal study of American internists, 84 percent were opposed to artificial feeding in nursing-home residents with feeding difficulties and with irreversible dementia.

Functionally, what happens to a person when he or she reaches the advanced stages of dementia? If you know someone with dementia, you may have noticed that he or she progressively loses his or her abilities to speak, ambulate, and eat. Research shows that about 50 percent of advanced dementia patients lose their ability to feed themselves within eight years of a diagnosis. Feeding difficulties in dementia patients stem from their reduced ability to feed themselves, impaired ability to swallow, or a combination of both. Swallowing becomes a problem because they can't chew or their tongue and jaw don't move normally. As a result, they experience coughing, choking, and delayed swallowing while eating. Selma Lyon experienced all these symptoms, as she pocketed food in her cheeks, choked, and coughed while being hand fed, according to her caregivers. Eventually, Selma was unable to swallow. Although a nasogastric tube (NGT) was used for a time, Selma's physicians ultimately applied the percutaneous endoscopic gastrostomy (PEG), which was surgically placed through the abdomen into the stomach.

If you're ever faced with the tough decision to start or stop artificial feeding for a loved one, consider these four bioethical principles.

> *Autonomy*—You have the right to refuse artificial nutrition and hydration (ANH), according to ethicists and the courts. If you're suffering from dementia and are unable to communicate your wishes about ANH but have furnished them in a medical power of attorney, your physician should respect your wishes.

> *Beneficence*—Your physician should at all times act in your best interests. Oftentimes feeding tube placement in dementia patients is justified to improve nutrition, prevent pressure ulcers, and reduce aspiration risk.

> *Nonmaleficence*—This Latin term means "First, do no harm." The physician should ask, "Will the patient be harmed by placing a feeding tube?" and, equally, "Will feeding tube placement not do harm to the patient?"

> *Futility*—In a bioethical context, *futility* means that a physician should base his or her decision to use a medical treatment according to his or her personal experience, his or her colleagues' shared experiences, or published empirical data in at least 100 cases. Based on these considerations, if a medical treatment

has been useless in the past, it should be regarded as
"futile."

The above concepts and considerations are especially relevant in making end-of-life decisions, given that current medical technologies allow us to live with physical and mental limitations almost indefinitely. Which brings us to one of the most difficult questions of all: If a patient's prognosis is irreversibly hopeless, such as when a patient falls into a persistent vegetative state (PVS), should ANH be withheld or withdrawn? Before addressing this burdensome question, let's define what PVS is.

According to the American Academy of Neurology (AAN), *persistent vegetative state (PVS)* is a "form of eyes open permanent unconsciousness in which the patient has periods of wakefulness and physiological sleep/wake cycles, but at no time is the patient aware of himself or his environment." On a functional level, PVS patients aren't terminally ill, they don't experience pain or suffering, and they're unable to swallow. As a result, it's generally accepted that medical treatment, such as artificial life support, may be initiated when the prognosis is unclear, but also may be stopped when the patient's situation is bleak. However, in patients with advanced dementia who are vegetative, the decision isn't always clear-cut.

According to an article titled "Tube Feeding Patients with Advanced Dementia: An Ethical Dilemma," several factors should be considered in making the decision to start or stop ANH, including race, cultural background, personal values, and so on. For example, in the Chinese culture, food is regarded as a gift from God. If you waste food, you will be punished by God. So Chinese nursing home residents are commonly forced to eat by one means or another. Moreover, practical considerations of artificially feeding should be taken into account. Once you start it, it's hard to withdraw it as was discovered in Selma's case.

The President's Council on Bioethics commissioned a working paper, "Treatment Decisions for Dementia Patients: The Search for Normative Boundaries," that explored standards of medical decision making for dementia patients. First is the *substituted judgment standard*, which instructs physicians and families to decide for a patient as if she were "miraculously lucid for an interval (not altering the existing prognosis of the condition to which she would soon return) and perceptive of her irreversible condition." Using this standard, a knowledge of the loved one's values, religious beliefs, attitudes toward medical treatment, and so on is required. In the absence of a clear advance directive, the patient's general values, religious beliefs, and attitudes toward medical care become the evidentiary basis for the treatment decision. This argument was put forward by several of Selma's family members who knew Selma's wishes, values, and thoughts toward artificial life support.

Second is *the best interest standard*, or *the benefit burden* or *reasonable person standard*. Here, objective standards are applied in the absence of the patient's past values and preferences, while also relying on community norms—that is, "a societal consensus, or the perspective of a reasonable person, choosing as most people would choose for themselves." This standard balances the benefits and burdens, such as pain, pleasure, enjoyment, suffering, and so forth, that an incompetent patient would experience if medical treatment were administered or withheld. As an example of the objective approach, after Mr. Gaines e-mailed Harper that Selma could no longer "recognize pain" due to her advanced dementia, Harper replied:

> "While it is comforting to believe that Aunt Selma is unaware of pain, it is also distressing to think that Aunt Selma is unable to experience any pleasure in life, such as comfort, joy, happiness, companionship, and so on—which is our family's biggest concern— and has not been able to benefit from these for some years now."

End-of-Life Decisions: A Legal Dilemma

According to the American Hospital Association (AHA), roughly 80 percent of individuals who die are patients in either hospitals or in health care facilities, while 70 percent of these deaths involve the decision to administer, withhold, or withdraw some type of care. On top of this, over 50 percent of these deaths include an end-of-life health care decision. For patients with advanced dementia who are unable to communicate their wishes, it's usually left up to families, physicians, and hospitals or nursing home staffs to decide on the adoption or suspension of life-sustaining procedures or treatments. In most cases, the parties can agree. But what happens if they disagree? Enter the courts.

The courts often rule on cases where there's disagreement between and among parties on the continuance of artificial feeding. In 1990 the U.S. Supreme Court first tackled the issue of withholding or withdrawing life support in the *Cruzan case*, which was heard in Missouri. Nancy Cruzan had been in a persistent vegetative state for seven years. Her parents requested to have her feeding tube removed. The court ruled that Missouri and other states must present "clear and convincing evidence" of the patient's wishes in the absence of an advance directive. In addition, the court accepted the principle that a competent person has the right to forego treatment such as ANH, a freedom protected under the Fourteenth Amendment to the Constitution.

Not even courts can agree on the right course of action to take in ruling on such cases and, in particular, in conservatorship cases. For example, in the *Matter of Claire C. Conroy*, Ms. Conroy was an 84-year-old nursing home resident who was receiving feedings through a nasogastric tube. When she lapsed into a near-vegetative state, Ms. Conroy's nephew requested that the tube be removed, claiming that his aunt would never wish to have such a treatment. First, the trial court allowed the feeding tube to be removed. However, the New Jersey appellate court reversed the original opinion. Then the New Jersey Supreme Court reversed the appellate court decision. The

New Jersey Supreme Court said that any life-sustaining treatment could be withheld if there was evidence that the patient would refuse it, when the decision maker feels the treatment is "long-suffering," and "when the burdens of continued life with the treatment clearly outweigh any benefits."

Now consider the *Conservatorship of Morrison case*. In 1988 the court held that the conservator, the daughter of the patient, could authorize the removal of a nasogastric tube from the conservatee, the daughter's mother, a 90-year-old patient who had been hospitalized since 1979 and who was in a persistent vegetative state. However, the court couldn't require the conservatee's physicians to remove the tube if the physicians objected on moral grounds. As a result, the patient's care would have to be transferred to a physician who would follow the conservator's instructions. This was a complex case in which the hospital medical director and the conservatee's physician sought an injunction to prevent the tube removal as they morally objected to this action. The court denied their request, concluding that the daughter was acting in good faith and, further, that her mother would not improve. The daughter was then able to authorize the tube removal.

Some experts question whether the courts are the right place to resolve treatment issues. For example, the California court in the *Conservatorship of Drabick case* concluded that "when the conservator desires removal of life-sustaining treatment, the court should intervene only if there is disagreement among the interested parties." Otherwise, the conservator's right to reject medical treatment on behalf of the conservatee would be "meaningless." The court reasoned that the patient retained the right to refuse treatment, so the patient's conservator can too. While the conservator must seek medical advice on a particular medical treatment, he or she isn't "ethically bound to follow it." Rather, the conservator should seek information that will help him or her to make an informed decision consistent with the patient's best interests.

This brings us to the polarizing issue of the right to a natural death. California was the first state to pass a law that allowed patients the right to refuse artificial life support. The California Natural Death Act of 1976 requires physicians to withhold or withdraw life-sustaining treatment when a terminally ill patient has furnished such instructions in an executed directive. The act states that if a physician refuses to comply with the wishes of the patient, he or she is required to transfer the patient to another physician who will follow the patient's directive.

In 2000 the California Health Care Decisions Law was enacted. The law gives an adult person the right to withdraw or withhold life-sustaining treatment, positing that adults can rightfully make their own medical decisions. The act acknowledges that medical technology has promoted "life beyond natural limits" and that "personal autonomy must be weighed against the duty of the state to preserve life." In preserving life, the duty of the state must recognize an individual's right to circumvent efforts "to sustain life which may demean or degrade humanity."

The Lyon Case: Death Without Dignity

Selma's conservator of the person was Mr. Gaines, who ran a fiduciary business. Mr. Gaines took control of Selma's personal and health care needs. Livingston asked his attorney to what extent Selma's family members would be allowed to participate in personal and health care decisions for Selma. The attorney replied, "In no way." Mr. Gaines would be making all these decisions for Selma. According to the settlement agreement, though, Livingston and certain family members ("interested parties") were allowed to ask Mr. Gaines for information on Selma's care, but they were not permitted to directly speak to Selma's doctors nor interfere with Selma's personal or medical care.

By all accounts, Selma had been medically neglected. According to Mr. Gaines, Selma's sugar levels were "horrifically" out of control. Selma had received very little medical treatment or follow up after her first stroke, and she had not gotten routine medical check-ups, according to a family representative.

Mr. Gaines selected a geriatric specialist to be Selma's primary care physician (PCP). Mr. Gaines's immediate concern was that Selma's diabetes had ravaged Selma's organs and, if left unchecked, would lead to blindness, strokes, and circulation problems, which could result in amputation.

Selma had difficulties adjusting to the changes in her household after Zachary was required to move out of Selma's home, which was a stipulation in the settlement agreement. During the temporary conservatorship, a revolving door of caregivers, who were selected by Selma's court-appointed attorney, Hall, were swinging through in shifts. After the conservatorship was made permanent, Mr. Gaines hired a live-in caregiver for Selma.

One day a social worker came to evaluate Selma in her home. The live-in caregiver said that Selma became enraged. "This was totally uncharacteristic behavior for my aunt [Selma]. She's usually quiet and agreeable," claimed Agatha. According to the live-in caregiver, Selma was resisting her health care regimen and was scratching and hitting her. As a result, Mr. Gaines had Selma committed to a geriatric psychiatric unit for older women.

When Agatha learned that Selma had been institutionalized, she called the facility to determine what had happened to her aunt. The staff refused to say, instructing her to contact Mr. Gaines. So Agatha called Mr. Gaines's office. She found out that Mr. Gaines had ordered that Selma be admitted to the unit on a 5150 (i.e., involuntary psychiatric hold). Agatha said, "My aunt was a sweet, nonthreatening person. Placing her on lockdown in a psych ward was grievous. But there was nothing we [the family] could do about it." Other family members were stunned by Mr. Gaines's decision, and questioned its validity.

Livingston visited Selma during her lengthy stay in the lockup unit. He found Selma to be downtrodden and in poor shape. When Agatha visited Selma at the psychiatric facility, Agatha also observed that Selma was despondent, frail, tearful, and generally not responding psychologically well to the environment. While the unit was clean and habitable, it was a sad place where older women with mental health problems would act out their symptoms, according to Agatha's observations.

Livingston, who had maintained contact with Hall early in Selma's conservatorship, said that Hall was furious when she learned that Selma had been placed on involuntary psychiatric hold. But not even Hall had a say in Selma's treatment.

During Selma's confinement, Selma underwent a series of medical tests and procedures. The origin of Selma's cognitive disorder was assessed further. Instead of a diagnosis of dementia, it was possible that Selma had *hydrocephalus*, also known as "water on the brain," a neurological disorder that might be reversible. But Mr. Gaines still needed to verify the diagnosis with his neurologist. Also, it was discovered that Selma was "impacted," with stool stored in her colon for nearly a year, which had backed up all the way to her stomach.

Eventually, Selma was returned home with a new live-in caregiver. Not long afterwards, Selma fell and fractured her hip. Hip surgery was performed, and Selma remained in the hospital during her lengthy recovery.

In the aftermath of Selma's hip surgery, the live-in caregiver said that Zachary and Sybil had accused her of negligence. They said they had a witness who would claim that she was outside the house when Selma fell. The couple caused a frenzy around the negligence claim, which was ultimately dropped.

Noah spoke discouragingly about Selma's overall prognosis, given her hip fracture, dementia, and chronic conditions. He believed that Selma would probably live only a few more years. The same prediction was made by Attorney Forte. Agatha disagreed. She felt sure that Selma would thrive for many more years—which she did.

Livingston visited Selma during her recovery period in the hospital. He observed that Selma was "very sick and hopeless." He further observed that Selma was experiencing new problems since the fall, including a twitching in her face, right shoulder, and right hand, plus a drooping on her right side. Livingston felt that something of a neurological nature may have occurred when Selma fell, although the MRIs came back normal. Moreover, Selma wasn't cooperating during her physical therapy nor was she eating.

Instead of returning Selma to her home after her hospitalization, Mr. Gaines sent Selma, who was now wheelchair bound, to a locked Alzheimer's and dementia care unit to complete her recovery.

Livingston visited Selma in the dementia care unit. "I found Selma slumped over in a wheelchair, drooling and incoherent— she was heavily sedated. While being handfed, she had difficulty swallowing," he observed.

Other family members paid Selma a visit at the dementia care unit. They witnessed that Selma was in the same sad state that Livingston had observed. While the unit was quaint and homey, it was nonetheless chilling. Several patients lay bedridden, some acted out, many languished in wheelchairs, several were treated harshly by impatient staffers, many appeared sedated, and some were left unsupervised to behave in ways that were unseemly. According to one of Selma's caregivers, "Even the Alzheimer's patients screamed to go home!"

Based on Livingston's and Agatha's observations, initial concerns were raised about the decisions Mr. Gaines was making for Selma. These concerns were communicated to Attorney Forte. In turn, Forte fired off a letter to Mr. Gaines stating that another doctor would be evaluating Selma and that a caregiver should be hired to motivate Selma during her rehabilitation.

Agatha and Livingston were also troubled that Selma was placed in "chemical restraints" (overmedicated). The rationale given by Mr. Gaines was that Selma had become "combative," which was not the Selma that Livingston, Agatha, and other family members knew.

Selma's chronic conditions were quickly piling up, according to Selma's brother. In addition to her dementia, high blood pressure, and diabetes, she developed chronic anemia, which also required intermittent hospitalizations. She experienced frequent bouts of aggressive urinary tract infections (UTIs), which also required hospitalizations. She had gastrointestinal tract bleeding and a neurogenic bladder. She developed a bed sore that required surgery. And she had episodes of congestive heart failure (CHF) and pneumonia.

In spite of it all, several family members felt that the best place for Selma to live out her days was in her home and not in the dementia care unit. However, Mr. Gaines and Selma's PCP disagreed. Using an analogy of the Black Flag commercial tagline, "The patients could check in, but they never check out."

By now, a full medical report was produced by Selma's PCP. Selma did not have hydrocephalus but instead vascular dementia/Alzheimer's for which there was no cure.

Agatha and Livingston continued to lobby for Selma to be returned home. On behalf of Livingston and Agatha, Attorney Forte wrote Mr. Gaines, requesting that Selma be moved home at the soonest opportunity. In the same correspondence to Mr. Gaines, Forte made it clear that "protecting Selma from what causes her anxiety" was a top priority. Forte wrote, "Please set in place a directive that prohibits contact with Sybil [...] I will, if necessary, obtain a restraining order to implement this prohibition." Zachary could still see and visit Selma, but Sybil would be prevented from doing so.

Mr. Gaines still would not embrace the idea of returning Selma home, and Livingston and Agatha would not give up on the idea. So Forte consulted experts to determine if Selma's catheterization had any bearing on Selma returning home. Forte also pursued the matter of Sybil's visitations, given that Selma was helpless and became stressed when Sybil was present.

At long last, Selma was cleared to go home by Mr. Gaines and his team of medical doctors. As a condition of her return, she was to be seen at least once a week by a nurse. Selma was to receive round-the-clock care through two regular caregivers who had bonded with Selma at the dementia care unit.

Several years passed as Selma, with dulled senses, sat wheelchair bound. According to Harper, Selma was badly contracted, with her limbs rigidly held in one position, and she was diapered. Selma was completely dependent on her caregivers for her basic needs.

Selma's dementia had advanced to the point that she could no longer swallow. To deliver nutrition and administer medications, Selma was eventually fitted with a gastrostomy tube.

Before long, Selma's sentience drifted into a repetitive wake/sleep cycle. Then something happened that was a game changer: Selma was diagnosed with cancer.

Selma's family included several medical practitioners. They asked for more information on Selma's cancer, specifically staging, location, and size. Of concern was that Selma, who lacked the ability to communicate, was in chronic pain and thus suffering in silence.

Mr. Gaines concluded that Selma's cancer would not endanger her life. However, a cousin who was a surgeon disagreed: "I think the conservator of the person is wrong as the cancer can kill her anytime if it erodes in a blood vessel." Moreover, both the cousin and Harper felt that Selma's cancer had not been properly staged and evaluated based on the information supplied by Mr. Gaines.

Mr. Gaines contended that Selma, who was about 90 years of age and was very fragile, would not be a good candidate for cancer surgery, and Selma's family members agreed. Still, concern over surrogate health care decisions being made for Selma by Mr. Gaines and his doctors were raised, as these decisions were contrary to the ones that Selma would have made for herself, according to family members.

Given that Harper was a palliative care specialist, Livingston asked her to conduct an informal assessment and evaluation on Selma. Harper reported her findings to Livingston in an e-mail. In it, she said:

> "Per your request I did a limited physical exam and asked Selma's caregiver some questions about her activities of daily living (ADL) and quality of life (QOL). Selma is completely immobile due to chronic, severe contractures of her extremities. According to the caregiver, Selma hasn't been able to move or assist with moving since she broke her hip about eight years ago. She was sitting upright in a wheelchair with her knees frozen at an angle. More recently her head has become

frozen in one position and she cannot move her neck or head from side to side. I also observed that her eyes did not track or have a blink reflex. It did not appear that she had vision or was able to communicate using her eyes. The caregiver confirmed that she believes that Selma has been blind for years... Based on my clinical judgment and palliative care expertise, it is my professional opinion that your aunt has a very poor QOL and been in this immobile, noncommunicative state for several years. She is completely unable to perform any ADL, either with or without assistance from her full-time caregivers. She cannot independently move any part of her body; she cannot chew, swallow, or speak; and now it appears that she may be blind as well. At this time, it would help to have a palliative care consult with a physician that has expertise in palliative care and end-of-life decision-making. He/she may be able to guide and assist your family in determining your aunt's QOL and what you believe would be her wishes at her end of life."

Harper's assessment was communicated to Selma's family members. One of Selma's sisters said, "We [Selma's family] felt the tube should be removed. My sister would not have wanted to live that way." However, Livingston remained neutral because of his fiduciary status, while one sister favored suspension but only if Selma was in pain. Some family members questioned G-tube placement to begin with. Noah summarized the family's position on tube feeding as follows:

"The most compassionate treatment would be withdrawal of feedings with control of any pain/discomfort with narcotics (either through her G-tube) or administered intravenously. I also know Selma, how proud she was, would be disgraced by any further continuation of support given her meager condition and dismal quality

155

of life. She has always been and continues to be the gleam of the best of the human spirit...Now is the time to assist her and not continue artificial support as I am SURE she would have desired."

Meanwhile, Selma's brother had found a Declaration to Withhold Life-Sustaining Treatment signed by Selma among Selma's trust documents. The declaration stated that Selma did not want artificial feeding. The document was shared with Mr. Gaines. It turned out that the declaration was nullified because it was signed around the time Selma was deemed incapable. The position taken by one of the attorneys involved in Selma's case was that even though Selma was unduly being influenced by her son Zachary on decisions concerning finances, that in and of itself did not mean that Selma lacked legal capacity to make medical decisions for herself at the time the declaration was signed. The attorney remarked, "It is clear that Selma's intent was not to remain in a vegetative state where she would never return to a meaningful life." According to Harper, the declaration was "irrefutable proof of Selma's wishes and suspension of ANH should be done without delay."

Harper pressed Mr. Gaines to have Selma assessed by an independent palliative care specialist. Mr. Gaines finally agreed to the assessment. He sent a doctor of his own choosing, a gerontologist, to perform the assessment and evaluation. The gerontologist's conclusion was that Selma was "medically stable." He recommended no change to Selma's current treatment plan.

Harper and Mason looked over the gerontologist's report and found gaps in it. Harper responded:

"... I found the gerontologist's report very interesting. Not so much for what was included, but for what was not included. First of all, both Mr. Gaines and the gerontologist referred to the consultation as an evaluation for 'hospice.' I don't believe anyone in the family suggested that Aunt Selma would meet the criteria for hospice, which is defined as a life expectancy of less than six months. The family's concern is that she could be maintained in her current state indefinitely with the use of artificial nutrition. It is literally the only thing keeping her alive. That is why I recommended a Palliative Care (PC) consultation. The focus of palliative care is to maintain comfort and dignity while not prolonging a natural death, especially when there is such poor quality of life (QOL). A Palliative Care Physician would be evaluating Aunt Selma from a QOL perspective. The gerontologist conducted a physical exam and barely mentioned her mental status, other than to say that she has advanced stage Alzheimer's Disease."

Given all this, Livingston requested that Mr. Gaines arrange for Selma to be seen by an independent palliative care specialist. Harper e-mailed Livingston: "A PC assessment is <u>incomplete</u> unless the family has an opportunity to discuss Selma with the consultant. Selma's cultural views about artificial nutrition also need to be considered. Selma is unable to communicate anything to the PC consultant, so he/she needs to talk to close family members to provide information on Selma (that does not include Mr. Gaines or the caregiver's opinion about her QOL)."

Mr. Gaines agreed to have Selma seen by a palliative care specialist, who "rubber-stamped" the gerontologist's assessment. Mr. Gaines supported the gerontologist's conclusion that discontinuing life supportive measures was "an ethical issue" and unwarranted.

Shortly thereafter, Livingston said that Mr. Gaines stopped communicating with him, refusing to return Livingston's calls or his e-mails. By now, some family members called for the removal of Mr. Gaines as Selma's conservator of the person. Mason and other family members questioned Mr. Gaines's "reasonableness," as he was making surrogate decisions for Selma that weren't in her best interests but instead appeared to be motivated by something else.

Weeks passed without any further discussion on Selma's situation. Harper broke the silence by e-mailing Mr. Gaines about the lack of family input in the palliative care assessment as well as Selma's poor quality of life.

> "Your communication to the palliative care MD should not have been in place of the family's ability to speak on behalf, and in the best interest, of Selma. A complete palliative care assessment should always include input from the family with special cultural considerations. It was also interesting that the palliative care MD never once mentioned Selma's quality of life (QOL) in his three-page report. The focus of palliative medicine is maximizing one's quality of life and minimizing suffering even if that means discontinuing artificial nutrition. When a patient's unable to speak on his or her own behalf and QOL is as poor as Selma's is, then it is the family's responsibility to speak on her behalf. The PC's palliative care assessment appears to be incomplete because it does not include the family's preference and cultural aspects. Your e-mail also indicated that the gerontologist believed that discontinuing the artificial nutrition was an 'ethical' issue. One could argue that it is unethical to allow Selma to suffer any longer. It is clear that artificial nutrition is the only thing preventing her from dying with dignity. Selma has many family members with medical degrees and not one of them believes that removing the artificial feeding is unethical."

Only days later Selma died from complications brought on by pneumonia. In the days leading up to Selma's death, family members struggled to obtain accurate information on Selma's status. The hospital staff overseeing Selma's care would only say that Selma was "stable." Beyond that, Selma's relatives were redirected to Mr.

Gaines. A family member said, "We had no idea Selma's situation had become life-threatening, because we weren't allowed to discuss Selma's medical treatment with her doctors. At Selma's dying moment, she was without her family by her bedside."

The conservatorship ended when Selma died. Livingston remarked that Selma's doctor made a very handsome sum on Selma's case. The doctor would not sign Selma's death certificate.

Selma was laid to rest next to her parents and her sister Minerva. Selma was an avid gardener and nature lover. Agatha reminisced, "It was only fitting that my aunt's final resting place was a private garden within a memorial park that sits on a seaward slope overlooking the Pacific Ocean." In attendance at her memorial service were immediate family members and a few close friends. Selma's son Zachary did not attend.

In the next chapter, we'll unmask "who" the conservator of the estate is, and reveal what duties and responsibilities he or she performs. Also, we'll look at the ways that the conservator of the estate spends other people's money. Finally, we'll take a walk on the gritty side of the protection industry.

CHAPTER 7

The Money Trail

Many articles about guardians gone wild have been published by the press. In California, one controversial conservator who has made news headlines is the high-flying Melodie Scott of C.A.R.E., Inc., a Redlands-based for-profit conservatorship firm. Scott was accused of fiduciary abuse by family members whose loved ones were under Scott's care and supervision.

A *Los Angeles Times* investigation into conservatorship abuse spotlighted Scott's alleged misdeeds. In one case, a conservatee filed a court complaint that accused Scott of frivolously spending $200,000 of the conservatee's life savings for things the conservatee didn't need nor want. In a different conservatorship case, Scott was accused of permitting an in-law to live rent-free in a mentally ill client's home. One complainant, who accused Scott of criminal misconduct on the grounds that Scott stole a large sum of the complainant's disabled husband's money, wondered why Scott wasn't doing jail time.

Another sensational *Los Angeles Times* story about conservator corruption was that of Planned Protective Services, Inc. (PPS), one of California's largest conservatorship firms. The judge who heard the case said, "I have never seen such overreaching... We have economic abuse of the elderly and the incapacitated." The allegations against PPS included kickbacks (one bank gave $223,809 to PPS for its business), double billing, and faulty accounting records.

These cases highlight the potential for financial abuse by crooked conservators who were appointed by the very courts that were entrusted with protecting vulnerable and dependent persons from mistreatment and exploitation. As a paternalistic system based on arcane rules and procedures, conservatorships and guardianships often fail.

In this chapter, we'll describe who the conservator of the estate is and what duties and responsibilities he or she performs. Also, we'll look at the standards by which conservators manage their conservatee's property. Finally, we'll probe into the dark side of the protection industry. For the sake of this discussion, the terms *conservatee* and *ward* and *conservator* and *guardian* may be used interchangeably.

What Is the Conservator of the Estate?

As you may recall, a *conservator* is a court-appointed person or an organization that handles the affairs for a person, a *conservatee*, who can no longer mange them for him- or herself. A probate court picks the conservator. He or she can be a family member, a friend, a relative, a neighbor, an interested party, a private conservator, or a public guardian.

The *conservator of the estate* manages the conservatee's finances and handles his or her estate matters. Let's say that you've been appointed as your uncle's conservator of the estate because he needs help with his financial affairs. As your uncle's conservator of the estate, you must initially carry out these responsibilities:

- Obtain your *Letters of Conservatorship*, also known as the *Letters*, which authorize you to act on the behalf of your uncle.
- Give a copy of the Letters to the financial institutions where your uncle holds his assets and to your uncle's employer if he still works.

- Contact individuals and organizations with which your uncle has a financial relationship, such as stockbrokers, insurance companies and agents, government agencies (such as the Social Security Administration), retirement plans, accountants, creditors, and debtors.
- Notify the post office if your uncle's mail will be forwarded to you. Also, furnish your address to any institution with which your uncle does business.
- Take possession of your uncle's assets, prepare an initial inventory and appraisal of these assets for the court, and develop a financial plan and budget that shows how you plan to manage your uncle's estate. Appraisals will reflect the value of an asset as of the date you were appointed your uncle's conservator.
- Maintain a surety bond for the protection of your uncle's estate unless the judge doesn't require it. The bond must be filed with the court clerk.
- Record a certified copy of the Letters with the County Recorder's Office in each county that your uncle owns or has an interest in any real property. By recording the Letters, you prevent the property from being sold, transferred, or used as collateral for a loan without your knowledge.

Local probate court rules may require other initial tasks. For example, if you've been appointed a conservator in California, you must sign and file an acknowledgment of the receipt of a statement of the duties and liabilities of the Office of Conservator as well as sign an oath, also referred to as "an affirmation," promising to fulfill these duties. If you're unclear about your duties, always check with a local probate court or a conservatorship attorney.

Let's return to Selma's conservatorship formation to demonstrate the prickly decision of designating conservators. When it was realized that Selma's conservatorship would be made permanent, several of Selma's family members campaigned to make Livingston Selma's conservator of the estate *and* trustee. This is largely because they knew that Selma would be very opposed to having a nonfamily member handle her affairs.

In some way, shape, or form, certain interested parties, mainly Zachary and Sybil, objected to Livingston playing the dual role. So a compromised solution was found, in which Livingston was made Selma's conservator of the estate. A professional fiduciary was selected as Selma's trustee. The court approved these nominations. Down the road, however, Livingston elected to curtail his role by becoming Selma's co-conservator of the estate alongside the trustee.

Know that if you have a properly constructed trust in place (a *trust* is a "fiduciary arrangement that allows a third party, or trustee, to hold assets on behalf of a beneficiary or beneficiaries"), you'll rarely need a conservator of the estate. Selma had established a trust. However, her incapacity, which resulted in the appointment of a conservator, triggered a change of trustees. As stated previously, Selma's family hoped that Livingston would be allowed to serve as Selma's conservator of the estate and trustee, thus reducing conservatorship costs and increasing a family presence. However, due to objections to Livingston's appointment, a third party was appointed as Selma's trustee, adding another layer to Selma's already cumbersome conservatorship.

What Are the Ongoing Duties and Responsibilities of the Conservator of the Estate?

According to the National Guardianship Association (NGA), as the guardian of the estate, you are bound to "act in a manner above reproach." At any given time, your actions may be open to scrutiny. You're required to manage the conservatee's estate only for his or her benefit, unless the court authorizes you to use estate assets to the benefit of others, such as a spouse or other relatives. For example, the judge, who approved Selma's permanent conservatorship, allowed Zachary and his new family to remain in Selma's home, without paying rent or contributing to household expenses, for a stated time period while Zachary and his new family found a new place to live.

Now let's look at some of your ongoing responsibilities as your uncle's conservator of the estate.

Inventory and Appraisal

Once you've located and taken control of your uncle's estate, take a complete inventory of all property and assets owned by your uncle. Assets may include cash; bank accounts; securities; promissory notes; real estate; pensions; life insurance policies; and personal possessions such as jewelry, furniture, antiques, artwork, and other valuables. In addition to finding your uncle's assets, take steps to protect them against loss. Finally, do an appraisal of your uncle's assets and property based on their market value at the time that you became your uncle's conservator.

Your uncle might have assets that are not included in the conservatorship estate, for which you won't be responsible. For example, assets sitting in a living trust are the trustee's responsibility to control as provided for in your uncle's trust documents.

Financial Plan and Budget

Prepare a financial plan and budget, which will include your uncle's expenses and income. The budget should correspond to your uncle's care plan and should consider free or low-cost services offered through community programs. For this reason, *you must communicate regularly with your uncle's conservator of the person if one exists and if that person is not you.* Of utmost importance is that you and the conservator of the person agree on the quantity and quality of care and comfort that your uncle can afford.

To what extent Selma's fiduciaries did any planning and budgeting are unknown. Livingston had done some forecasting. He said, "At an average 'burn rate' of roughly \$250,000 per year, Selma's assets would be depleted in ten years or less." Livingston kept in touch with Mr. Powell to discuss the disposition of Selma's assets as well as to obtain infusions of cash when Selma was low on money. Livingston also remained in close contact with Mr. Gaines. Mr. Gaines retained medical providers, caregivers, and ancillary services for Selma, but Livingston was responsible for paying their fees.

Collections and Disbursements

Oversee all income and disbursements as well as apply for any public benefits programs to which your uncle may be entitled. Pay your uncle's bills and expenses in a timely fashion. You might need to make claims against other parties on behalf of your uncle's estate, while also guarding against actions that could cause a loss to it. For example, Livingston received and accounted for all of Selma's income and also paid for all of Selma's expenses. He used accounting software to regularly record and process every transaction.

Keep an eye on how the trustee or someone else in control of your uncle's assets is managing your uncle's funds. For instance, Livingston worked alongside the trustee to ensure that Selma's assets were working for her. At one point they had to consider whether to mortgage or to sell Selma's investment property, given that Selma's income did not sufficiently cover Selma's outsized caregiving costs, continuing conservator fees, ongoing legal fees, and other costs.

Investments and Insurances

Follow two investment principles when you invest your uncle's money. The first is the *Prudent-Person Rule*—a legal term that limits "the discretion in a client's account to investments that a prudent person seeking reasonable income and preservation of capital might buy for his or her own portfolio." The second is the *Prudent Investor*

Rule—a general rule of thumb that "requires a fiduciary to invest trust assets as if they were his own." Overall, make safe investments that will fulfill your uncle's needs and satisfy the court's requirements.

Make certain your uncle has sufficient health insurance. In the last chapter, we discussed the different ways that your uncle can obtain affordable health insurance. If your uncle has a life insurance policy, check on the amount of coverage as well as your uncle's named beneficiaries. Finally, if your uncle owns real property, make certain that he has the appropriate types of insurance coverage.

Taxes and Accounting

File your uncle's income tax returns on time. You might wish to hire an accountant to prepare and file the returns. Also, inform the Internal Revenue Service that you are the responsible party for tax filings and payments on behalf of your uncle.

Use careful accounting procedures, and keep your uncle's money separate from your own—do not comingle your money with that of your uncle's! File periodic accountings with the court and share them with other interested parties as required. For example, all accountings produced by Livingston and his attorney were shared with Selma's immediate family. Mr. Powell furnished all trust accountings with Selma's beneficiaries.

Payments to Lawyers and Aides

A conservatorship is a legal process, which means hiring attorneys. Your attorney is paid from your uncle's estate. If your uncle has a court-appointed attorney, he or she is paid from your uncle's estate. If your uncle has a conservator of the person and a trustee, their attorneys are paid from your uncle's estate. But a judge must first approve these fees before disbursal. You can pay certain administrative fees, such as court filing fees, from your uncle's estate without court approval.

For example, Selma's conservatorship involved several attorneys, including Selma's court-appointed attorney, Livingston's attorney, Mr. Powell's attorney, and Mr. Gaines's attorney. Attorney fees were recurring and consumed a chunk of Selma's estate.

If your uncle needs professional help with his personal and physical needs, you can hire a home health aide or a caregiver to assist him with these. If your uncle has a conservator of the person, he or she will likely hire the aide, but you will be responsible for paying the aide directly or paying the agency that employs the aide.

Finally, as your uncle's conservator of the estate, compensating others for services rendered and reimbursing yourself for overhead expenses can get tricky. When in doubt, check with your attorney.

Other Things to Do or to Think About

First, contact your uncle's attorney to find out if your uncle has a *will and/or a living trust*. In the will, important information will be provided, such as the name of your uncle's executor, his funeral and burial preferences, the names of his beneficiaries, any special gifts he'd like to leave to particular individuals, and so on. Likewise, your uncle might have set up a trust that contains some or all of his assets, or the trust may distribute money to your uncle.

Second, your uncle may be in the habit of *gift giving*. He might still wish to gift others during the conservatorship. But you can't give away anything without first getting court approval.

Third, *borrowing and loaning money* from your uncle's estate is prohibited unless you receive prior court approval. You can loan money to your uncle's estate and get repaid. But if you want to charge interest on the loan, get court approval first.

Fourth, open a *burial trust account* for your uncle and make *funeral arrangements* for when your uncle passes away. In Selma's situation, Selma had already bought a cemetery plot, and Livingston made funeral arrangements for Selma.

Finally, managing and protecting a conservatee's estate is a huge responsibility. To familiarize yourself with the duties and responsibilities of a conservator, you can obtain user's manuals from your local probate court or take conservator education classes that may be offered there. How-to books on guardianships and conservatorships are another good source, such as *The Conservatorship Book for California*. Finally, a number of Web resources are provided by the courts, organizations (such as Family Caregiver Alliance), government agencies (such as Federal Housing Finance Agency), and other sources. A list of helpful sources is provided in Chapter 9.

Property Management and Sale

Probably one of your biggest challenges as your uncle's conservator of the estate is handling your uncle's real property. As a general rule, you must petition the court to order the sale of any of your uncle's assets, from his car to his home. If you don't do that and a loss results, you're on the hook for it!

Let's say that your uncle owns rental property, or you decide to rent out his home instead of selling it. As your uncle's conservator of the estate, you become legally responsible as the landlord. For example, Selma owned rental property. Livingston managed it by collecting rent and handling all aspects of maintaining and improving it. Selma also owned a primary residence. Livingston handled Selma's home expenses, repairs, maintenance, and improvements.

What happens if your uncle starts running out of cash? If he owns a home but doesn't want to move or sell the property, you can make the property work for him. In lieu of selling your uncle's home, you can do several things.

- Sell the remaining interest in your uncle's home, where a portion of the home is sold and your uncle becomes a free tenant.

- Do a sale with a leaseback, where your uncle's home is sold for full value and he becomes a rent-paying tenant.
- Rent the home, which may be better than selling it if the sale would trigger a capital gains tax.
- Consider a home equity loan or a *reverse annuity mortgage (RAM)*, where a lender will give your uncle monthly loan installments.

Regardless of which approach you take, you should ask your lawyer and accountant about the advantages and disadvantages of each.

As a word of warning, do not dispose of your uncle's real or personal property "without judicial, administrative, or other independent review," according to the NGA. You may not sell, encumber, convey, or transfer your uncle's property unless doing so is in the *best interest* of your uncle. Remember that the best interest standard of decision making requires you to adopt a course of action based on a knowledge of your uncle's wishes. Before taking any action, then, you should ask yourself:

- Does selling your uncle's property benefit or improve his life?
- Will your uncle need the property or benefit from it at some future time?
- What is/was your uncle's views about the disposition of the property?
- What does your uncle's estate plan say about the property?
- What are the tax implications of a property sale?
- How does the property sale affect your uncle's heirs?
- Would the property sale or borrowing against the property affect your uncle's eligibility for public benefits programs?
- What is the overall condition of the estate?
- Are there alternatives to the property sale?
- What are the benefits versus the risks of looking after the property if you don't sell it?

If you ultimately decide to sell your uncle's property, you must follow certain court rules and procedures to complete the sale. First, you must show that the sale was for a purpose authorized by law. Second, if you sell the property a year or more after your appointment, you must prepare a Reappraisal for Sale. Third, to sell some kinds of property, you must post "a notice of intent to sell in the courthouse and publish the notice in a newspaper." Finally, you must get court approval for the terms of the sale.

Conservator Services and Fees

In the last chapter, we discussed the issue of *conflict of interest* as it relates to the conservator of the person's actions. Here again, as the conservator of the estate, avoid giving the appearance of a conflict of interest or impropriety when discharging your obligations. According to the NGA, "Impropriety or conflict of interest arises when the guardian has some personal or agency interest that might be perceived as self-serving or adverse to the position or best interest of the ward." Here are some do's and don'ts to follow:

- Do not combine your uncle's money with yours unless the court allows you to use combined accounts. This general rule doesn't usually apply to professional fiduciaries who handle several conservatees' funds.
- Charge a reasonable fee for your services. A judge must approve your fees before you pay yourself. If you don't get prior court approval, you may be out-of-pocket (plus interest) to your uncle's estate or the surety company that holds your bond. Moreover, you may be removed as your uncle's conservator. The average range for conservatorship fees is between $50 and $135 an hour and even higher. In Selma's case, Livingston waived his fees. Mr. Gaines charged for everything from case management, to a case assistant, to document preservation like filing, and other activities. Mr. Powell earned a percent

per annum of Selma's estate, plus he charged hourly fees for bill paying and other administrative tasks. Each fiduciary used an accountant and an attorney, and their fees were paid through Selma's estate. Other service providers retained by the fiduciaries also received payments through Selma's estate.

- Conserve your uncle's assets as much as possible, as your actions will be subject to court review and approval. In an attempt to conserve Selma's estate to cover her outsized care needs, Livingston proposed that an amendment be made to the original settlement agreement that would eliminate layers of fiduciaries and their helpers and instead install a single trustee/conservator of the person and one attorney to handle Selma's case. This proposal withered on the vine, as a consensus among the parties couldn't be reached.

- Pay legal fees, court filing fees, and the first year's surety bond premium. A *surety bond* protects your uncle against loss if you fail to meet his financial obligations. These costs don't require court approval because they are regarded as "an expense of administration." Other routine costs, such as for telephone use, postage stamps, mileage and travel, and so on, are reimbursable. Document everything by maintaining detailed records and billings, given that a judge will review your requests and those of your lawyer to assess their appropriateness.

In Selma's case, all accountings were approved ("rubberstamped") by the court, according to a family representative. In an example of lax court oversight, Selma's court-appointed attorney was supposed to be discharged after the approval of the conservator's first accounting as stipulated in the settlement agreement that the attorney signed. Instead, the court-appointed attorney stayed on Selma's case for several more years—and billed for it. Livingston and his attorney filed an objection to the new fees. The judge reduced the court-appointed attorney's fees by half, but allowed her to bill a few thousand dollars for defending her fee request.

Accountings and Accountability

One of the most important administrative tasks undertaken by the conservator of the estate is the preparation and filing of periodic reports and accountings that show and describe how he or she is managing the conservatee's estate. Let's briefly discuss your accounting responsibilities as your uncle's conservator of the estate.

The first court filing of a report and an accounting must occur no later than one year after your appointment and then no less than every two years thereafter. The report must be drafted into a petition. The accounting, which lists all transactions and actions taken during the reporting period, accompanies the petition. Also contained in the petition are requests for your conservator fees and those of your lawyer. At the end of the conservatorship, a final accounting will be submitted to the court.

In preparing an accounting, detail each transaction and explain or provide clarification for any sales or other adjustments to your uncle's estate. Each accounting shows a beginning and an ending date. It includes the value of assets on hand, income received by the estate, gains and losses from the sale of assets, and disbursements from available funds. The final accounting will cover the period from the last accounting to the date that the conservatorship ends. When Selma died, for example, each conservator and the trustee prepared and filed a final accounting, which included requests for conservator and lawyer fees and showed disbursements and income, with the court.

Accountings must follow a specific format unique to probate court accountings. So if you use an accountant to produce the accountings, find one who does estate accounting. Or your lawyer may prefer to do the accountings. For example, Livingston prepared the accountings, and his lawyer drafted the petition and the report.

Courts set hearing dates to monitor the filings of reports and accountings. Your lawyer will usually attend these hearings to address any questions the judge may have about the report and accounting, and you may be asked to accompany him or her. Your lawyer will send out a notice of the hearing and also the report and accounting to interested parties before the hearing date. For example, Selma's close relatives received a mountain of petitions, reports, and accountings over the course of Selma's conservatorship.

If there are no objections to the accounting and report from interested parties, you and your lawyer won't need to attend the scheduled hearing. Rather, the judge will just approve the report and accounting without a hearing. But if an interested party files a written objection to the accounting and report or attends the hearing and tells the judge he or she plans to object in writing, then the matter will be held over for another hearing, making the report and accounting a "contested matter."

During Selma's conservatorship, some family members questioned the appropriateness or reasonableness of how Selma's money was being spent and how her care was being managed, yet none filed an objection in court. A family representative reasoned, "We [the family] figured a bunch of lawyers would get in the ring and duke it out in court. Her [Selma's] estate was eroding—fast. The last thing we wanted to do was waste Selma's money on attorneys when she badly needed it for her care."

The Dark Side of the Protection Industry

In Michigan, a 23-year-old barroom janitor was appointed as a public guardian. He had no training or experience in a field that would prepare him for the job. In one year's time, he took control of the lives of 80 wards and their combined income and assets worth $350,000. He was later convicted of embezzling $130,000 from his wards. Stories like this one aren't a rarity. Still, most conservators and guardians manage the lives and the assets of incapacitated loved ones and vulnerable and dependent persons with care, compassion, and respect. But what happens when they don't? Let's find out.

The courts usually appoint a family member to be a conservator or a guardian for an elderly loved one who needs help. In fact, 70 percent of conservators and guardians to the elderly are family members. However, most family members are ill-equipped to play their roles as conservators or guardians. One survey found that fewer than 20 percent of courts furnished conservators and guardians with instructions on carrying out their duties and legal responsibilities.

When no suitable family member is available to serve as conservator, the courts may appoint a *professional fiduciary*, "a person who acts as conservator of the person, the estate, or person and estate, or guardian of the estate, or person and estate, for two or more individuals at the same time who are not related to the professional fiduciary." A professional fiduciary often manages many clients, plays a paternalistic role in their lives, and demonstrates no or limited interest in their well-being. Some critics say that "they [fiduciaries] profit off mostly helpless people."

A conservator or a guardian must manage the incapacitated person's estate for the benefit of him or her. Yet localized studies on conservatorship and guardianship proceedings found "little benefit to the incapacitated persons" but instead suggested that many petitions were filed for "the benefit of third persons," according to a report titled "Wards of the State: A National Study on Public Guardianships. One empirical study found:

> "Under the present system of the 'Estate Management by Preemption,' we divest the incompetent of control of his property upon the finding of the existence of serious mental illness whenever divestiture is in the interest of some third-party person or institution. The theory of incompetency is to protect the debilitated from their own financial foolishness or from the fraud of others who would prey upon their mental weaknesses. In practice, however, we seek to protect the interests of others... All of these motives may be honest and without any intention to cheat the aged, but none of these proceedings are commenced to assist the debilitated."

Instead of appointing a family member or a professional fiduciary as a conservator or guardian for an incapacitated person, the court may appoint a *public guardian*. Even public guardians who are government officials aren't immune to tripping up in meeting their responsibilities to their wards. As an example, in a study of the Los Angeles County Office of Public Guardian (LAPG), some troubling findings surfaced.

- The office was able to "petition for its own incapacitated persons, which creates potential for self-aggrandizement."
- The office improperly prioritized its inquiries and acceptance of clients on the basis of their ability to pay fees for services.
- The office infrequently visited clients, while reporting lags existed in several cases.

The key takeaway is that even local government programs that are responsible for helping the helpless can't always be depended on to adequately assist them.

Critics of the guardianship system have long complained about guardianship abuse. In an article titled "Guardianship Gone Bad," the author states that many guardians strip the elderly of their life savings; overcharge for menial tasks; sell elders' homes right from under their feet; toss away elders' personal possessions and memorabilia; fail to pay bills; and cash and pocket elders' Social Security checks. In many instances, elders are thrown into nursing homes against their protests, their families are barred from seeing them, and they're kept in chemical straightjackets (overmedicated). With elders' life savings diverted to guardians and lawyers, elders are often left with nothing and may be forced to go on Medicaid.

The public outrage over guardianship abuse has taken to the Internet. For example, the National Association to Stop Guardian Abuse (NASGA) is an organization that posts, blogs, tweets, and reports on guardianship abuse. The NASGA calls the guardianship system "a growing menace which feeds on greed." It criticizes the judicial system for its complicity in usurping people's liberties and property. The NASGA claims that judges are often inclined to appoint faceless fiduciaries on the basis of cronyism. After taking control of their wards' assets and property, the fiduciaries go to town by selling the wards' property, often below market value, to their friends or relatives and then move their wards to nursing homes, where the wards are placed on "inappropriate antipsychotic drugs which hasten their deaths—but not until all the money is gone!" According to the NASGA:

> "These 'protectors' are now free to bill for 'services' whether actually rendered or not even billable at all—and at inflated rates. With the cooperation of an uncaring (or possibly even corrupt) judiciary, they are free to bleed an estate to death, then dump their newly impoverished wards onto the taxpayers' backs and the Medicaid rolls."

When family members complain to the courts about guardian wrongdoing, they often find themselves fighting an uphill battle. Even when a family member doesn't fight the good fight, it can be costly to him or her after his or her loved one is absorbed into the "system." For example, Agatha spent thousands of dollars of her own money to keep pace with the plethora of petitions and legal actions spun by Selma's conservatorship.

The incidents and instances of fiduciary abuse and fraud committed by conservators, guardians, and personal representatives of the elderly are difficult to quantify. Qualitatively, the harm done to vulnerable elderly persons is incalculable. Let's look at some recorded examples.

- In a report to the Chairman of the U.S. Senate's Special Committee on Aging produced by the U.S. Government Accountability Office (GAO), several episodes of exploitation of the elderly by their guardians were documented. Here are some.

❖ A former case manager in a Nevada public guardian's office became a professional guardian. She was accused of ripping off her wards to the tune of $200,000 to partly subsidize her gambling habit.

❖ A New York lawyer, who served as a court-appointed guardian, stole over $4 million from 23 wards, many of whom were impaired elders.

❖ Two Michigan public guardians were accused of embezzling $300,000 from at least 50 wards. One of the embezzlers used the wards' money to buy supplies for her farm.

• A San Jose father-and-son team was "charged with five felony counts including four counts of grand theft and one count of conspiracy to cheat and defraud," according to Mortgage Fraud Reporter. The father, who was the personal representative and executor of the estate to an elderly widow (the victim), was accused of "illegally misappropriating over $260,000 and using the money for personal uses."

• An Irvine, California, attorney overcharged his elderly client's estate for serving as her attorney, trustee, packer, groundskeeper, and supervisor, according to a *Los Angeles Times* article. For example, the attorney charged $288,000 in legal fees in 1990—in one instance, billing the client's estate for working 21.9 hours in a single day. Also, he charged the client outlandish fees for "reviewing properties," billing the client's estate for 216 hours in 1990. When an independent court-appointed attorney reported the billing irregularities to the state attorney general, the attorney accused of overbilling admitted to "inadvertent" irregularities in his billing process but denied any wrongdoing.

• A well-connected Laguna Hills, California, attorney made himself the beneficiary of several elderly clients' estates. As a result, he inherited millions in cash, stock, and real estate from these estates. The attorney even accepted a $3.5 million bequest from one estate in spite of a California Supreme Court ruling that states an attorney may accept only a "modest" gift from a client. To answer for his unethical conduct, the attorney was brought before State Bar prosecutors and asked to surrender his license to practice law. Several clients' heirs have sued the attorney for malfeasance.

- Several stories about guardianship abuse appear on the National Association to Stop Guardian Abuse (NASGA) website. Here are a few.

  ❖ Two former guardians failed to meet their fiduciary duty to their ward, a New York judge. The guardians failed to pay the judge's bills. They also neglected to file the judge's tax returns, resulting in the judge's estate receiving a $1 million tax bill for a failure to file. When the judge's home burned to the ground, the judge's estate had to absorb the loss because the guardians failed to pay the judge's homeowner's insurance.

  ❖ A daughter filed for an emergency conservatorship for her father when a distant cousin took control over her father's life, isolated him from his family, and revoked his existing power of attorney. Instead of solving the problem through the conservatorship, a new problem was created when the court-appointed guardian isolated the father, denied him access to a phone, and moved him without telling his family. Along the way, the guardian nearly depleted the father's life savings. When her father passed away, the daughter said, "there was no life insurance, no stock portfolios, or any other assets." Her mother (the elderly widow) was left "nearly destitute."

  ❖ A 50-something musician and composer's estranged brother and the estranged brother's attorney used fraudulent means to "work" the conservatorship system in order to place the musician/composer in a conservatorship. The judge made the estranged brother the conservator to the musician/composer (the conservatee). The judge allegedly "aided and abetted" the conservator by permitting him to exhaust the conservatee's $2.5 million estate. The conservatee was then plunged into debt.

- The *Los Angeles Times* reviewed 2,400 California conservatorship cases between 1997 and 2003. In their investigative reports on the "broken conservatorship system," conservatorship abuses were documented. Here are just a few.

  ❖ A conservator charged an elderly woman "$170 in fees to have an employee bring her $49.93 worth of groceries."

  ❖ In only 15 months, a conservator managed to spend $265,000 of an elderly conservatee's estate <u>with</u> court approval.

  ❖ An elderly man with Parkinson's was put in a conservatorship. Within five years, the conservator charged the conservatee $1.1 million in fees. The elderly man's relatives tried to get rid of the conservator by hiring a lawyer and going to court. But the conservator hired six attorneys—paid through the elderly man's estate—to successfully fend them off. The elderly man's son said, "You can't fight them if they're using his money to fight you."

  ❖ A public guardian billed his blind elderly ward "$18 to write a check for $5.79."

  ❖ A public guardian's male ward died. Prior to the ward's death, the agency sold the ward's home, paid itself, and compensated the attorney working on the ward's case. The public guardian never notified relatives that the ward had died. The ward was cremated in the county crematory, with his unclaimed ashes dumped in a common grave for indigents. The only thing etched on his gravestone was the year of his cremation.

Also reported in the *Los Angeles Times* was the yardstick by which conservators tended to hand-pick their cases. Most professional conservators look for clients with money. Some professional conservators set a floor of $300,000 before they'll even consider a case. Oftentimes these conservators bring with them a cadre of property managers, attorneys, accountants, case managers, and so on. In fact, probate attorneys say that conservatorships chew up estates, and many of these attorneys discourage their clients from going down this road.

After hearing these chilling stories about conservators and guardians behaving badly, you'd probably not be surprised to learn that conservators say that they would never want to be conserved. "It's the biggest imposition on your civil liberties short of being imprisoned," says a conservator in a *Los Angeles Times* interview.

Fortunately, the government is doing more to stamp out guardianship abuse, in part, due to greater press exposure. As an example, the Associated Press (AP) launched a lengthy probe into adult guardianships in 51 jurisdictions. In its six-part national series, "Guardians of the Elderly: An Ailing System," it concluded that the guardianship process is "a crucial last line of protection for the ailing elderly, [that] is failing many of those it is designed to protect." In response to the AP's investigation, the U.S. House Select Committee on Aging convened a hearing, which in turn spurred an interdisciplinary National Guardianship Symposium sponsored by the American Bar Association (ABA) and which later led to a rash of guardianship reforms.

In spite of an overhaul of guardianship practices through legislative changes, there's still room for improvement. The critical problem of poor judicial oversight is still a stain on the system, which the federal government is finally addressing. In 2012 the Senate Judiciary Committee approved the Guardian Accountability and Senior Protection Act. If Congress approves this bill, states will be able "to provide the better oversight over guardianships and conservatorships of vulnerable and elderly adults."

As a final note, the postlude to the book *Public Guardianship After 25 Years: In the Best Interest of Incapacitated People?* highlights the stark reality of the concept of guardianship. It states:

> "Recognize guardianship for what it really is: the most intrusive, non-interest serving, impersonal legal device known and available to us and as such, one which minimizes personal autonomy and respect for the individual, has a high potential for doing harm and raises at best a questionable benefit/burden ratio. As such, it is a devise to be studiously avoided."

The Lyon Case: Given A Blank Check

Selma worked hard all her life. She carved out a career as a respected academician. She lived simply. She saved. She invested in real estate. She was frugal.

Selma was extremely family-oriented. She deeply loved and fervently supported her son. According to Selma's brother, she sent money overseas to assist family members and relatives, and also met requests for assistance by other immediate family members.

Zachary was financially dependent on Selma and on Selma's sister Minerva. After Selma's first stroke, he helped Selma with her finances. Livingston said, "As Selma began to lose her ability to pay her bills and manage her money, Zachary did these chores for her." Yet Zachary did not have a background in a field that would prepare him to properly advise Selma and invest her money. Other family members had strong professional backgrounds in finance and accounting and were able to offer Selma financial advice. But Selma put her full trust in Zachary.

According to a family source, Zachary first met Sybil when she took over the position of Minerva's regular home health aide—the stage was set for Sybil to enter the lives of the Lyon family.

Zachary was smitten with Sybil, according to one family observer. He wanted to impress her. One way to do that was by meeting Sybil's requests for money. So Zachary gave her money, Selma's money.

Zachary and Sybil wed a few weeks after Minerva died. After the nuptials, Sybil did not live with Zachary.

After his marriage to Sybil, Zachary continued to live with Selma, who was helpless and dependent due to the onset of dementia. One of Selma's sisters realized that Zachary was neglecting Selma and abandoning her for long periods of time. When other family members became aware of Selma's bad situation, they intervened. Doing so triggered Sybil and her family to move into Selma's home.

When evidence emerged that Zachary and his new family were isolating and allegedly exploiting Selma, her family intervened. They explored legal options by consulting attorneys who specialized in elder law. On the whole, the attorneys suggested that the family should pursue a conservatorship for Selma, which they did and were successful in obtaining. At first, a temporary conservatorship was approved by the probate court that heard Selma's case, with a permanent conservatorship to follow.

Prior to the conservatorship, a settlement agreement that contained a series of stipulations laid the foundation for the pending conservatorship. In pursuing a legal remedy to Selma's situation, the up-front outlays (both in dollar and material terms) to Selma's estate ran around $150,000. Of that figure, legal fees alone were about $55,000 for only a few months of legal activities.

The court-appointed trustee Mr. Powell prepared the first trust account that showed Selma's beginning inventory was a few million dollars, with a substantial amount of cash on hand. Selma's annual income was over six figures.

Early in the conservatorship, Selma's estate was low on cash. So Selma's real property was sold. Following that, her investment property was mortgaged.

Selma had no liabilities and low household expenses. In spite of this, the conservatorship caused Selma's annual total costs to hover around $250,000 annually and even higher in some years. That meant that a lot of money was going to expenses that had nothing directly to do with Selma's care, such as attorneys and fiduciary fees.

Selma's biggest ongoing expense was for caregiving. Selma required 24/7 care and supervision, as she was completely dependent on others to provide for her physical and basic needs. Mason and Harper discussed Selma's medical situation as well as her home care costs with Livingston. Mason and Harper were surprised to learn that the caregiving costs ran around $150,000 per year, plus additional disbursements were being regularly made to one of Selma's caregivers for chores like grocery shopping and personal care—which later became a bone of contention. Harper suggested that a live-in caregiver be hired instead of using shift caregivers, a common arrangement for situations like Selma's. Doing so would be more cost effective to Selma in the long run.

Livingston also sought a second opinion on Selma's care needs and costs by consulting a care management expert. The expert said that Selma's current caregiving costs were excessive due to the use of "shift billing." The expert recommended hiring a live-in caregiver and also provided efficient care management strategies.

Based on expert advice, then, Livingston approached Mr. Gaines to see whether something could be done to lower caregiving costs while maintaining the highest possible quality care for Selma. Livingston said, "Mr. Gaines would not budge from the current care plan."

A few years into the conservatorship, Livingston and Attorney Forte came up with a conservatorship arrangement whereby one fiduciary and one attorney would handle Selma's case. Livingston said, "If we could get rid of the chain of fiduciaries, we could reduce overhead expenses—which would be a huge cost savings to Selma."

Forte suggested using a well-regarded fiduciary and trustee, a doctor with a background in geriatrics. Livingston and other family members spoke to the doctor, liked her, and felt she would do an excellent job for Selma.

Forte drafted an amendment, which contained the conservatorship changes, to the original settlement agreement. Getting buy-in from the various parties would be a necessary first step. The parties included Selma's court-appointed attorney, Selma's trustee, Selma's conservator of the person, Zachary, Sybil, and other interested parties.

Livingston and Forte recognized that going forward with the proposed changes would be difficult if Zachary wasn't willing to cooperate. Livingston also had another concern: all changes required a petition. A petition ignited not only legal fees but also fiduciary fees. One petition, then, could set off thousands of dollars in legal fees.

The amendment was moving through the channels and parties, and then it hit a snag. Livingston said, "Sybil wouldn't go for it. She harangued Gaines and Powell about the amendment and the issue of money." Both Messrs. Gaines and Powell didn't have an objection to the change. In the end, the proposed amendment was squashed due to growing opposition from various parties.

Years passed while Selma's estate shrank. Some family members were concerned that Selma's estate assets would be drained to the point that she would be forced to move from her home and be returned to the dementia care unit where she had been placed earlier and where she had done poorly. By now, Selma was deaf, blind, crippled, vegetative, terminally ill, and tube fed. Yet some expert advisors believed that before Selma's situation got to that point, Selma's doctors and her conservator of the person would "pull the plug [i.e., remove the feeding tube]" because the financial incentive would be removed.

After several years as Selma's conservator of the estate, Livingston stepped down from his day-to-day duties but remained as Selma's overseer (co-conservator of the estate) to ensure that Selma's best interests were being served within the constraints of the conservatorship. Mr. Powell then took over bill paying for Selma. Livingston had done his best to conserve Selma's funds for her care. However, he couldn't control decisions made by other fiduciaries who dictated how Selma's money was being spent and for what.

When the conservatorship ended with the death of Selma, Mr. Gaines and his attorney filed their final report and accounting, while also petitioning the court for Mr. Gaines's fees and those of his attorney for the reporting period. Livingston and his attorney felt that many entries in Mr. Gaines's accounting were too vague; it was hard to tell what Selma was being billed for. Instead of going to court to resolve the disputed fees, Mr. Gaines agreed to a slight few reduction.

The conservatorship lasted less than a decade. During that time, Selma's conservatorship eroded Selma's estate. To wit, one of the attorneys involved in Selma's case commented, "Selma's estate has been subjected to enormous costs and fees, far beyond shocking."

The final account prepared by Mr. Powell was for a one-year period, of which Selma was alive only two months. Disbursements were over a million dollars to cover expenses and repay obligations.

In Mr. Powell's prayer for relief, he included an open-ended request to the court for additional fees for him and his attorney in the future.

Mr. Powell had no sooner petitioned the court to terminate the trust than an attorney who had worked on Selma's case requested new fees, which were disputed by the attorney's own client. The fee dispute proceeded to a court hearing.

At the time of this writing, the matter of Selma's estate is not closed.

In the next chapter, we'll explain why it's important to do advance planning. Also, we'll present alternatives to a conservatorship, including powers of attorney, bill payer programs, banking arrangements, trusts, living wills, estate planning, and other options.

PART IV
Change Agents

CHAPTER 8

The Advocates

Abraham Lincoln said, "You cannot escape the responsibility of tomorrow by evading it today." Indeed, procrastination can be a stubborn habit when you don't want to face inevitable realities like preparing for your death and what happens afterwards. Being proactive by taking steps to get your affairs in order can preempt family conflict and confusion over what you want to happen in the event of death, a health care crisis, or mental incompetency.

If you've postponed doing any advance planning, such as organizing your records, making health care decisions in advance, or doing estate planning, you're not alone. In fact, about 70 percent of all American adults have done no estate planning, such as drafting a will, setting up a trust, or establishing powers of attorney, according to the author of *The Procrastinator's Guide to Wills and Estate Planning*.

Why do people fail to do advance planning to ensure that their wishes are carried out? P. Mark Accettura, the author of *Blood and Money: Why Families Fight Over Inheritance and What to Do about It*, has some answers for us. First, many people are gripped by a fear of death. One way to deal with that fear is simply not to think about it and thus avoid planning for it. Also, many people put off planning because they don't want to spend money on a professional, or they feel that their estate is too small to justify professional assistance. Moreover, many people don't want to discuss their personal and financial affairs with others. Finally, some people feel that by planning for death, they'll hasten its arrival.

In this chapter, we'll explain why it's important to do advance planning. Also, we'll highlight alternatives to a conservatorship or a guardianship. As before, the terms *conservatorship* and *guardianship* may be used interchangeably, although these terms can vary according to elder law and state law.

Why Should You Plan Ahead?

First, accidents happen and illnesses befall us with little or no forewarning. To prepare for an unexpected occurrence that may prevent you from handling your personal or financial affairs, you should furnish formal instructions for loved ones or whomever you've selected to make surrogate decisions. By not doing that, you could leave family members, relatives, or friends in a quandary, which could lead to arguments or uncertainty over how best to handle a particular situation.

Second, in instances where you can anticipate that a dispute may be unavoidable due to dysfunctional family dynamics, it's doubly important that you plan ahead. For instance, death can bring out the absolute worst behavior in some people, often unexpectedly. Siblings who seem to get along when you're alive can become quarrelsome when you're gone. Distant family members may come out of the woodwork to stake a claim on your estate. Such situations can lead to ugly family disagreements that may result in legal actions and, in turn, costly litigation.

Third, advance planning can guard you against being conserved, and even if you were conserved, you'd have named the individual(s) in advance whom you'd like to serve as your conservator(s). By building a "safety net" of legal tools, then, you cannot only protect yourself but also dodge the conservatorship card.

Finally, just because you do advance planning and have your affairs in order, that in and of itself does not guarantee that your instructions will be followed, nor that an unusual situation will be covered. In Selma Lyon's case, for example, she had done estate planning, but nothing in her estate plan adequately addressed the unusual situation that ultimately endangered her physical safety and financial security. In building your estate planning arsenal, then, choose your agents wisely and address every conceivable "what-if" scenario.

Let's relook at a conservatorship as a protective measure before discussing alternatives to one.

To Conserve or Not to Conserve?

Let's say your elderly mother is making really poor financial decisions. You feel that your mother needs help or else she'll deplete resources needed for her lifelong care. Someone tells you about a conservatorship, which sounds like a good way to prevent your mother's own undoing. However, it's important to remember that *"Eccentric or unusual choices are not grounds for conservatorship,"* according to one authority. After all, every adult has the right to make bad decisions. However, if your mother is making harmful decisions and she doesn't understand the ramifications of these decisions, then a conservatorship might be the only way to protect her.

In determining whether a person is competent to make reasonable decisions, you should consider:

- The difficulty of the decision
- Whether the decision is consistent with the manner in which the person lives or manages his or her life
- Whether the person understands the risks or consequences of acting or not acting

To illustrate, if your mother is mentally competent to make decisions and she comprehends the risks involved in her choices, then it would be inappropriate to employ a conservatorship because it would infringe on her personal autonomy and right to self-determination. Equally, if your mother can't make rational decisions and a conservatorship is employed, the danger is that it might give someone a window to substitute his or her judgment in handling your mother's affairs. At best, then, conservatorships can be a Catch-22.

As a cautionary note, according to one legal expert, conservatorships should be avoided, as court-appointed fiduciaries can be a "nightmare"—their sole interest is in creating fees. In all instances, it's recommended that you contact an attorney specializing in elder law or estate planning to discuss options to a conservatorship if you're considering one. This is especially important because alternatives to a conservatorship vary from state to state. You can contact the National Academy of Elder Law Attorneys (NAELA), an organization that specializes in legal matters affecting the elderly, for advice on finding and selecting an appropriate attorney if you don't have or know one.

Alternatives to a Conservatorship/Guardianship: Financial Management

You may have heard of a *power of attorney*, also known as a *POA*, as a legal tool that delegates decision-making authority to another person. Let's describe what powers of attorney are and introduce other common planning tools.

Powers of Attorney (POA): In a power of attorney, one person, *the principal*, authorizes another person, *an agent* or *an attorney-in-fact*, to act or function on the principal's behalf. By appointing an agent, you can pick a trusted person to manage your affairs, which will reduce anxiety over what will happen to you if you become disabled or incapacitated. A power of attorney is legally binding and can be implemented without the involvement of the court. More to the point, you can avoid a conservatorship by executing a power of attorney while you're competent.

You can give power of attorney only if you possess legal capacity. A power of attorney takes effect if you ever lose capacity. You can revoke or change a power of attorney as long as you have capacity. When you pass away, a power of attorney ends.

Not just one type of power of attorney exists. The general types of power of attorney are as follows:

- *General Power of Attorney*—gives permission to your agent to make all personal and financial decisions for you.
- *Limited Power of Attorney*—authorizes your agent to handle only those matters specified.
- *Durable Power of Attorney (DPA)*—grants your agent the legal authority to handle some aspects of your personal and/or financial matters. Unlike a general or limited power of attorney, a durable power of attorney remains effective even in the event of disability or incapacity, and it takes effect upon a certain occurrence or an event, such as a physician's diagnosis of incapacity. One type of durable power of attorney is a *springing power of attorney*, also referred to as a *conditional power of attorney*, which goes into effect after certain conditions are met, such as when the principal becomes disabled or incompetent.

How does a power of attorney for finances work? Let's say that you want to make your brother your agent. You must determine what powers you want to give your brother. You can give him limited powers with the legal authority to handle only some financial matters, such as bill paying or overseeing brokerage accounts. Or you can give your brother general powers with the legal authority to handle all your financial affairs. Also, you can determine the timing of the powers. For example, you might wish your brother to take over immediately or at a later date when you need help with finances or you become incapacitated.

You should consider the actions you'd like your brother to take on your behalf. Transaction categories that can be included in your agent's general authority are:

- Banks and other financial institutions
- Real and personal property
- Securities (stocks, bonds, commodities, etc.)
- Insurance and annuities
- Pension plans
- Taxes
- Claims and litigation
- Government benefits
- Estates and trusts

You can grant additional powers to your brother, such as creating, amending, revoking, or terminating a revocable trust; creating or changing beneficiary designations; and so on. Think carefully before granting such powers because your estate plan might be significantly altered.

Daily Money Management: If you simply need help taking care of your daily financial needs, a *bill payer program* may just be the ticket. A bill payer can help manage your income and expenses, write checks for your signature, and assist in organizing your bills and related paperwork. Bill payer programs and services include:

- *Representative Payee* or *Substitute Payee*—If you're receiving Social Security benefits or other state or federal benefits, you can ask the appropriate agency to appoint a representative payee to help you manage your benefit checks. For example, you can contact the Social Security Administration (SSA), and ask that a representative payee be appointed to manage your Social Security benefits if you're unable to manage them yourself. In addition to the SSA, other agencies that allow the use of a representative payee include the Department of

Veterans Affairs, the Department of Defense, the Railroad Retirement Board, and the Office of Personnel Management. Other persons or institutions can also receive benefit checks on your behalf, including a family member, friend, social service agency, care facility, or nursing home. Checks are made payable to the payee. The money must be used for your benefit, and the payee must account for how your money is being used. The payee is held liable for any irregularities. Assigning a representative payee is a relatively simple process that doesn't require court involvement. This alternative to a conservatorship/guardianship might be adequate if the only income you receive is from a public agency.

- *Direct Deposits and Automatic Deductions*—If you're concerned that your benefit or payroll checks might get stolen or misplaced, you can arrange for your checks to be directly deposited into your bank accounts. You can also arrange for your monthly bills, such as utilities or mortgage, to be paid through one of your bank accounts.

- *Bill Paying Services*—A convenient way to handle your transactions is to use an online bill-paying service or program, which is faster and more secure than paying bills through the mail. There is a whole slew of bill-paying services from which to choose. For example, Quicken, a leader in accounting software, offers Quicken Bill Pay that allows you to pay your bills and manage several accounts simultaneously online.

Banking Arrangements and Joint Property Arrangements: A few easy banking options can be used in lieu of a conservatorship/guardianship. Arrangements include:

- *Banking Arrangements*—To maintain control over your finances, you can ask your bank to arrange bank account features to help manage your money, such as direct deposit, automatic bill pay, or banking by mail, phone, or online.

- *Joint Bank Accounts*—You can easily and inexpensively set up joint bank accounts with a trusted family member or a friend by adding his or her name to the accounts, which requires no court supervision. By doing so, the family member or friend can write checks, make withdrawals, and make deposits for you. Both you and the family member or friend would have ownership of the accounts. *Proceed with extreme caution here: joint accounts can be risky and inflexible because of the control you're handing over to the co-owner.* For example, Selma's son had set up several joint bank accounts with Selma, which opened the door to the alleged fiduciary abuse that followed.
- *Joint Property Ownership*—To ensure that your home or other real property is being properly managed, you can place property in a joint ownership under your name and that of a family member or a trusted person. Here again, you should give careful consideration to this option. For example, let's say you and your daughter concurrently hold title to your home. Depending on the type of joint ownership, if your daughter never contributed to the purchase of the home, there might be tax consequences. Also, if your daughter is married and then gets divorced, her spouse might be able to claim a portion of the property in a community property settlement. Moreover, if your daughter becomes hamstrung by financial difficulties and isn't able to pay her bills, a creditor might be able to go after joint property to pay off her debts. Finally, if you were deemed incapable by the court at some point, the joint property can't be sold without court approval.

Trusts: You've probably heard of a trust. The legal definition of a *trust* is "a relationship created at the direction of an individual, in which one or more persons hold the individual's property subject to certain duties to use and protect it for the benefit of others." If you're the person setting up the trust, you're called a *trustmaker, settlor, trustor,* or *grantor.* The written agreement is called the *trust instrument* or the *trust agreement.* Finally, *property* includes real or personal property, such as real estate, money, stocks and bonds, personal possessions, and other tangible assets.

A trust can be an excellent planning tool because it's established and controlled when you're mentally competent. If you become incapacitated or impaired, the trust continues in operation under your *successor trustee*, the person or institution who would become trustee when the original trustee has died or become incapacitated.

Usually, one person sets up a trust for the benefit of another. In this type of trust, at least three parties are involved: the *trustor*—the individual establishing the trust; the *trustee*—the person or financial institution that holds and manages the assets for the benefit of the trustor and others; and the *beneficiary*—the person who reaps the benefits of the trust. In most instances, the creator of the trust is all three—the trustor, trustee, and beneficiary—until his or her death. As the trustee, you hold legal title to the property transferred into the trust (i.e., vesting property in a trust), and you have the legal duty to use the property as stipulated in the trust agreement; in other words, the trust is the owner of the property. Finally, you must be mentally competent to establish a trust because capacity is a condition for creating one.

If you set up a *revocable* or *living trust*, you can change or terminate your trust anytime, which you can't do with an irrevocable trust. With a living trust, you assign a trustee to manage your property to better ensure that your assets will be protected if you become incapacitated or impaired. Your trustee has a legal or fiduciary duty to use your trust assets as specified in your trust.

In setting up your trust, you can name more than one trustee at a time. Each cotrustee must choose the best way to discharge his or her fiduciary duty. Say that you and your sister have been named as cotrustees of your mother's trust. If your sister breaches her fiduciary duty, you can be held responsible for her actions. So if you're a cotrustee, it's important that you keep a watchful eye on the administration of the trust; and if a disagreement occurs, that you document it. After all, you don't want to be responsible for your sister's faulty judgment or breach of duty.

If you've been named as a successor trustee of your mother's trust, give careful consideration before accepting the position. By consenting to the job of trustee, you agree to several responsibilities as well as hold similar liabilities as those of a cotrustee.

Once you've drawn up the trust agreement, you must transfer property to the trustee, the legal owner of the property. Amazingly, many people establish a trust but fail to fund a trust (vest the assets to a trust), which in turn can become their successor trustee's problem: if the initial trustee can no longer function, is unwilling to resign, or dies, the successor trustee would have no control over assets sitting outside of the trust. Every trust, then, should include a *companion will* or *pour over will*, which guarantees that any assets sitting outside the trust become assets to the trust upon the trustee's death.

A different problem arises when an incapacitated person continues to act as trustee and refuses to or won't resign, which happened in the Lyon case. Selma Lyon remained trustee even after it was clear to family members (and later to the court) that she could no longer function due to the onset of dementia. Selma would not voluntarily step down as trustee, and she refused to be evaluated by a doctor to determine her capacity. Consequently, Selma's intractability made it difficult for family members to help her and left her vulnerable to undue influence.

Finally, in 90 percent of living trusts, trust administration after death is usually simple and fairly inexpensive, and it requires no courts and massive fees. For example, let's say that your dad has passed away, and he has made you the trustee of his trust, which means you'll need to administer your father's trust. For uncomplicated estates, post-death trust administration typically includes the following general tasks:

- Obtain all your father's trust documents and records to administer your father's trust and certify its validity.
- Consult with an estate planning attorney who can guide you through the administration process.
- Collect any monies owed the trust.
- Pay off creditors and trust expenses.
- Manage trust assets and investments.

- Acquire appraisals and valuations of the trust assets.
- Dispose of trust assets.
- Maintain accurate records of trust income and disbursements.
- File tax returns.
- Furnish the trust accounting to beneficiaries.
- Distribute trust assets and property to beneficiaries.
- Close the trust at the end of the administration.

The whole administration process may take about three to four months and cost as little as $1,000. For more complicated estates, it may take longer to complete the process and may cost somewhere between $5,000 to $10,000. Any way you stack it up, a solidly written trust can save you time and money and avoid the future need for a conservatorship.

Limited Conservatorship/Guardianship—Property: A *limited conservatorship/guardianship* is a legal arrangement that grants specific powers to a conservator/guardian, while allowing the incapacitated person to make some types of decisions. By law, the court must only grant powers to a conservator/guardian that are required to fulfill the conservatee's/ward's needs. A chief advantage of a limited conservatorship/guardianship is that the conservatee/ward retains certain rights and autonomy over his or her life.

Standby Conservatorship/Guardianship—Property: To prepare for an unforeseeable event that may impede your capabilities, you can establish a *standby conservatorship/guardianship*. The standby conservatorship/guardianship would take effect if a particular event occurs or a particular condition exists (e.g., mental or physical decline) as set forth in a verified petition. As the petitioner, you can revoke the petition as long as you're of sound mind. Also, you can maintain control over your affairs until the specified event or described condition occurs.

Fiduciary Services and Concierge Client Services: Remember that a fiduciary is a person or legal entity appointed and authorized to hold and manage assets for the benefit of another. You can retain a professional fiduciary to perform a variety of tasks, such as trust management and administration; management of a *special needs trust* (a trust designed to benefit a person with a disability); an executor or administrator of a decedent's estate; and so forth.

In addition to fiduciary services, *concierge client services* can support personal care and/or financial management. Former conservatees or wards who transition to self-management; trust beneficiaries; and other individuals who need assistance with their basic needs might benefit from this type of service. Know that these services don't come cheap, as billing rates can be as high as $145 per hour.

Alternatives to a Conservatorship/Guardianship: Personal Care

In addition to establishing financial safeguards, your safety net of planning tools should include provisions for your future personal care. In this section, we'll discuss the most common life planning tools as alternatives to a conservatorship/guardianship.

Advance Directives: *Advance directives* are written instructions to be followed in the event that you're unable to communicate them to health care providers and loved ones. Like other legal documents, advance directives must be prepared while you're mentally competent. Let's glance at common types of advance directives.

- *Durable Power of Attorney for Health Care*—Just as you can set up a durable power of attorney for financial management, you can establish a *durable power of attorney for health care (DPAHC)*, also referred to as a *health care proxy*. A DPAHC is a legal document that allows you to appoint a health care agent to make medical decisions for you. A DPAHC takes effect when your doctor determines that you're unable to make medical decisions for yourself, regardless if the situation is temporary or permanent.

In a DPAHC, your agent must make health care decisions according to your instructions. Be explicit in your instructions! If you're unclear, your agent will decide what's in your best interests, which might not reflect your true preferences. For example, Selma had a vague durable power of attorney for health care. She was not specific about end-of-life care and preferences. As a result, Selma's conservator of the person and his doctors made all of Selma's end-of-life decisions, which did not harmonize with Selma's values, preferences, cultural beliefs, and attitudes toward death and dying.

Think carefully about whom you pick to serve as your agent for health care. After all, your agent will have the legal authority to make life-and-death decisions for you. You want someone who will honor your wishes in making these decisions. Finally, discuss advance care planning, specifically end-of-life care, with your agent ahead of time.

- *Advance Medical Directive*—You may have been asked on a patient intake form whether you have an *advance medical directive (AMD),* which authorizes a trusted person to be your health care representative or agent. An AMD gives your agent the power to make medical decisions on your behalf in case you're unable to make them yourself. For the most part, an AMD has replaced the durable power of attorney for health care. Persons who may not be appointed as your agent on an AMD include doctors and staff members of a health facility or operators of a community care facility, unless that person is a blood relative or a relative by marriage or through adoption. An AMD does not expire unless it contains a time limit, and it can be revoked. Neither courts nor government agencies supervise an AMD. You can easily obtain the forms from most hospitals or online. An AMD allows your agent to do the following:

  - Hire and fire doctors and other health care providers and professionals

- Consent to or withhold or withdraw a specific procedure and treatment, such as artificial nutrition and hydration
- Access and release medical records
- Drop off and pick up prescriptions
- Request an autopsy and determine the disposition of bodily remains, such as making an anatomical gift

Living Will: A *living will* is a written document that provides specific instructions to health care providers and to your family on certain medical treatments that you wish to receive or refuse and under what conditions, including withholding or withdrawing life-sustaining procedures that can extend the dying process. A living will takes effect only if specific medical criteria are met, such as the written opinion of the treating doctor confirmed by another doctor.

Physician Orders for Life-Sustaining Treatment (POLST): To improve end-of-life care, many states allow the use of *Physician Orders for Life-Sustaining Treatment (POLST)*, also called *medical orders for life-sustaining treatment (MOLST); medical orders on scope of treatment (MOST); physician's orders on scope of treatment (POST); or transportable physician orders for patient preferences (TPOPP)*. Here, your doctor will discuss your end-of-life care preferences in the event of a medical crisis. POLST is a standardized form that documents the discussion with your doctor and creates medical orders based on your end-of-life wishes. POLST can be revoked or changed at any time.

Limited Conservatorship/Guardianship—Person: A *limited conservatorship/guardianship* gives your conservator/guardian only those special powers granted under a court order. A limited conservator/guardian of the person would make specific health care decisions for you based on your particular medical care needs, some of which might require court approval such as the administration of psychotropic drugs. Under a limited conservatorship/guardianship, you might still retain control over some medical decisions if a judge allows.

Standby Conservatorship/Guardianship—Person: You can establish a *standby conservatorship/guardianship* by preselecting a person to serve as your conservator/guardian if a conservatorship/guardianship becomes necessary at some future time. The standby conservatorship/ guardianship will go into effect only upon the occurrence of an event or the presence of a certain mental or physical condition, which is spelled out in the petition. With a standby petition, you retain control over your health care decisions until such time that the specified event happens. You must be of sound mind to establish a standby conservatorship/guardianship, which can be revoked.

Other Alternatives to Personal Care: In addition to the legal tools already mentioned, other services and resources are available to help with your care needs. The existence and availability of each alternative depends on where you live. Let's take a peek at your options.

- *Community-Based Services*—Your community may offer a wide variety of community-based services that will allow you to continue to live independently at home, including caregivers, companions, or home health aides; homemakers; home delivered meals; mental health services; transportation; and others. For example, case management services can assist a frail or vulnerable elder and his or her family make long-term care choices and thus avoid institutionalization for the elder. These services provide an assessment of the elder's environment as well as his or her social, financial, and medical needs. In addition, adult services and aging specialists can develop a care plan and coordinate needed services, such as setting up home care assistance.
- *Legal Case Management*—Here, a legal case manager does an in-home assessment with an elder and his or her family before coordinating services and making appropriate referrals to an attorney or other service providers. Services include an initial consultation that supplies resources and referrals for powers of attorney and guardianships and conservatorships;

assistance with issues concerning Medicaid programs; handling concerns over dependent elder abuse; and so on.

- *Adult Day Care Services*—These programs provide supportive day care in a group setting to people who need supervision and assistance. Services include some or all of the following: personal care; transportation; social and recreational activities; and preventative or restorative services.

- *Respite Care*—This service provides family caregivers with temporary relief from caring for an elderly, dependent adult. The respite may be for a short duration, such as for 2 to 3 hours, or for periods longer than 24 hours. Respite care may take place within the home or someplace else.

- *Other Supportive Services*—In the next chapter, we'll discuss a wide variety of resources and services that can be tapped for elder care. Among the government programs and services that are available are *Area Agencies on Aging (AAAs)*. Each state has designated AAAs that administer programs for people 60 and older aimed at helping them to remain healthy, independent, and financially secure. In addition, *community mental health centers* furnish mental health services to people, including the elderly, who are not coping well with life issues or who suffer from serious mental illnesses. Services include counseling and medication management.

Estate Planning

You've probably heard of an estate plan. Think of it as a briefcase filled with essential planning tools, including a will, powers of attorney, a living trust, and an advance medical directive. Very importantly, a properly drafted estate plan can help avoid a conservatorship. If you decide to put together an estate plan, you should consult an estate planning or elder law attorney. He or she will not only guide you through the estate planning process but will also know and understand both federal and state laws governing estates.

What exactly is your *estate*? Very simply, your estate contains everything you own, from car to home, bank accounts to investments, and furniture to personal possessions. Even if your estate is modest, you should decide to whom your assets and personal possessions will go, what each beneficiary will receive, and when each beneficiary will acquire it.

According to EstatePlanning.com, estate planning does more than simply specify who gets what and when. Good estate planning also does the following:

- Provides instructions for "passing your values (religion, education, hard work, etc.) in addition to your valuables"
- Furnishes direction for your care if you become incapacitated or impaired
- Appoints fiduciaries and also someone to manage the inheritance that your minor children will get someday
- Provides for family members who have special needs, are spendthrifts, or require future protection of some sort (e.g., protecting assets from creditors)
- Includes life insurance, disability income insurance, and/or long-term care insurance
- Supplies instructions for the transfer of business interests at the time of your retirement, if you become disabled, or you die
- Reduces taxes, minimizes possible court costs, and avoids unnecessary legal fees

Know that estate planning is an ongoing process. Because your priorities and circumstances are apt to change over your lifetime, you should review and update your plan accordingly.

What happens if you don't have an estate plan? Should you become incapacitated and your name is on the title of your assets, the court will determine how your assets would be used for your care through a conservatorship/guardianship—you know all about the pitfalls of that happening after reading this book. In addition, if you die without an estate plan, probate laws in your state will determine how your assets would be distributed. The length of the probate process depends on the size of your estate; it can take several months or several years. Due to legal fees, executor fees, and court costs, the probate process can become quite expensive.

In addition to avoiding court hassles, estate planning forces you to pull together your financial records, take an inventory of your assets, and assign beneficiary designations. Since many people put off doing these tasks, estate planning places you in a frame of mind to take care of them.

As mentioned earlier, some people postpone doing estate planning because they're worried about the expense. But ask yourself: Can you afford not to do estate planning, given the dangers presented in this book? Probably not. Bear in mind that not all estate plans require a bunch of planning tools. As a starting point, you may only need a will and powers of attorney; you would then keep adding to your plan as your situation changes. Again, don't try this alone—consult an experienced estate planning or elder law attorney who can guide you through the planning process and properly prepare the legal documents.

P. Mark Accettura offers sound general advice on estate planning. Accettura recommends doing the following:

- *Hire a qualified attorney.* For elders doing estate planning, hire a qualified elder law attorney. This is particularly important because elder laws can be complicated and, thus, require a legal specialist in this practice area.
- *Do not dispose of old wills and trusts.* These documents demonstrate a pattern of behavior and provide a documented history. That way, if changes were gained through fraud or undue influence, they can be better identified. In Selma's case, Livingston discovered that Zachary destroyed Selma's original will that placed someone other than him in charge of Selma's estate.
- *Assign two agents for financial powers of attorney.* By appointing an agent, you're creating a fiduciary relationship between you

(the principal) and the person whom you appoint (the agent). To add another layer of protection, you might wish to appoint coagents who must work together. This official arrangement provides you with a legal cushion should one of your agents engage in misconduct. Bear in mind that while two minds are better than one, two minds can also lead to potential problems when disagreements arise between the agents.

- *Appoint one health care advocate.* While Accettura recommends the use of two agents for financial management, he suggests that you use only one health care advocate. Accettura says, "A single healthcare advocate who shares the principal's views on life and death is able to make urgent health care decisions without the potential for conflict that may arise with coadvocates." Furthermore, because health care professionals are bound by a strict ethical code, you're generally protected from any misguided decisions made by your advocate.

- *Handle your personal possessions separately.* Create a separate list of personal possessions, often called a *Personal Property Memorandum*, that states who will inherit what. Be sure to describe each item being gifted. This is particularly important because personal possessions can be a source of conflict and even tear families apart.

- *Update your estate plan.* A change to your estate plan should be made whenever a key change in your circumstances occurs, such as the death or divorce of your spouse. Most states' matrimonial laws invalidate beneficiary designations and will stipulations that favor former spouses. However, a former spouse may continue to have authority under your health care or financial powers of attorney.

- *Keep your estate plan private.* To ensure your chosen fiduciaries and agents are willing to act on your behalf if and when they're needed, it's probably a good idea to share your thoughts and preferences with them. However, it's inadvisable to share particulars of your plan with them, especially family members. That way, you can avoid bruised feelings among family members who would have benefited at the time of your death but ultimately do not because you changed your mind.

- *Specify gifts versus loans.* If you financially help an adult child or advance gifts or loans to him or her, you should state whether these transfers and other advances will be forgiven after your death. If a loan must be repaid, loan documentation should be included in your estate plan. Repayment should be made at the time of your death, which can be an offset to the borrower's inheritance.

- *Fund your trust.* As stated earlier, people often establish a trust but forget or put off funding it. To prevent confusion over your intent and to avert probate, fund all assets into your trust and retitle them in the name of the trust.

- *Make your funeral arrangements.* Furnish written funeral plans to spare your family worry and uncertainty.

- *Include a no-contest clause.* Insert a *no-contest clause*, also known as a *forfeiture clause*, in your will or trust, especially if you expect that one of your beneficiaries might not be pleased with what you left him or her. By doing this, you can discourage will challenges depending on how your state treats no-contest clauses.

Accettura also provides tips on executing an estate plan. These include:

- *Watch out for undue influence.* Elders with declining mental competency can be at greater risk for manipulation and more vulnerable to undue influence. If the divisor of the estate plan, say an elder, is accompanied to an attorney's office by someone, the attorney should speak to the elder alone so that the attorney can determine if the elder fully grasps his or her specific intentions. In Selma's situation, Zachary carted Selma to a series of attorneys in an attempt to change Selma's trust to benefit him. The attorney who altered Selma's estate plan said that he thought Selma had capacity at the time that the changes were made; thus, Selma was not being unduly influenced. Livingston said, "Selma didn't know she had an attorney—not even when the guy was in the same room with her. She had no recollection that she changed her estate plan. And she had no idea that Zachary was solely in charge of her estate and that Sybil would be involved in her care." So the whiff of undue influence was a big factor in Selma's case.

- *Review the documents before signing them.* Your attorney should review and summarize all estate planning documents with you before execution. You should understand what you're signing. In addition, to meet the capacity requirement and demonstrate the absence of undue influence, your attorney will probably ask you a series of questions, such as "Have you come here of your own free will?" and "Do you realize that you are signing your will, trust, and powers of attorney?

- *Videotape the execution ceremony.* Though controversial, videotaping the execution ceremony can show the circumstances of the signing.

- *Store your estate planning documents in a safe place.* These are sensitive documents that should be kept in a safe place and away from prying eyes.

Facilitative Mediation

As described in the Lyon case, a settlement agreement was voluntarily reached by the disputing parties. The settlement agreement called for a conservatorship. The conservatorship protected Selma, but it also created barriers to Selma's family's involvement in making or participating in decisions for Selma. Also stipulated in the settlement agreement was the revocation of the changes made to Selma's estate plan by Zachary and the attorney whom Zachary hired for Selma. At the same time, Selma's trust was reverted back to the original trust that was executed while Selma retained capacity. Selma was removed as trustee, and a new trustee was named. Later on, one of the attorneys involved in Selma's case felt that the conservatorship could have been avoided if the parties would have agreed to facilitative mediation. Let's take a moment to discuss it.

Facilitative mediation, also known a *problem-solving resolution*, is a method for efficiently and inexpensively resolving family disputes. Facilitative mediation is voluntary, nonbinding, private, and confidential. In facilitative mediation, a trained mediator (a neutral third party) assists the parties to reach a mutual agreement. According to Mediate.com:

> "The mediator asks questions; validates and normalizes parties' points of view; searches for interests underneath the positions taken by parties; and assists the parties in finding and analyzing options for resolution. The facilitative mediator does not make recommendations to the parties, give his or her own advice or opinion as to the outcome of the case, or predict what a court would do in the case. The mediator is in charge of the process, while the parties are in charge of the outcomes."

While mediation can be an effective tool in such situations as will contests, trust disputes, guardianship and conservatorship cases, and other situations, it may not be suitable in others, such as alleged abuse and capacity issues of key parties, according to Accettura. Ultimately, if the involved parties can reach an agreement, the mediator will ordinarily draft a *memorandum of understanding (MoU)*, a document that states the terms and details of the agreement. No court or legal fees are necessary.

The important thing is to enter mediation at the first sign of a problem. Over time, family members can become inflexible, bellicose, and fractionalized. In Selma's situation, family members began to take sides. Zachary, whom the family was trying to help, became paranoid, according to one family observer. He concocted the idea that the family was against him and that they were trying to usurp his position and have him disinherited. When Zachary barred family communications and isolated Selma, the situation went downhill quickly. While facilitative mediation could have been a solution to Selma's situation, which would have been far more cost-effective and far less emotionally traumatizing to Selma and other family members, the barriers to communication precluded it from happening.

Years after the family dispute, several family members are still not speaking with one another. Just maybe, mediation could have prevented the family dissolution that followed in the wake of Selma's conservatorship.

In the next chapter, we'll discuss places where people can go for assistance and support to prevent and stop elder neglect, abuse, and exploitation. Also, we'll provide most everything you need to know to prepare you, or a loved one, for the unknowns of the Golden Years.

CHAPTER 9

The Agencies

By now you realize that elder mistreatment is a complex issue influenced by the interplay of a number of factors, including sociocultural attitudes toward aging, life cycle stages, family dynamics, cultural issues, demographics, and other factors. As you've learned through the Lyon case, Selma's worst fears became a reality when she placed her trust in her son who she believed would protect her from harm and exploitation. Instead, the son was party to the injuries and manipulations employed to undo Selma. When family members tried to reason and help the son with Selma's health care and financial management, he responded by perpetuating and intensifying the harmful behavior toward Selma. Selma's grim situation only compounded when the son opened the door to a family of predators.

Had Selma's family better understood Selma's risk for mistreatment and employed intervention strategies to stamp it out before it redoubled, there might have been a very different outcome to Selma's story that better matched what Selma wanted for herself during her twilight years.

In this chapter, we'll discuss places where you can go for assistance and support to prevent and stop elder neglect, abuse, and exploitation. We'll also provide general information and resources for seniors and their families on a variety of elder issues and topics.

Detecting and Reporting Elder Mistreatment

Elder mistreatment usually occurs without witnesses, making the detection of the abuse or neglect more difficult. To demonstrate the complexity of detecting and reporting elder mistreatment, let's return to Selma's situation.

One of Selma's sisters observed that Selma wasn't being well provided for after her son became Selma's primary caretaker. The sister sounded the alarm by contacting a niece who was close to Selma. Initially, the niece tried to improve Selma's situation without involving a third party, which would have spooked the son and scared Selma.

When the niece's informal attempts to improve Selma's situation didn't work, the niece contacted her attorney. She advised the niece to report the son's neglect of Selma to Adult Protective Services (APS). However, Selma's sister advised against doing this. She claimed that APS could remove Selma from her home, put her in a shelter, and then place her in a nursing home, which Selma would never want. While Selma's sister's advice considered Selma's wishes, it was nonetheless poor, given the extent of the neglect. Instead of calling APS, then, the niece contacted a nephew to help persuade the son to retain outside help for both him *and* Selma. The son agreed to this several times but never followed through. Other relatives also tried to convince the son to arrange for home health care and appropriate medical care for Selma. Again, he agreed but later reneged.

In frustration, Selma's sister and the niece wrote Selma's doctor to tell him that Selma's son was neglecting Selma's basic needs. The niece said, "I never heard back from the doctor. So I called him. He refused to address the neglect issue. He treated me like a meddler instead of a concerned family member."

With the continuation of the son's and now his wife's pattern of neglecting, isolating, and allegedly exploiting Selma, it was the nephew who filed a complaint against Selma's son and his wife with APS. "The agency investigated the complaint but did not do an intervention," said the nephew. As a result, the neglect and exploitation continued unabated. Later on, APS was called again. Since whistleblowers remain anonymous, no one knew who contacted APS the second time. The agency investigated the new complaint and again did not perform an intervention, with no available explanation.

In Selma's situation, both Selma's doctor and APS received reports of Selma's suspected neglect and exploitation but somehow did not detect it and thus did nothing to prevent it.

One of the stumbling blocks in Selma's case and elder abuse cases like hers is that Selma denied that the abuse was taking place. According to the literature on elder mistreatment, abused elders rarely report or confirm suspected abuse or neglect. The reasons for elder's failure to report include fear of retaliation or abandonment; fear of being moved into an institutional setting; belief that the abuse was deserved; a feeling that nothing can be done to stop the abuse; or a sense of shame that a loved one committed the abuse. Oftentimes the elderly victim prefers to remain within the home in an abusive situation rather than to be moved into a nursing home.

In the book *Elder Abuse: Conflict in the Family*, the authors explain why elders, loved ones, friends, and neighbors often fail to report neglect or abuse:

> "The older adult may be unable to recognize or report neglect or abuse because of severe illness, depression, immobility, or dementia. Further, the myth of 'senility' may cause older adults to hesitate to report abuse and risk having their credibility questioned when they do try to report it. In either instance, elders' fear of retaliation may be reinforced. The privacy and intimacy norms of the family result in members' reticence to share information about abuse, and strangers hesitate to violate these norms in pursuit of evidence. Relatives, neighbors, and friends are also reluctant to report suspected abuse out of fear, anxiety about how to handle the problem, or ambivalence about becoming involved."

To illustrate this point, let's go back to Selma's circumstances. Selma was a dementia sufferer who was very attached to her son, and he was financially dependent on her. He converted the home into a guarded fortress. He blocked Selma from seeing relatives or convinced relatives to stay away. Selma's closest living relatives, her siblings, recognized that Selma needed help and that Zachary was overwhelmed. However, they did not get directly involved in remedying Selma's situation.

First Responders to Reports of Elder Mistreatment

Should you suspect that a family member or a relative is being neglected, abused, or exploited, your first call should be made to Adult Protective Services (APS). Under Elder and Dependent Adult Abuse Reporting laws, county APS agencies investigate reports of suspected elder abuse, neglect, or exploitation. State Adult Protective Services laws determine what types of abuse APS must investigate and whether APS must "cross-report" with law enforcement.

Let's say you call APS to report the suspected abuse of a relative. If the situation is an emergency, APS will pass along the information to the police or emergency medical staff. If your report doesn't meet APS's parameters, you might be given further information on appropriate community-based services. If APS investigates your report, it will be assigned a priority response time, such as 24 hours, 48 hours, and so on, based on the victim's risk. Your report will then be assigned to an APS caseworker. The caseworker will conduct an investigation to substantiate your claims. He or she will also evaluate your relative's capacity to understand the situation and to consent to services provided through APS, such as counseling, money management, out-of-home placement, and so on. If your relative consents to these services, the caseworker will create a service plan, with the participation of the client (your relative), family members, and caregivers. Finally, APS will implement the plan and monitor the case until it's closed.

If your relative retains the capacity to understand his or her circumstances, he or she can refuse services, no matter what his or her risk level is. In Selma's situation, it was clear to several family members that Selma lacked mental capacity, and several third parties believed this as well. Had the APS caseworkers who investigated the complaints agreed with these observations, Selma would not have been able to deny consent to APS services.

Community-Based Efforts to Address and Prevent Elder Mistreatment

While Adult Protective Services is the real locus of community-based efforts to respond to elder mistreatment, other community services are available to victims and their families. The nature of the abuse will determine the type of services that are appropriate in any given situation. The book *Abuse, Neglect, and Exploitation of Older Persons: Strategies for Assessment and Intervention* provides a list of community resources where you can go for help if you or a family member finds him- or herself in an abusive situation or is an overburdened caregiver.

- *Long-Term Care Ombudsman*—This federal program was established to investigate complaints reported by residents of nursing homes and residential care facilities. In states with mandatory abuse reporting laws, the long-term care ombudsman investigates allegations of abuse and neglect occurring in institutional settings and adult day health centers.
- *Law Enforcement*—In an abuse situation where a crime was committed, such as battery, domestic violence, theft, and fraud, the abusive act must be reported to the police. Some states have passed laws that enhance penalties for physical and financial crimes against the elderly.

- *Medicaid Fraud Control Units*—A Medicaid Fraud Control Unit is a state program that investigates and prosecutes health care providers that defraud the Medicaid program, as well as probes complaints of abuse or neglect of residents in an institutional setting.

- *Area Agencies on Aging*—Under the federal Older Americans Act (OAA), each state has instituted a state unit on aging known as *Area Agencies on Aging (AAAs)*. AAAs serve small geographical regions, such as cities, counties, or clusters of counties. In addition to delivering aging services and referral sources, AAAs serve as hubs for health and human services that can be deployed to decrease the risk of elder mistreatment or treat its effects.

- *Legal Services*—The OAA has created a network of free legal services for older adults, which handles abuse cases; assists in issuing restraining orders; files lawsuits to recover stolen money or property; and provides other services.

- *Victim Services*—Victim services' units are usually housed within prosecutors' offices. These units provide information about the court process to crime victims and their families, as well as notify victims and their families on the status of their cases.

- *Domestic Violence Programs*—According to the National Center on Elder Abuse (NCEA), late life domestic violence "occurs when a person uses power and control to inflict physical, sexual, emotional, or financial injury or harm upon an older adult with whom they have an ongoing relationship." Domestic violence prevention programs, including shelters, 24-hour help/crisis hotlines, support groups, and legal advocacy groups, offer assistance to elderly victims. Some communities have established special shelters, emergency housing, and "safe houses" in private homes with foster families for elderly victims.

- *Financial Management*—If a family member loses his or her capacity to make financial decisions, he or she might unintentionally hand over financial decision making to an untrustworthy individual. Or the family member might become susceptible to being coerced, manipulated, or duped into signing away property or other assets. In the last chapter, we discussed ways that a family member can get help with his or her finances through a representative payee, a bill paying service, a financial power of attorney, and so on.

- *Mental Health Services*—These services provide crisis intervention and counseling for victims of elder abuse, their abusers, and their families.

- *Family and Caregiver Support Services and Groups* and *Respite Care*—A family caregiver who becomes abusive or neglectful toward an elderly parent or a relative can seek relief through support services aimed at lessening the elder's dependency on the family caregiver. These support services include home-delivered meals and dependent care. Also, support groups for caregivers provide tips and information to help manage caregiver stress and to avoid burnout. Finally, respite care programs, which lessen the risk of abuse or neglect by alleviating caregiver stress, provide family caregivers with a breather from their caregiving responsibilities.

- *Dependency Reduction*—When an abuser is financially dependent on an elderly victim, minimizing the abuser's dependency on the victim can ease the situation. For example, providing the abuser with job training or placement can lessen his or her financial dependence on the elder.

Mandatory Reporting Laws for Elder Abuse

Let's discuss mandatory reporting laws that have been passed by most states. First, reports of suspected elder abuse, neglect, or exploitation are usually referred to the agency responsible for investigating the complaints. For example, in Georgia, the Division of Aging Services (DAS) investigates reports of the abuse or neglect of adults 65 years and older. If a crime has been committed, the agency will turn the matter over to a criminal justice agency. In the attorney general's office, some states have special units that investigate crimes against the elderly. For example, in Pennsylvania, the Attorney General's Elder Abuse Unit investigates elder abuse complaints and prosecutes the offenders.

Second, the people and professionals who must report elder abuse vary by jurisdiction. For example, everyone must report suspected elder abuse in some jurisdictions, whereas only specific professionals are required to report in other areas. In a number of states, some professionals are exempt from reporting abuse or neglect because they're bound by confidentiality, such as clergy, lawyers, therapists, and physicians. Finally, some states have no statutory provisions for reporting elder abuse, including Colorado, North Dakota, and New Jersey.

Third, mandated reporters generally include the following professionals:

- Health care professionals
- Registered nurses, nurse's aides, certified nursing assistants, caregivers, home health aides, and employees of a home health service
- Psychologists, licensed clinical social workers, licensed professional counselors, licensed marriage and family therapists
- Law enforcement, firefighters, and emergency medical technicians
- Physical therapists, speech therapists, and occupational therapists
- Senior center employees
- Any public official who comes in contact with older adults in the course of performing his or her official duties
- An administrator, employee, or person who furnishes services in or through an unlicensed community-based facility

Fourth, the types of abuse or neglect that must be reported and about whom differs from state to state. Take Connecticut's mandated reporter laws. Mandated reporters include licensed physicians and surgeons, registered and licensed practical nurses, medical examiners, dentists, and others. The law requires that when a mandated reporter has "reasonable cause to suspect or believes that someone age 60 or over (1) has been abused, neglected, exploited, or abandoned, or is in a condition caused by one of these or (2) is in need of protective services (services designed to protect elderly individuals from such harm), he/she must report this to the Connecticut Department of Social Services (DSS), Protective Services for the Elderly (PSE) within five days." If a mandated reporter does not report, he or she will be fined not more than $500. Also, nonmandated reporters are urged to report suspected elder mistreatment.

Fifth, states with mandatory reporting laws often punish those who fail to report elder abuse. The punishment can be in the form of a fine, incarceration, and/or license revocation. For example, under Alabama law, if a mandated reporter doesn't report suspected abuse or neglect, he or she may be charged with a misdemeanor, pay a criminal fine, or be jailed. In Massachusetts, a mandated reporter who fails to report elder abuse or neglect will be fined an amount that doesn't exceed $1,000. Moreover, states differ on the time allowed between the detection of the abuse or neglect and reporting it. For example, under Illinois law, professionals and state employees must report suspected abuse or neglect within 24 hours.

Sixth, states usually offer "good faith immunity" for reporters and protect their confidentiality. For example, under Oregon law, "anyone reporting adult abuse with reasonable grounds is immune from civil liability."

Seventh, according to the book *Elder Mistreatment: Abuse, Neglect, and Exploitation in an Aging America*, third parties report elder abuse most often, as compared to self-reporting by the victim. Hospitals, physicians, nurses, and clinics were responsible for 25.7 percent of reports, 20 percent of reports came from family members, and 14.8 percent of reports came from home service providers, according to the National Elder Abuse Incidence Study (NEAIS). The study also found that most reports of financial abuse came from friends and neighbors (15 percent), followed by hospitals (14.2 percent), and finally, by family members (14 percent).

Lastly, given the number of different professions and persons who are required to report suspected elder abuse, it's surprising that elder mistreatment is underreported. According to the National Center on Elder Abuse (NCEA), in spite of the presence of APS in every state and the existence of mandatory reporting laws, "an overwhelming number of cases of abuse, neglect, and exploitation go undetected and untreated each year." In fact, only one in 14 instances of elder abuse gets reported to the authorities, according to the House Select Committee on Aging.

Online Resources for Family Caregivers

If you're a family caregiver who is seeking information resources on assisting and caring for an aging loved one, you don't have to go very far for guidance: just let your fingers do the walking across your computer keyboard. To help you get started, an alphabetized list of general Web resources that you can tap into is provided, several of which are jumping-off points for other helpful links and resources. Also, a number of professional websites are listed, which provide the consumer with valuable information on aging and age-related issues. Finally, you might wish to check government websites in your state or locality to explore community-specific programs and resources that offer helpful assistance and advice.

A to C

American Association of Retired Persons (AARP) <http://www. aarp.org>: AARP is a nonprofit organization that supports the needs of older Americans. The organization produces several publications that provide news, lifestyle advice, and educational information, including *AARP The Magazine*, *AARP Bulletin*, and AARP books.

Administration on Aging (AoA) <http://www.aoa.gov>: The AoA is an agency under the United States Department of Health and Human Services that provides home- and community-based care for older adults and supplies information on age-related topics.

AgingStats.gov <http://www.agingstats.gov>: Known as the Federal Interagency Forum on Aging-Related Statistics, the Forum provides useful and quality aging-related data.

Alliance for Aging Research <http://www.agingresearch.org>: This nonprofit organization is a leader in aging research. The Alliance strives to "advance science and enhance lives" through a variety of programs and initiatives, such as grassroots education campaigns and health education materials.

Alzheimer's Association <http://www.alz.org>: This nonprofit association is a leading voluntary health organization dedicated to the care, support, and research of Alzheimer's disease and related dementias.

American Association for Geriatric Psychiatry <http://www.aagponline.org>: This national association advances the mental health and well-being of older adults through public advocacy, professional education, and other aims.

American Bar Association (ABA) Commission on Law and Aging <http://www.americanbar.org/groups/law_aging.html>: The Commission is dedicated to supporting and securing "the legal rights, dignity, autonomy, quality of life, and quality of care of elders." It explores a broad range of legal issues that affects older persons, such as health and long-term care; professional ethical issues; elder abuse; planning for incapacity; and other relevant issues.

American Federation for Aging Research (AFAR) <http://www.afar.org>: AFAR provides the latest information on the biology of aging, common age-related diseases, and ways to promote healthy aging.

American Society of Aging (ASA) <http://www.asaging.org>: The ASA offers continuing education and professional development, publications, and resources to professionals working in the field of aging.

Assisted Living Federation of America (ALFA) <http://www.alfa.org>: ALFA provides resources, education, research, publications, and other information on resident-centered senior living communities.

Benefits.gov <http://www.benefits.gov>: This government website offers easy online access to government benefit and assistance programs.

Care.com <https://www.care.com>: This website offers products and services to help families "find quality care solutions" for their elderly loved ones, including housing arrangements, transportation services, home care, end-of-life care, and other care needs.

Caregiver Action Network (CAN) <http://cargiveraction.org>: The CAN is a leading family caregiver organization that aims to enhance family caregivers' quality of life.

Centers for Disease Control and Prevention (CDC) <http://www.cdc.gov/ViolencePrevention>: The CDC's Division of Violence Prevention provides general information on elder abuse, including risk and protective factors, consequences, and prevention strategies.

The Clearinghouse on Abuse and Neglect of the Elderly (CANE) <http://www.cane.udel.edu>: Housed in the University of Delaware Center for Community Research and Service, CANE is the largest database on elder abuse literature.

D to F

Disability.gov <https://www.disability.gov>: This government website furnishes complete information on disability programs and services nationwide.

Elder Abuse Forensic Center <http://www.elderabuseforensiccenter. com>: The Center is committed to the prevention of elder mistreatment, the education of professionals who handle crimes against the elderly, and the creation of intervention strategies, while also raising public awareness of elder abuse.

Eldercare Locator <http://www.eldercare.gov>: As a public service of the Administration on Aging, this website offers useful information and resources aimed at helping older persons lead safe, independent lives. Its extensive database links older persons and their families to a number of agencies and programs serving the elderly, including Area Agencies on Aging; aging information and referral programs; Aging and Disability Resource Centers; legal services; elder abuse prevention; the Long-Term Care Ombudsman Program; and others.

Family Caregiver Alliance (FCA) <http://www.caregiver.org>: The FCA is a community-based nonprofit organization that offers programs aimed at supporting family caregivers.

The Federal Bureau of Investigation (FBI) <http://www.fbi.gov/ scams-safety/fraud/seniors>: The FBI furnishes resources on frauds affecting seniors.

The Fisher Center for Alzheimer's Research Foundation <http://www. alzinfo.org>: The Fisher Center provides a wealth of information on Alzheimer's disease.

Foundation Aiding the Elderly <http://www.4fate.org>: This nonprofit organization provides information, counseling, and referrals for those who need assistance in caring for the elderly, as well as offers help in dealing with the abuse of the elderly.

G to I

Geriatric Mental Health Foundation <http://www.gmhfonline.org >: Created by the American Association for Geriatric Psychiatry, the Foundation strives to raise awareness of psychiatric and mental health disorders presented in the elderly, improve access to quality mental health care for the elderly, and other aims.

HealthCare.gov <http://www.hhs.gov/healthcare/>: Sponsored by the U.S. Department of Health & Human Services and created under Obamacare, this health insurance exchange website serves as a clearinghouse where people can do comparison shopping for health insurance plans, among other things.

HealthFinder.gov <http://www.healthfinder.gov>: This government website provides information and tools, including topics on elder care, to help people stay healthy.

Healthinaging.org <http://www.healthinaging.org/>: Formed by the American Geriatrics Society Foundation for Health in Aging (FHA), this website furnishes consumers and caregivers with the latest information on health and aging.

J to M

Medicaid.gov <http://www.medicaid.gov>: This federal government website is managed by the Centers for Medicare and Medicaid Services, an agency of the U.S. Department of Health and Human Services (HHS). The website outlines services covered by the Medicaid program and describes services provided by nursing homes and other care facilities.

Medicare.gov <http://www.medicare.gov>: This government website gives consumers access to information on Medicare funding and the Affordable Care Act (ACA), as well as contact information for the Centers for Medicare & Medicaid Services, which operates the Medicare program.

N to P

National Academy of Elder Law Attorneys, Inc. (NAELA) <http://www.naela.org>: The NAELA is a professional association mostly comprised of private and public sector attorneys who handle legal issues that affect seniors and the disabled. In addition, the NAELA offers support to organizations that serve the elderly and those with special needs.

National Adult Protective Services Association (NAPSA) <http://www.napsa-now.org>: The NAPSA provides Adult Protective Services (APS) programs, agencies, and professionals with a platform to exchange information, solve problems, and enhance "the quality, consistency, and effectiveness of APS programs across the country."

National Association to Stop Guardian Abuse (NASGA) <http://www.stopguardianabuse.org>: This public benefit civil rights organization addresses guardianship and conservatorship abuse.

National Cancer Institute (NCI) <http://www.cancer.gov>: NCI's Cancer Information Service (CIS) provides the latest information on a range of cancer topics, including cancer research, cancer prevention, risk factors, symptoms, and early detection.

National Caregivers Library <http://www.caregiverslibrary.org>: The library is a rich source of information and tools for caregivers and seniors.

National Center on Elder Abuse (NCEA) <http://ncea.aoa.gov>: Funded through the Administration on Aging, the NCEA is a chief source of information, research, training, best practices, news, and resources on elder mistreatment.

National Center for Victims of Crime (NCVC) <http://www. victimsofcrime.org>: The National Center is a leading resource and advocacy organization dedicated to "advancing victims' rights and helping victims of crime rebuild their lives."

National Clearinghouse on Abuse Later in Life (NCALL) <http://www.ncall.us>: The NCALL provides information and resources on domestic violence, sexual assault, and elder mistreatment.

National Committee for the Prevention of Elder Abuse (NCPEA) <http://www.preventelderabuse.org>: The NCPEA is a nonprofit organization made up of researchers, practitioners, educators, and advocates who are committed to the prevention of elder abuse among vulnerable and dependent adults. The NCPEA enhances prevention and intervention strategies; conducts research on elder mistreatment; furnishes information to professionals and advocates in the field of elder mistreatment; and engages in other activities.

National Council on Aging (NCOA) <http://www.ncoa.org>: The NCOA is a nonprofit service and advocacy organization that works with organizations that help seniors find jobs and benefits, while also enhancing seniors' well-being and independence. The organization offers a number of resources on age-related topics to professionals, advocates, and older adults and their caregivers.

National Criminal Justice Reference Service (NCJRS) < https://www. ncjrs.gov>: Sponsored by the U.S. Department of Justice (DOJ), the NCJRS offers services and resources on a number of topics, such as substance abuse, victim assistance, public safety, law enforcement, and elder abuse.

National Senior Citizens Law Center (NSCLC) <http://www.nsclc. org>: The NSCLC provides advocacy, litigation, education, and counseling for local advocates who work with older adults, focusing on health care, economic security, and judicial activism.

National Institutes of Health SeniorHealth <http://nihseniorhealth. gov>: As part of the National Institutes of Health (NIH), this website provides older adults with aging-related health information.

National Institute on Aging (NIA) <http://www.nia.nih.gov>: The NIA is a leading supplier of research on health and aging.

NursingHomeMonitors.org <http://www.nursinghomemonitors. org/>: This nonprofit organization is committed to enhancing "the lives of the American elderly by fighting abuse, neglect, and exploitation in our nation's nursing homes."

Office for Victims of Crime (OVC) <http://www.ovc.gov>: As part of the U.S. Department of Justice (DOJ), the OVC supports various programs and services designed to help victims of crime, including elderly victims, rebuild their lives.

Q to S

The Rosalynn Carter Institute for Caregiving (RCI) <http://www. rosalynncarter.org>: The RCI offers support to both family and professional caregivers through advocacy, education, research, and advice.

SeniorLiving.org <http://www.seniorliving.org>: This website informs seniors and their caregivers about senior care, including senior living, assisted living, nursing homes, home care, and other topics.

Seniors Resource Guide <http://www.seniorsresourceguide.com>: This website furnishes databases that address topics on senior housing, home health, health services, care management and referral services, community services, and others topics.

The Social Security Administration (SSA) <http://www.ssa.gov>: The official website of the Social Security Administration provides vital information about Social Security services nationwide.

T to Z

USA.gov <http://www.usa.gov>: This federal government portal provides an array of resources and information that addresses the needs of seniors, including money management, health, housing, consumer protection, retirement, elder laws, and so on.

U.S. Department of Housing and Urban Development (HUD) <http://portal.hud.gov>: HUD helps seniors find affordable housing through HUD-funded programs, including public housing, multifamily subsidized houses, and voucher housing programs.

U.S. Department of Veteran Affairs (VA) <http://www.va.gov>: This government website furnishes information on VA benefits and services, including those for older veterans.

U.S. Food and Drug Administration (FDA) <http://www.fda.gov>: This government website provides information on a broad range of health issues, such as cancer treatment, diabetes treatment, drug information, and nutrition.

United States Senate Special Committee on Aging <http://www. aging.senate.gov>: The Committee regularly reviews and studies issues concerning health care for seniors, long-term care, elder fraud and abuse, affordable senior housing, and other issues.

The Lyon Case: Selma's Twilight Years

Thanks to the loving care that Selma's caregivers gave Selma and because of the resources Selma's family was able to consult, Selma seemed to achieve peace and tranquility during the final years of her life, even as the ravages of dementia progressively stripped Selma of her faculties. For a short while, Selma appeared to be aware of her environment and the people within it. Selma's family was able to spend precious unobstructed time with Selma during her conservatorship. As onerous as the conservatorship was on Selma and on her family, it accomplished at least two objectives: to ensure Selma's care and protection and to let Selma quietly and safely live out her last days at home, one of Selma's greatest wishes.

EPILOGUE

Selma died in 2012. Her death certificate stated that her immediate cause of death was cardiopulmonary arrest, with aspiration pneumonia and senile dementia listed as underlying causes resulting in her death.

The court-appointed professional conservators and their attorneys and service providers benefited handsomely from Selma's estate, which was chewed up during the conservatorship. Whereas Selma's fiduciaries ordinarily exercised due diligence, they made surrogate decisions that oftentimes ran afoul of Selma's values, preferences, and wants.

As Selma's family conservator, Livingston served Selma with love, compassion, and prudence. He remained vigilant throughout Selma's conservatorship. Livingston and his attorney went to bat for Selma right to the very end when situations arose that flew in the face of Selma's best interests.

Agatha and Attorney Armstrong continued to advocate alongside Livingston on Selma's behalf. Agatha, along with other relatives and close friends, visited and kept in regular contact with Selma until her death.

After moving out of Selma's home, Zachary, his wife Sybil, and her family took up residence in a neighboring town. Zachary cut off all ties with Selma and the family. Years later, the family learned that Sybil had left Zachary, only to return to him after the announcement of Selma's death. Zachary had inherited Selma's home. Based on county records, Zachary signed a quitclaim deed, making Sybil the sole owner of the home but not guaranteeing Zachary a place in the household. Zachary has begun divorce proceedings against Sybil, according to a neighbor.

It took a family crisis to bring distant family members together, many of whom had had no contact with one another for over 30 years. They formed a coalition for a common cause: to save Selma from ruination at the hands of a family insider and a team of predators. Along the way, however, *they unwittingly swapped domestic oppression for institutional paternalism.*

After the dustup of Selma's conservatorship and following Selma's death, the Lyon legacy of hard work, steely discipline, and solid citizenship fell into obscurity.

Selma's memory is enshrined in the hearts of the people on whom she had a direct and lasting impact, not just her family, but also the thousands of students who directly benefited from her teaching of engineering, many of whom are today's engineers, scientists, physicists, mathematicians, lawyers, physicians, architects, and engineering professors like Selma.

REFERENCES

Accettura, Mark P. *Blood & Money: Why Families Fight Over Inheritance and What to Do About It.* Farmington Hills: Collinwood Press, 2011. Print.

"Ageism in America: As Boomers Age, Bias Against the Elderly Becomes Hot Topic." *NBCNews.com*, 7 Sept. 2004. Web. 10 Oct. 2013.

"Aging Statistics." Administration on Aging, n.d. Web. 5 Oct. 2013.

Ahmad, Mahnaz, and Mark S. Lachs. "Elder Abuse and Neglect: What Physicians Can and Should Do." *Cleveland Clinic Journal of Medicine* 69.10 (2002): n. pag. Web. 10 Oct. 2013.

Alzheimer's Association. "New Alzheimer's Association Report Reveals 1 in 3 Seniors Dies with Alzheimer's or Another Dementia." 19 Mar. 2013. Web. 5 Oct. 2013.

American Bar Association Commission on Law and Aging. "Consumer's Toolkit for Health Care Advance Planning." n.d. Web. 5 Oct. 2013.

American Bar Association Commission on Law and Aging. "Elder Abuse." n.d. Web. 5 Oct. 2013.

The American Bar Association. "Giving Someone a Power of Attorney for your Health Care: A Guide with an Easy-to-Use, Legal Form for All Adults." 2011. PDF file. Web. 5 Oct. 2013.

American Geriatrics Society. "Feeding Tubes in Advanced Dementia Position Statement." May 2013. PDF file. Web. 10 Oct. 2013.

American Psychological Association. "Elder Abuse and Neglect: In Search of Solutions." 2006. Web. 10 Oct. 2013.

Anders, Sarah, et. al. "Conservatorship Reform in California: Three Cost-Effective Recommendations." Goldman School of Public Policy University of California, Berkeley, May 2009. PDF file. Web. 10 Oct. 2013.

Anderson, Doug, and Laurel Kennedy. "Baby Boomer Segmentation: Eight Is Enough." ACNielsen, 2006. PDF file. Web. 5 Oct. 2013.

The Arc Tennessee Advocacy Committee. "Conservatorship and Alternatives to Conservatorship: A Guide for Families." 2011. PDF file. Web. 5 Oct. 2013.

Arenella, Cheryl. "Coma and Persistent Vegetative State: An Exploration of Terms." America Hospice Foundation, 2005. Web. 10 Oct. 2013.

Assisted Living Federation of America. "1 in 8 Seniors Report Memory Loss, Survey Finds." n.d. Web. 5 Oct. 2013.

Assisted Living Federation of America. "4 in 10 US Adults Are Caregivers, Report Finds." n.d. Web. 5 Oct. 2013.

Assisted Living Federation of America. "15 Percent of Seniors Live in Poverty, Analysis Finds." n.d. Web. 5 Oct. 2013.

Assisted Living Federation of America. "Researchers Find Three Causes to Ageism." n.d. Web. 5 Oct. 2013.

Assisted Living Federation of America. "2013 Senior Health Rankings Highlight Health Problems of Aging Population." n.d. Web. 5 Oct. 2013.

"Baby Boomer." *Wikipedia*. Last modified: 6 September 2013. Web. 5 Oct. 2013.

"Baby Boomers: From the Age of Aquarius to the Age of Responsibility." Pew Research Social & Demographic Trends, 8 Dec. 2005. Web. 5 Oct. 2013.

Beck, Melinda. "Starting to Feel Older? New Studies Show Attitude Can Be Critical." *The Wall Street Journal* 17 Oct. 2009: n. pag. Web. 5 Oct. 2013.

Beinhocker, Eric D., Diana Farrell and Ezra Greenberg. "Why Baby Boomers Will Need to Work Longer." *The McKinsey Quarterly* Nov. 2008: n. pag. Web. 5 Oct. 2013.

Bernanke, Chairman Ben S. "Causes of the Recent Financial and Economic Crisis." Board of Governors of the Federal Reserve System. Financial Crisis Inquiry Commission. Washington, D.C., 2 Sept. 2010. Testimony. Web. 10 Oct. 2013.

Blumenthal, Susan, and Katherine Warren. "Baby Boomers: Public Health's Biggest Challenge." *The Huffington Post* 1 Apr. 2011. Web. 10 Oct. 2013.

Bonnie, Richard J., and Robert B. Wallace, eds. *Elder Mistreatment: Abuse, Neglect, and Exploitation in an Aging America*. Washington: The National Academies Press, 2003. Print.

"Boomers Are 'The Most Valuable Generation For Marketers, Nielsen Report Finds." *The Huffington Post* 17 Aug. 2012: n. pag. Web. 5 Oct. 2013.

Boshoff, Alison. "£1m on Drugs in Three Years, a £500,000 Hotel Bill and £1,000 a Month on Her Kittens: How Amy Winehouse Squandered £10 Million." *Daily Mail* 30 Mar. 2012. Web. 10 Oct. 2013.

Brenner, Joanna, and Aaron Smith. "72% of Online Adults are Social Networking Site Users." Pew Internet & American Life Project, 5 Aug. 2013. Web. 5 Oct. 2013.

Buhai, Sande L., and James W. Gilliam, Jr. "Honor Thy Mother and Father: Preventing Elder Abuse Through Education and Litigation." *Loyola of Los Angeles Law Review* 36.2 (2003): 565-588. PDF file. Web. 10 Oct. 2013.

Byron, Ellen. "From Diapers to 'Depends': Marketers Discreetly Retool for Aging Boomers." *The Wall Street Journal* 5 Feb. 2011: n. pag. Web. 5 Oct. 2013.

California Department on Aging. "California State Plan on Aging 2013-2017." 6 May 2013. PDF file. Web. 5 Oct. 2013.

California Judicial Branch. "Conservatorship." n.d. Web. 5 Oct. 2013.

"Caregiver Scams Target Most Vulnerable Victims," *Scambusters.org*, n.d. Web. 10 Oct. 2013.

Carlozo, Lou. "How the Sandwich Generation Can Avoid Getting Squeezed." *Reuters* 6 Jul. 2012. Web. 5 Oct. 2013.

Carmichael, Matt. "Study Finds Striking Trends in How Growing Subset Stays Connected the Most?" *AdAge* 11 Nov. 2010: n. pag. Web. 10 Oct. 2013.

---."Which Boomers Are Using Social Media the Most?: Study Finds Striking Trends in How Growing Subset Stays Connected," *AdAge* 11 Nov. 2010: n. pag. Web. 5 Oct. 2013.

Centers for Elders and Courts. "Elder Abuse Laws." n.d. Web. 5 Oct. 2013.

"Charlie Sheen's Family Seeks Conservatorship over Him: Report." *The New York Post* 1 Feb. 2011: n. pag. Web. 10 Oct. 2013.

Cohn, D'Vera, and Paul Taylor. "Baby Boomers Approach 65 – Glumly." Pew Research Social & Demographic Trends, 20 Dec. 2010. Web. 5 Oct. 2013.

"Cohorts: Age-Based Marketing." Bidwell, 2009. PDF file. Web. 5 Oct. 2013.

Coleman, Nancy, et al. "Facts about Law and the Elderly." American Bar Association Commission on Law and the Elderly, 1998. PDF file. Web. 10 Oct. 2013.

Colvin, Geoff Colvin. "How Long Will You Live?" *Fortune Magazine* 10 Jun. 2008: n. pag. Web. 5 Oct. 2013.

"Common Fraud Schemes." *FBI.gov*, n.d. Web. 10 Oct. 2013.

"Conservatorship of Drabick (1988) 200 Cal. App. 3d 185 [245 Cal. Rptr. 840]." *Justia*, n.d. Web. 5 Oct. 2013.

"Conservatorship of Morrison (1988) 206 Cal. App. 3d 304 [253 Cal. Rptr. 530]." *Justia*, n.d. Web. 5 Oct. 2013.

"Conservatorship of Wendland v. Florence Wendland et al., Objectors and Respondents; Robert Wendland, Appellant." *Find Law*, n.d. Web. 5 Oct. 2013.

"Conservatorships and Adult Guardianships." *Nolo*, n.d. Web. 10 Oct. 2013.

"Consumers of Tomorrow: Insights and Observations About Generation Z." Grail Research, Nov. 2011. PDF file. Web. 5 Oct. 2013.

Coyne, Andrew C., W.E. Reichman and L.J. Berbig. "The Relationship Between Dementia and Elder Abuse." *American Journal of Psychiatry* 150.4 (1993): 643-46. Web. 10 Oct. 2013.

"The Demographics of Aging... Characteristics of our Aging Population." *Transgenerational Design*. n.d. Web. 5 Oct. 2013.

DiSomma, Anthony V. "In Re Drabick." *Issues in Law & Medicine* 4.4 (1989): n. pag. Web. 5 Oct. 2013.

Dolliver, Mark. "Marketing to Today's 65-plus Consumers." *Adweek* 27 Jul. 2009: n. pag. Web. 5 Oct. 2013.

Dresser, Rebecca. "Treatment Decisions for Dementia Patients: The Search for Normative Boundaries." President's Council on Bioethics, Dec. 2004. Web. 10 Oct. 2013.

Duke, Alan. "Mickey Rooney Seeks Career Revival Under New Conservatorship." *CNN.com*. 25 Mar. 2011. Web. 10 Oct. 2013.

Eichler, Alexander. "Millions Of Senior Citizens Can't Afford Basic Living Expenses: Study." *The Huffington Post* 2 March 2012: n. pag. Web. 5 Oct. 2013.

Eisenberg, Jon B., and J. Clark Kelso. "Legal Implications of the Wendland Case for End-of-Life Decision Making." *Western Journal of Medicine* 176.2 (2002): 124–127. Web. 5 Oct. 2013.

"Elder Justice: Section 6703 of the Patient Protection and Affordable Care Act." *Health Reform Issue Briefs* 6:10 (2011): n. pag. PDF file. Web. 10 Oct. 2013.

"Elderly Abuse Statistics." *Statistic Brain.com*, n.d. Web. 10 Oct. 2013.

El Nasser, Haya, and Paul Overberg. "Nation's Aging Population Booms." *USA Today*, 26 May 2011: n. pag. Web. 10 Oct. 2013.

Elton, Catherine. "The Fleecing of America's Elderly." *Consumers Digest*, Nov. 2012: n. pag. Web. 10 Oct. 2013.

Ersek, Mary. "Artificial Nutrition and Hydration: Clinical Issues." *Journal of Hospice and Palliative Nursing* 5.4 (2003): n. pag. Web. 10 Oct. 2013.

Esri. "Is 'Seniors' One Demographic Group? An Analysis of America's Changing Demographics." 2012. PDF file. Web. 5 Oct. 2013.

Experience Corps. "Fact Sheet on Aging in America." n.d. PDF file. Web. 5 Oct. 2013.

"Father and Son Arrested in Probate Fraud case." *The Mortgage Fraud Reporter* 15 Apr. 2005: n. pag. Web. 5 Oct. 2013.

"Favorite Brands of the Boomer Generation." *CNBC.com.* n.d. Web. 5 Oct. 2013.

Federman, Allen. "Conservatorship: A Viable Alternative to Incompetency." *Fordham Urban Law Journal* 14.4 (1985): n. pag. Web. 5 Oct. 2013.

"Feeding Tubes in Patients with Severe Dementia." *American Family Physician* 65.8 (2002): 1605-1611. Web. 10 Oct. 2013.

"50 and Over: What's Next?" *AdAge Insights* 4 April 2011. PDF file. Web. 5 Oct. 2013.

Fields, Robin, Evelyn Larrubia and Jack Leonard. "For Most Vulnerable, a Promise Abandoned." *Los Angeles Times* 16 Nov. 2005: n. pag. Web. 10 Oct. 2013.

---. "When a Family Matter Turns into a Business." *Los Angeles Times* 13 Nov. 2005: n. pag. Web. 10 Oct. 2013.

"Financial Crisis of 2007-08." *Wikipedia*. Last modified: 20 Sept. 2013. Web. 5 Oct. 2013.

Fox, Susannah. "Older Americans and the Internet." Pew Internet & American Life Project, 28 Mar. 2004. Web. 5 Oct. 2013.

"Generation Y." *Wikipedia*. Last modified: 22 September 2013. Web. 5 Oct. 2013.

"Generation Z." *Wikipedia*. Last modified: 23 Sept. 2013. Web. 5 Oct. 2013.

"Get Ahead of Your Estate Planning," *CNN.com*. n.d. Web. 5 Oct. 2013.

Gigante, Shelly. "How Boomers Will Impact the Health Care Industry." *CNBC.com*. 22 Feb. 2010. Web. 5 Oct. 2013.

Gilmartin, Jim. "Position Your Product as a Gateway to Desired Experiences." Coming of Age Incorporated, n.d. Web. 5 Oct. 2013.

Glink, Ilyce. "Baby Boomer Real Estate Trends." *CBSNews.com*. 17 Oct. 2011. Web. 5 Oct. 2013.

Goetting, Marsha, and E. Edwin Eck. "Power of Attorney." Revised Mar. 2013. Montana State University Extension. Web. 10 Oct. 2013.

Gorbien, Martin J. and Amy R. Eisenstein. "Elder Abuse and Neglect: An Overview." Section of Geriatric Medicine, Department of Internal Medicine, Rush University Medical Center, Clin Geriatr Med 21 (2005) 279– 292. PDF file. Web. 31 May 2014.

Grinberg, Emanuella. "Boomers Will Redefine Notions of Age." *CNN.com.* 9 May 2011. Web. 5 Oct. 2013.

---."Caregiving for Loved Ones the 'New Normal' for Boomers." *CNN.com.* 9 Apr. 2012. Web. 5 Oct. 2013.

Grodnitzky, Gustavo. "Ready or Not, Here They Come! Understanding and Motivating the Millennial Generation." n.d. *PowerPoint* file. Web. 5 Oct. 2013.

Gross, Jane. "Forensic Skills Seek to Uncover Elder Abuse." *The New York Times* 27 Sept. 2006: n. pag. Web. 10 Oct. 2013.

"Growing Old in America: Expectations vs. Reality." Pew Research Social & Demographic Trends, 29 Jun. 2009. Web. 5 Oct. 2013.

Haas, Jane Glenn. "Survey: Caregiving Issues a Top Concern for Seniors." *Orange County Register* 21 Aug. 2013: n. pag. Web. 5 Oct. 2013.

Hafemeister, Thomas L. *Financial Abuse of the Elderly in Domestic Setting.* National Academies Press, 2003. Web. 10 Oct. 2013.

Hall, Ryan C.W., and Marcia J. Chapman. "Exploitation of the Elderly: Undue Influence as a Form of Elder Abuse." *Clinical Geriatrics* 13.2 (2005): n. pag. PDF file. Web. 10 Oct. 2013.

Hamilton, Brady E., Joyce A. Martin and Stephanie J. Ventura. "Births: Preliminary Data for 2012." *Centers for Disease Control and Prevention* 62:3 (2013): 1-33. PDF file. Web. 5 Oct. 2013.

Hartsell, Z.C. and J.S. Williams. "Is It Ethical to Provide Enteral Tube Feedings for Patients with Dementia?" *Journal of the American Academy of Physician Assistants* 23(2010): 55-6. Web. 10 Oct. 2013.

Harvey, Kay. "Challenges and Change Confront the Boomers." *MinnPost* 10 Apr. 2012: n. pag. Web. 5 Oct. 2013.

Hindman, Susan. "Guardianship Gone Bad: Isolate. Medicate. Take the Estate." *Silver Planet*, n.d. Web. 5 Oct. 2013.

Howden, Lindsay M., and Julie A. Meyer. "Age and Sex Composition: 2010." U.S Census Bureau, May 2011. PDF file. Web. 5 Oct. 2013.

Howe, Neil. "What Makes the Boomers the Boomers?" *Governing the State and Localities*. Sept. 2012. Web. 5 Oct. 2013.

Howe, Neil, and William Strauss. "The Silent Generation Passes into History." *The Seattle Times* 23 Feb. 1992: n. pag. Web. 5 Oct. 2013.

"How Retiring Baby-Boomers Could Hurt the Economy." *InvestorGuide* 10 Oct. 2012: n. pag. Web. 5 Oct. 2013.

Hughes, Sandra L. "Can Bank Tellers Tell?—Legal Issues Relating to Banks Reporting Financial Abuse of the Elderly." American Bar Association Commission on Law and Aging, 2003. Web. 5 Oct. 2013.

Hupp, William. "The Misunderstood Generation: By Lumping Them Together, Marketers Fail to Understand Baby Boomers." *AdAge* 5 Feb. 2008: n. pag. Web. 10 Oct. 2013.

Husebo, Bettina, et al. "Who Suffers Most? Dementia and Pain in Nursing Home Patients: A Cross-sectional Study." *Journal of the American Medical Directors Association* 9 (2008): 427-433. Web. 10 Oct. 2013.

"In-Home Care: A Solution for Baby Boomers Now and in the Future." *Comfort Keepers*. n.d. Web. 5 Oct. 2013.

Johnson, Kelly Dedel. "Financial Crimes against the Elderly." U.S. Department of Justice Office of Community Oriented Policing Services, 4 Aug. 2004. Web. 10 Oct. 2013.

Jones, Bethany. "What You Need to Know about Probate Conservatorships in California." California Advocates for Nursing Home Reform, Summer 2005. PDF file. Web. 10 Oct. 2013.

Jones, Jeffrey M. "Pensions Are Top Income Source for Wealthier U.S. Retirees: Social Security Top Source for Less Wealthy Retirees." *Gallup*, 21 May 2013. Web. 5 Oct. 2013.

Judicial Council of California. *Handbook for Conservators*. 2002 Revised Edition. PDF file. Web. 10 Oct. 2013.

Karp, Naomi, and Erica Wood. "Guardianship Monitoring: A National Survey of Court Practices." AARP Public Policy Institute, Jun. 2006. Web. 5 Oct. 2013.

---."Guarding the Guardians: Promising Practices for Court Monitoring." AARP Public Policy Institute, Dec. 2007. Web. 5 Oct. 2013.

Kelly, Jeff, Maggie Kowalski and Candice Novak. "Courts Strip Elders of Their Independence: Within Minutes, Judges Send Seniors to Supervised Care." *The Boston Globe* 13 Jan. 2008: n. pag. Web. 5 Oct. 2013.

Kerschner, Edward M., and Michael Geraghty. "The Next American Dream." Citigroup Global Markets, Apr. 2004. PDF file. Web. 5 Oct. 2013.

Kincaid, Linda. "Conservatorships in Crisis: Civil Rights Violations & Abuses of Power." Research Paper De Anza College, Dec. 2012. Print.

King, Steve M. "Guardianship Monitoring: A Demographic Imperative." *Future Trends in State Courts*, 2007. Web. 5 Oct. 2013.

Knickman, James R., and Emily K. Snell. "The 2030 Problem: Caring for Aging Baby Boomers." *Health Services Research* 37.4 (2002): 849–884. Web. 5 Oct. 2013.

Kohn, Robert, and Wendy Verhoek-Oftedahl. "Caregiving and Elder Abuse." *Medicine & Health Rhode Island* 94.2 (2011): n. pag. Web. 10 Oct. 2013.

Larrubia, Evelyn, Jack Leonard and Robin Fields. "Missing Money, Unpaid Bills and Forgotten Clients." *Los Angeles Times* 15 Nov. 2005: n. pag. Web. 10 Oct. 2013.

---."Judge Orders Review of Vet's Contested Will." *Los Angeles Times* 16 Nov. 2005: n. pag. Web. 10 Oct. 2013.

Laumann, Edward O., Sara A. Leitsch and Linda J. Waite. "Elder Mistreatment in the United States: Prevalence Estimates from a Nationally Representative Study." *Journal of Gerontology* 63B. 4 (2008): n. pag. Web. 10 Oct. 2013.

Leonard, Jack, Robin Fields and Evelyn Larrubia. "Justice Sleeps While Seniors Suffer." *Los Angeles Times* 14 Nov. 2005: n. pag. Web. 10 Oct. 2013.

LeTrent, Sarah. "Companies Target Baby Boomers' Changing Tastes." *CNN.com*. 16 Apr. 2010. Web. 5 Oct. 2013.

Levens, Michael. *Marketing: Defined, Explained, Applied*. 2nd ed. Upper Saddle River: Prentice Hall, 2012. Print.

"Licensed Fiduciaries Are Working Hard to Combat Elder Financial Abuse – a $3 Billion a Year Problem." *Reuters* 6 Oct. 2011. Web. 10 Oct. 2013.

"License to Steal from Seniors: How to Protect the Elderly from the People They've Chosen to Trust." *Business Week* 31 May 2006: n. pag. Web. 10 Oct. 2013.

Loope, Lance. "How Generation Z Works." *HowStuffWorks*. n.d. Web. 5 Oct. 2013.

Lorin A. Baumhover, Lorin A., and S. Colleen Beall, eds. *Abuse, Neglect, and Exploitation of Older Persons: Strategies for Assessment and Intervention*. Baltimore: Health Professions Press, Inc., 1996. Print.

Luce, John M., and Ann Alpers. "Legal Aspects of Withholding and Withdrawing Life Support From Critically Ill Patients in the United States and Providing Palliative Care to Them." *American Journal of Respiratory and Critical Care Medicine* 162.6 (2000): 2029-2032. Web. 10 Oct. 2013.

Lynott, William J. "10 Things You Should Know About Living Trusts." *AARP Bulletin* 15 Sept. 2010: n. pag. Web. 5 Oct. 2013.

The MacArthur Foundation Research Network on an Aging Society. "Facts and Fictions About an Aging America." 2009. PDF file. Web. 5 Oct. 2013.

Madden, Mary. "Older Adults and Social Media." Pew Internet & American Life Project, 27 Aug. 2010. Web. 5 Oct. 2013.

"Maharaj, Davan. "Lawyer Resigns after Probe of Bequests: Law: James D. Gunderson, Who Allegedly Was the Beneficiary of Millions of Dollars from His Leisure World Clients, Had Faced Conflict-of-Interest Charges from the State Bar." *Los Angeles Times* 11 Jan. 1994: n. pag. Web. 10 Oct. 2013.

---."Lawyer Collected Big Fees from Estate: Lloyd G. Copenbarger Allegedly Overcharged His Client for Tasks such as Packing Her Belongings and Inspecting Her Orange Groves and Properties." *Los Angeles Times* 7 Feb. 1993: n. pag. Web. 10 Oct. 2013.

"Majority of Seniors Postpone Doctor Visits Due to Financial Concerns: New Survey Finds Close to Half of Seniors Also Postpone Filling Prescriptions." *PRNewswire-USNewswire* 30 Nov. 2011: n. pag. Web. 5 Oct. 2013.

Martin, Joyce A., et al. "Births: Final Data for 2010." *Centers for Disease Control and Prevention* 61.1 (2012): 1-72. PDF file. Web. 5 Oct. 2013.

Massachusetts Guardianship Association. "Alternative to Conservatorship: A Durable Power of Attorney." n.d. Web. 5 Oct. 2013.

Mateja, Jim. "What Will Baby Boomers Drive?" *Cars.com*. 1 Jul. 2012. Web. 5 Oct. 2013.

Mayoras, Andrew, and Danielle Mayoras. "Do Lindsay Lohan and Charlie Sheen Need Conservatorships?" *The Probate Lawyer Blog*, 23 Feb. 2011. Web. 10 Oct. 2013.

---."Oops!... Britney Spears' Conservator Did It Again." *Forbes* 12 Mar. 2012: n. pag. Web. 10 Oct. 2013.

McCarrick, Pat Milmoe. "Withholding or Withdrawing Nutrition or Hydration." *National Reference Center for Bioethics Literature*, 1988. Web. 10 Oct. 2013.

McCartney, Anthony. "*Columbo* Actor Peter Falk Placed in Conservatorship." *The Huffington Post* 2 Jun. 2009: n. pag. Web. 10 Oct. 2013.

McKay, Hollie. "Lindsay Lohan Could Get Court Appointed Conservatorship, Experts Say." *Fox News*.com. 26 Sept. 2010. Web. 10 Oct. 2013.

McNamara, Edel P. and Nicholas P. Kennedy. "Tube Feeding Patients with Advanced Dementia: An Ethical Dilemma." *Proceedings of the Nutrition Society* 60 (2001): 179–185. Web. 10 Oct. 2013.

MetLife Mature Market Institute. "Demographic Profile America's Younger Boomers." 2013. PDF file. Web. 5 Oct. 2013.

MetLife Mature Market Institute. "The MetLife Study of Caregiving Costs to Working Caregivers." Feb. 2010. PDF file. Web. 5 Oct. 2013.

The MetLife Mature Market Institute. "The MetLife Study of Caregiving Costs to Working Caregivers, Double Jeopardy for Baby Boomers Caring for Their Parents." Jun. 2011. PDF file. Web. 5 Oct. 2013.

The MetLife Mature Market Institute. "The MetLife Study of Elder Financial Abuse: Crimes of Occasion, Desperation, and Predation Against America's Elders." 2011. PDF file. Web. 5 Oct. 2013.

"Mickey Rooney's Conservatorship Is Permanent." *National Association to Stop Guardian Abuse*, 28 March 2011. Web. 5 Oct. 2013.

Mindlin, Jessica E., and Bonnie Brandl. "Respecting Elders, Protecting Elders: Untangling the Mystery of What Sexual Assault Advocates Need to Know About the Mandatory Reporting of Elder Abuse." Reshape: The Newsletter of the Sexual Assault Coalition Resource Sharing Project 27 (2011): n. pag. Web. 5 Oct. 2013.

Mitchell, Susan. "Geodemographics: Birds of a Feather Flock Together." *American Demographics*, Feb. 1995: n. pag. Web. 5 Oct. 2013.

Moffatt, Mike. "The Baby Boom and the Future of the Economy." *About.com*, n.d. Web. 5 Oct. 2013.

Moffit, Robert E., and Alvene Senger. "Medicare's Demographic Challenge—and the Urgent Need for Reform." The Heritage Foundation, 21 Mar. 2013. Web. 10 Oct. 2013.

Montana Supreme Court Commission on Self-Represented Litigants and Montana Legal Services Association. "How to Create an Advance Directive." Last updated: 26 Jan. 2010. PDF file. Web. 10 Oct. 2013.

Morgan, Sean P., and Jason M. Scott. "Prosecution of Elder Abuse, Neglect, & Exploitation: Criminal Liability, Due Process, and Hearsay." Bureau of Justice Assistance, 2003. Web. 10 Oct. 2013.

Moriarty, Sandra, Nancy Wells and William Wells. *Advertising & IMC: Principles and Practice*. 9th ed. Upper Saddle River: Prentice Hall, 2012. Print.

"Most Middle-Aged Adults Are Rethinking Retirement Plans." Pew Research Social & Demographic Trends, 28 May 2009.Web. 5 Oct. 2013.

National Academy of Social Insurance. "How Will Boomers Affect Social Security?" n.d. Web. 5 Oct. 2013.

National Center on Elder Abuse. "Fact Sheet: Elder Abuse Prevalence and Incidence." 2005. Web. 10 Oct. 2013.

National Center on Elder Abuse. "15 Questions & Answers about Elder Abuse." Jun. 2005. PDF file. Web. 10 Oct. 2013.

National Center on Elder Abuse. "Frequently Asked Questions." n.d. Web. 5 Oct. 2013.

National Center on Elder Abuse. "Statistics/Data." n.d. Web. 5 Oct. 2013.

National Committee for the Prevention of Elder Abuse. "Mental Capacity, Consent, and Undue Influence." Mar. 2003. Web. 10 Oct. 2013.

The National Conference of Commissioners on Uniform State Laws. "Adult Guardianship and Protective Proceedings Jurisdiction Act." n.d. Web. 5 Oct. 2013.

National Guardianship Association. *National Guardianship Association Standards of Practice*. 4th ed. 2013. Web. 5 Oct. 2013.

Neuhausen, Carolyn. "The Sandwich Generation, Baby boomers Feel the Squeeze of Caring for Aging Parents and College-Age Children in a Down Economy." *Pasadena Weekly* 29 April 2010: n. pag. Web. 10 Oct. 2013.

"New Baby Boomer Budget Item: Taking Care of the Parents." *AccountingWEB*. 16 Jun. 2011. Web. 10 Oct. 2013.

"New Record-High U.S. Life Expectancy." *The Huffington Post* 16 Mar. 2011: n. pag. Web 5 Oct. 2013.

"The Next Challenge for Baby Boomers Is Taking Care of their Parents: Overcoming Alzheimer's With a Single Tool." *PRWeb*. 30 Aug. 2010. Web. 5 Oct. 2013.

Nielsen, Jakob. "Seniors as Web Users." Nielsen Norman Group, 28 May 2013. Web. 5 Oct. 2013.

O'Brien, Sharon. "Caregiving for Aging Parents Strains Baby Boomer Marriages." *About.com*. n.d. Web. 10 Oct. 2013.

---."Sandwich Generation: Number of Aging Parents and Dependent Adult Children on the Rise," *About.com*. n.d. Web. 10 Oct. 2013.

---."What is Generation X?: Generation X Struggles with Economic Uncertainty and the Boomer Legacy," *About.com*. n.d. Web. 5 Oct. 2013.

Otto, Joann, and Patricia Ianni Stanis and Kevin W. Marlatt. "Survey Report: State Adult Protective Services Program Responses to Financial Exploitation of Vulnerable Adults 2003." The National Center on Elder Abuse, Jul. 2003. PDF file. Web. 10 Oct. 2013.

Parker, Kim, and Eileen Patten. "The Sandwich Generation: Rising Financial Burdens for Middle-Aged Americans." Pew Research Social & Demographic Trends, 30 Jan. 2013. Web. 5 Oct. 2013.

Pelan, Janet. "California's Professional Fiduciaries Bureau Appears Ineffective in its Mission." *San Bernardino County Sentinel* 19 Nov. 2010: n. pag. Web. 5 Oct. 2013.

---."Questions Continue to Surround Redlands (CA) Conservator Industry." *Scamraiders.com*. 4 Jan. 2010. Web. 10 Oct. 2013.

---."State of California and Failure to Protect? Funding Shortage Inhibiting PFB's Effectiveness." *San Bernardino County Sentinel* 19 Nov. 2010: n. pag. Web. 5 Oct. 2013.

Pillemer, Karl A., and Rosalie S. Wolf, eds. *Elder Abuse: Conflict in the Family*. Dover: Auburn House Publishing Company, 1986. Print.

Pillemer, Karl, and J. Jill Suitor. "Violence and Violent Feelings: What Causes Them Among Family Caregivers?" *Journal of Gerontology* 47: 4 (1992): n. pag. Web. 10 Oct. 2013.

Post, Stephen G. "Tube Feeding and Advanced Progressive Dementia." *Hastings Center Report* 31.1 (2001): 36-42. Web. 10 Oct. 2013.

"Probate Code Sections 1400-1499." *Official California Legislative Information*. n.d. Web. 10 Oct. 2013.

"Probate Information." *USA-Probate*. n.d. Web. 5 Oct. 2013.

Quinn, Mary Joy, and Susan K. Tomita. "Elder Abuse." Johnson County Family Crisis Center, 1986. Web. 10 Oct. 2013.

Ramnarace, Cynthia, "Congress Passes Elder Justice Act: A Piece of the Health Care Reform Bill Aims to Help Older Americans." *AARP Bulletin* 25 Mar. 2010: n. pag. Web. 5 Oct. 2013.

Reaney, Patricia. "Older Americans Upbeat about Aging, Future: Survey." *Reuters* 7 Aug. 2012. Web. 5 Oct. 2013.

Renfro, Adam. "Meet Generation Z." *Getting Smart.com*. 5 Dec. 2012. Web. 5 Oct. 2013.

Renoire, Elaine. "Boomers, Beware!—Your 'Golden Years' May Never Come! Your Nest Egg and Your Very Freedom May be in Jeopardy." National Association to Stop Guardian Abuse, n.d. Web. 5 Oct. 2013.

Rice, Faye. "Making Generational Marketing Come of Age: Does the Music in that Ad Ring a Bell? Sellers are Finally Learning to Exploit the Life Experiences that Define Each Generation. What Took Them so Long?" *Fortune Magazine* 26 Jun. 1995: n. pag. Web. 5 Oct. 2013.

Ridgway, Martha L. "Abuse, Neglect and Financial Exploitation of the Elderly and Disabled." 20 Apr. 2009. PDF file. Web. 10 Oct. 2013.

Robb, David. "Wire the Money and Run." *Hollywood Today.net*. 19 Aug. 2010. Web. 10 Oct. 2013.

Rosenberg, Matt. "Names of Generations." *About.com*. n.d. Web. 5 Oct. 2013.

---."Baby Boom: The Population Baby Boom of 1946-1964 in the United States." *About.com*. 27 Mar. 2009. Web. 5 Oct. 2013.

Rowley, Laura. "Baby Boomers Will Transform Aging In America, Panel Says." *The Huffington Post* 2 Apr. 2012: n. pag. Web. 5 Oct. 2013.

Ryder, Randall J. "Data on Elderly Population Suggest Challenges for the Future." *ElderParentHelp.com*. n.d. Web. 5 Oct. 2013.

---."How Boomers Will Change the Economy." *U.S. News & World Report* 15 Jan. 2013: n. pag. Web. 5 Oct. 2013.

"Sandwich Generation." *Investopedia*, n.d. Web. 5 Oct. 2013.

San Francisco Superior Court. "Alternatives to Conservatorship." 2006. PDF file. Web. 5 Oct. 2013.

Sightings, Tom. "What Baby Boomers Worry About." *U.S. News & World Report* 28 May 2013: n. pag. Web. 5 Oct. 2013.

Solomon, Michael R. *Consumer Behavior: Buying, Having, and Being*. Upper Saddle River: Prentice Hall, 2009. Print.

Steinberg, Brian. "Nielsen: This Isn't Your Grandfather's Baby Boomer." *AdAge* 19 Jul. 2010: n. pag. Web. 5 Oct. 2013.

Stiegel, Lori A. "Elder Justice Act Becomes Law, But Victory Is Only Partial." *Bifocal* 31.4 (2010): n. pag. Web. 5 Oct. 2013.

"Schwarzenegger Vetoes Conservatorship Reform Funding." *Metropolitan News-Enterprise* 27 Aug. 2007: 1. Web. 5 Oct. 2013.

Schroer, William J. "Generations X, Y, Z and the Others." *The Social Librarian Newsletter,* n.d. Web. 5 Oct. 2013.

Schwartz, Ken. "Top 6 Policy Issues Affecting Seniors in 2012." National Council on Aging, 23 Jan. 2012. Web. 5 Oct. 2013.

"Senior Citizen." *Wikipedia.* Last modified: 18 Aug. 2013. Web. 5 Oct. 2013.

"Senior Fear Factors: What Aging Americans Fear Most." *PR Web* 24 Mar. 2010. Web. 5 Oct. 2013.

"Services." *CA.gov.* California Department of Social Services, n.d. Web. 5 Oct. 2013.

Seta, Lauren. "Baby Boomers: A Burgeoning Customer Market." *IBISWorld Reports* 8 Apr. 2013: n. pag. Web. 5 Oct. 2013.

Sexton, Connie Cone. "Baby Boomers in the Middle, Caring for Two Generations." *The Republic* 7 Sept. 2012: n. pag. Web. 5 Oct. 2013.

"Silent Generation." *Wikipedia.* Last modified: 15 September 2013. Web. 5 Oct. 2013.

Smart Spending Editor. "If You Lived Here, You'd Live Longer." *MSN Money.com.* n.d. Web. 5 Oct. 2013.

Soble, Ronald L. "Audit of Conservator Alleges Kickbacks, Financial Abuses." *Los Angeles Times* 6 Jun. 1989: n. pag. Web. 10 Oct. 2013.

Span, Paula. "Will Boomers Be Any Different?" *The New York Times* 4 Mar. 2010: n. pag. Web. 10 Oct. 2013.

State of California Dept. of Consumer Affairs. *The Professional Fiduciaries Bureau Website.* 2013. Web. 5 Oct. 2013.

Steinberg, Brian. "Nielsen: This Isn't Your Grandfather's Baby Boomer: Research Titan Claims Demographic's Retirement Upends Old Notions, Younger Consumers Are Losing Dominance." *AdAge* 19 Jul. 2010: n. pag. Web. 5 Oct. 2013.

Stiegel, Lori, Ellen Klem and Laura Remick. "Penalties for Failing to Report Elder Abuse: Comparison Chart with Provisions from Adult Protective Services Laws, by State" and "Penalties for Making a False Report of Abuse: Comparison Chart with Provisions from Adult Protective Services Laws, By State 'Charts.'" American Bar Association Commission on Law and Aging, 2009. PDF file. Web. 5 Oct. 2013.

Stiegel, Lori A., and Pamela B. Teaster. "Final Technical Report to the National Institute of Justice on "A Multi-Site Assessment of Five Court-Focused Elder Abuse Initiatives." American Bar Association on Law and Aging, 30 Jun. 2010. PDF file. Web. 10 Oct. 2013.

Strauss, William, and Neil Howe. *Generations: The History of America's Future, 1584 to 2069*. New York: William Morrow and Company, Inc., 1991. Print.

The Substitute Decision Makers Task Force for the Iowa Department of Elder Affairs. "Alternatives to Guardianship and Conservatorship for Adults in Iowa." 2001. *Microsoft Word* file. Web. 5 Oct. 2013.

Tatara, Toshio, and Lisa M. Kuzmeskus. "Reporting of Elder Abuse in Domestic Settings." Elder Abuse Information Series No. 1. National Center on Elder Abuse, March 1999. PDF file. Web. 10 Oct. 2013.

---."Trends in Elder Abuse in Domestic Setting." Elder Abuse Information Series No. 2. National Center on Elder Abuse, Nov. 1997. PDF file. Web. 10 Oct. 2013.

Taylor, Liz. "Our New Attitude Toward Aging—and Some Changes to Reflect It." *The Seattle Times* 5 Nov. 2007: n. pag. Web. 5 Oct. 2013.

Teaster, Pamela B. *When the State Takes Over a Life: The Public Guardian as Public Administrator.* Diss. Virginia Polytechnic Institute and State University, 1997. Web. 5 Oct. 2013.

Teaster, Pamela B., et. al. "Public Guardianship After 25 Years: In the Best Interest of Incapacitated People?" The Retirement Research Foundation, 2007. PDF file. Web. 5 Oct. 2013.

---."The 2004 Survey of State Adult Protective Services: Abuse of Adults 60 Years of Age and Older." The National Center on Elder Abuse, Feb. 2006. PDF file. Web. 10 Oct. 2013.

---."Wards of the State: A National Study of Public Guardianship." The Retirement Research Foundation, 2005. PDF file. Web. 5 Oct. 2013.

Turkat, Ira Daniel. "Psychological Aspects of Undue Influence." American Bar Association, Feb. 2005. Web. 10 Oct. 2013.

United States. Administration on Aging. "A Profile of Older Americans: 2012." PDF file. Web. 5 Oct. 2013.

United States. Administration on Aging. "Online Statistical Data on the Aging." n.d. Web. 5 Oct. 2013.

United States. Census Bureau. "Aging Boomers Will Increase Dependency Ratio." 20 May 2010. Web. 5 Oct. 2013.

United States. Census Bureau. "As Baby Boomers Age, Fewer Families Have Children Under 18 at Home." 25 Feb. 2009. Web. 5 Oct. 2013.

United States. Census Bureau. "Census Bureau Releases Comprehensive Analysis of Fast-Growing 90-and-Older Population." 17 Nov. 2011. Web. 5 Oct. 2013.

United States. Census Bureau. "Census Bureau Reports World's Older Population Projected to Triple by 2050." 23 June 2009. Web. 5 Oct. 2013.

United States. Census Bureau. "2010 Census Report Shows More Than 80 Percent of Centenarians Are Women." 10 Dec. 2012. Web. 5 Oct. 2013.

United States. Census Bureau. "U.S. Census Bureau Projections Show a Slower Growing, Older, More Diverse Nation a Half Century from Now." 12 Dec. 2012. Web. 5 Oct. 2013.

United States. Congressional House Select Committee on Aging and Subcommittee on Health and Long-Term Care. *Abuses in Guardianship of the Elderly and Infirm: A National Disgrace.* Washington: GPO, 1988. Web. 5 Oct. 2013.

United States. Government Accountability Office. *Guardianships: Cases of Financial Exploitation, Neglect, and Abuse of Seniors.* Report to the Chairman, Special Committee on Aging, U.S. Senate. Sept.2010. PDF file. Web. 10 Oct. 2013.

United States. Senate Committee of the Judiciary. *Elder Abuse Victims Act of 2011*, 112ᵗʰ Congress, 2011-2013. Web. 5 Oct. 2013.

United States. The Social Security Administration. "When People Need Help Managing Their Money." n.d. Web. 5 Oct. 2013.

University of Missouri Extension. "Silent Generation/Traditionalists (Born Before 1946)." n.d. PDF file. Web. 5 Oct. 2013.

The University of North Carolina School of Government. "Guardianship and Public Health Directors: Some Questions and Answers." 22 April 2010. PDF file. Web. 5 Oct. 2013.

Vestergaard, Alice Jacobs. "The Sandwich Generation: Boomers Feel the Squeeze." *PRNewswire* 21 May 2013. Web. 5 Oct. 2013.

Villarreal, Pamela. "How Are Baby Boomers Spending Their Money?" National Center for Policy Analysis. Policy Report No. 341, Sept. 2012. PDF file. Web. 5 Oct. 2013.

Warren, Katherine. "Baby Boomers: Public Health's Biggest Challenge." *The Huffington Post* 1 Apr. 2011: n. pag. Web. 5 Oct. 2013.

"What Is Estate Planning?" *EstatePlanning.com.* n.d. Web. 5 Oct. 2013.

"When Baby Boomers Become Caregivers." CG Financial Services. n.d. Web. 5 Oct. 2013.

Winerman, Lea. "A Healthy Mind, a Longer Life: Can the Right Attitude and Personality Help You Live Longer? Psychologists are trying to find out." American Psychological Association. 37.10(2006): n. pag. Web. 5 Oct. 2013.

Winsten, Jay A., et al. "Reinventing Aging: Baby Boomers and Civic Engagement." Harvard School of Public Health, 2004. PDF file. Web. 10 Oct. 2013.

Wood, Erica F. "State-Level Adult Guardianship Data: An Exploratory Survey." American Bar Association Commission on Law and Aging, Aug. 2006. PDF file. Web. 5 Oct. 2013.

Zickuhr, Kathryn, and Mary Madden. "Older Adults and Internet Use." Pew Internet & American Life Project, 6 Jun. 2012. Web. 5 Oct. 2013.

"Zsa Zsa Gabor's Daughter Files for Conservatorship, Calls Frederic von Anhalt's Actions into Question." *NYDaily News.com*. 20 Mar. 2012. Web. 10 Oct. 2013.

INDEX

D

E

226
National Adult Protective Services
Association (NAPSA) 226
National Aging Network 55
National Association to
Stop Guardian Abuse
(NASGA) 175, 176, 178, 226,
247, 251
National Cancer Institute (NCI) 226
National Caregivers Library 226
National Center for Victims of Crime
(NCVC) 227
National Center on Elder Abuse
(NCEA) 42, 44, 46, 63, 66, 86,
217, 221, 227, 248, 249, 250,
254, 255
National Clearinghouse on Abuse
Later in Life (NCALL) 227
National Committee for the
Prevention of Elder Abuse
(NCPEA) 63, 78, 227, 249
National Council on Aging
(NCOA) 15, 16, 227, 253
National Criminal Justice Reference
Service (NCJRS) 227
National Guardianship Association
(NGA) 132, 136, 138, 139, 140,
141, 142, 163, 169, 170, 249
National Institute on Aging
(NIA) 35, 228
National Institutes of Health
(NIH) 51, 228
National Reference Center for
Bioethics Literature
(NRCBL) 142, 246
National Research Council
(NRC) 43, 52
National Senior Citizens Law Center
(NSCLC) 228
neglect xv, xvii, 35, 39, 40, 41, 42, 43,
44, 45, 46, 47, 52, 55, 56, 57, 58,
64, 66, 101, 109, 119, 121, 211,
212, 213, 214, 215, 216, 217,
218, 219, 220, 221, 223, 228,
233, 234, 235, 241, 245, 248,

251, 256
See also elder abuse
active neglect 47
passive neglect 46, 47
self-neglect 42, 46, 47, 109
NursingHomeMonitors.org 228

O

Office for Victims of Crime
(OVC) 228
Older Americans Act (OAA) 55, 217

P

Patient Protection and Affordable
Care Act (PPACA) 55, 239
peer personality 2
petition 60, 93, 103, 106, 107, 109,
110, 111, 112, 114, 125, 126,
127, 132, 136, 168, 172, 173,
174, 175, 176, 184, 199, 203
petitioner 93, 109, 110, 125, 199
Physician Orders for Life-Sustaining
Treatment (POLST) 202
medical orders for life-sustaining
treatment (MOLST) 202
medical orders on scope of
treatment (MOST) xiii, xv,
xvi, 8, 13, 16, 18, 21, 23, 27,
29, 31, 41, 45, 46, 47, 52, 53,
54, 61, 63, 65, 67, 70, 79, 80,
81, 82, 85, 87, 102, 105, 107,
109, 117, 129, 133, 134, 140,
142, 145, 146, 147, 155, 172,
173, 174, 180, 181, 197, 200,
201, 202, 207, 211, 218, 220,
236, 237, 240, 242, 248, 253
physician's orders on scope of
treatment (POST) 6, 115,
121, 162, 170, 198, 202, 235,

V

W

U

CPSIA information can be obtained at www.ICGtesting.com
Printed in the USA
BVOW05s1227050715

407445BV00002B/334/P